A Better Place to Live

A Better Place to Live
New Designs for Tomorrow's Communities
by Michael N. Corbett

editorial assistance by Judy Corbett and John Klein
illustrations by Paul Harris

foreword by Denis Hayes, Director, Solar Energy Research Institute

Rodale Press
Emmaus, Pennsylvania

Book design by Barbara Field

Printed in the United States of America on recycled paper, containing a high percentage of de-inked fiber.

Library of Congress Cataloging in Publication Data

Corbett, Michael N
  A better place to live.

  Includes bibliographical references and index.
  1. Human settlements — Philosophy.   2. Human settlements — Planning.   I. Corbett, Judy, joint author.   II. Klein, John, joint author.   III. Title. HT65.C67   307   80-27973
ISBN 0-87857-348-8   paperback

2   4   6   8   10   9   7   5   3   1   paperback

Dedication

This book is dedicated to my children, Lisa and Christopher, who have enriched my life immensely. My concern for them, as well as all children, has prompted the writing of this book.

Contents

Foreword

At the turn of the twentieth century, as the Petroleum Age was dawning, none of the world's cities contained as many as 5 million people. Today, there are 26 cities that are this size or larger. United Nations experts expect 750 million people to inhabit such megalopolises by the year 2000.

But those experts may be wrong. Huge cities, with their attendant vast demand for transportation, run on oil. Now the oil is running out. United States' oil production peaked in 1970 and then began to decline. In 1973, world per capita oil production peaked.

As supplies of petroleum tightened up over the last ten years, the world price of oil increased more than tenfold. Coal- and shale oil-derived synthetic substitutes for oil may ease the supply situation but they will be twice as expensive as oil to produce. While it might be theoretically possible for life to continue largely unchanged for some decades, the simple economics of skyrocketing fuel prices will strongly dictate a much more efficient husbanding of energy resources.

Patterns of human settlement have always been influenced by the sources of energy the community relied upon. The first towns were made possible by agricultural surpluses obtained using draft animals and irrigation. Early industrial communities were generally located near flowing streams that could be harnessed with dams. Later, these waterways were used to transport coal to fuel industrial boilers. These industrial cities grew along radial spokes, following rail transit systems served initially by horse-drawn trolleys and then by electric trams.

In the early twentieth century, the automobile began to appear in urban areas, but initial penetration was slow. Five-mile-per-hour speed limits retarded early auto use, as did laws requiring nighttime drivers to be preceded by men on foot carrying lanterns. Yet by 1907, 140 automobile companies had taken root in the United States, and within five years they were joined by hundreds more. Another transformation of the city was underway.

Automobiles had advantages over rival modes of transport. While they produced pollution, this was considered less objectionable than the horse manure that earlier fouled city streets. And while they required roads, cars were far more flexible than vehicles that needed rails. A person with a car and some gasoline was not at the mercy of transit schedules or transit strikes. If a rail line became obstructed, transit ceased; if a road got blocked, the automobile merely detoured around the problem area.

After Ford's Model T made personal automobiles within the means of many, subtle changes began to appear in the urban landscape. First, the spaces between the radial spokes of the railways began to fill with dwellings and businesses. Later, suburban developments began to encircle urban centers in concentric rings, leading to new patterns of urban organization.

Today, as we move into the post-petroleum era, we are likely to see the birth of new kinds of communities that are influenced as much by new energy supplies and technologies as earlier cities were affected by railways and automobiles. This strikes fear in certain hearts, but hope in others. As a West Virginian folk saying would have it, "America ain't perfect, but we ain't done yet." To risk understatement, our cities have room for improvement.

Cities have always drawn upon the surrounding countryside for food and raw materials. In return, they provided education, protection, commerce, religion, art, and industry. But in this century, as large cities grew from populations of thousands to millions, they found they couldn't support themselves as they had in the past. They have had to reach out sometimes halfway around the world for much of their food, fuel, and other necessities. The growth, coupled with greater dependency on outside sources, comes only at tremendous expense, putting drains on energy supplies and consuming local dollars that could have instead been spent to improve deteriorating city services, like education, and legal and medical systems.

Mike Corbett is well aware of the struggles and limitations of today's cities. And, happily for us all, he has some very good ideas about how to prevent future problems caused by city growth and suburban sprawl. In *A Better Place to Live* he goes beyond the bad news with his logical, detailed, and optimistic blueprint for new city and community designs.

Mike Corbett was a prime mover in the remarkable and inspirational advancement of Davis, California, to the leading edge of the 1970's solar revolution. His Village Homes project demonstrates that we can build far better places to live — creating beauty while we reduce waste and pollution. At the same time he has proven that we can dramatically slash our dependence on conventional fuels while heightening our quality of life.

If Mike Corbett's dream — which is also my own — is realized, the postpetroleum community will be a very attractive place in which to live. It will place a renewed emphasis on neighborhoods, with their own services and organs of commerce. It will stress the efficient use and reuse of resources, from water to steel. It will return the nutrients of its "wastes" to the soil where they belong, and it will raise much of its own food. It will substitute communications for much transportation, renewable energy for fossil fuels, and perhaps most important, strive for a higher degree of self-reliance. Few communities will ever be entirely self-sufficient, but most will see an advantage in assuming a high

degree of control over their own basic sources of sustenance.

A Better Place to Live is a political treatise as much as it is a tour of technologies, and it has a ready-made constituency waiting for it. An important phenomenon of the 1970s was the creation of new, locally based organizations throughout the country. With a diversity of memberships and purposes, these groups began to look for ways to touch the institutions of daily life. The results included the establishment of day-care centers, food cooperatives, environmental organizations, health care coalitions, women's organizations, minority caucuses, senior groups, consumer action networks, handicapped advocacy organizations, and a multitude of block- or neighborhood-based civic action groups. There are about a quarter-million such organizations in the United States today. Most have a natural inclination toward decentralized applications, and many have been active in advocacy or development.

A Better Place to Live is an excellent handbook for this effort in individual interest and action. For those who want to have more of a say in how they will live their lives, how they will provide energy, food, and other necessities, this book will be indispensable.

It is at the local level that many global problems must be resolved. Someone once said that, "People don't have birth rates; they have babies. Pontificating about birth rates won't affect behavior unless it somehow ties into the direct implications for a family of having additional children." Similarly, the problems of food shortages, fuel vulnerabilities, sewage, water, recycling, and so forth, cannot really be solved on a world-wide or even a national basis. They will be solved only when local communities perceive that they have a real choice and begin to act on it.

Mike Corbett's accomplishment is to show us that the choice is real. A few years ago, he began building a successful, integrated, future-oriented subdivision that gave new direction to the city he inhabits. Now, in *A Better Place to Live,* Mike spells out the details of that choice — what it requires, and what it can yield — for the whole world.

Denis Hayes
Director
Solar Energy Research Institute

Acknowledgments

I'm extremely grateful to all the people who have assisted me in one way or another with the production of this book, and particularly to John Klein and Judy Corbett.

John Klein has worked with me for the past seven years as an active partner in my Village Homes project. His writing skill and his supportive understanding of my ideas have often enabled him to put them into words more clearly and fully than I could have myself. In doing so, he has contributed many ideas and insights of his own.

My wife Judy has been as concerned with appropriate planning and design as I have, and many of the ideas present here have been developed through our discussions over the past 18 years. Her contributions to my understanding of the social and psychological impact of design (the subject of her graduate study under Robert Sommer) have been particularly valuable, as have her work and comments on the manuscript.

My editor Carol Stoner of Rodale Press has been extremely important in providing advice, direction, and editing assistance. In addition to John, Judy, and Carol, many others worked on the book:

General assistance: Kimberly Davenport — research, writing, and coordination; Richard Sacks — Agriculture, Water, and Recycling; Mack Walker — Recycling; Bruce Melzer — Energy; David Sausjord — Garden Cities; Robert Sterling — Grass-Roots Action; Richard Kline — Energy and Grass-Roots Action; and, Ken McEldowney — Housing and Energy.

Graphics: Paul Harris, assisted by Robert Boles, Sandra Stills, and Mairy de Witt; design by Barb Field of Rodale Press.

Typing: Carol Van Alstine of The Secretariat.

And finally, I would like to extend my deep appreciation to those people who reviewed the manuscript and offered ideas: Robert Sommer, Jack Wynns, Valerie Anderson, Richard Farrell, Manfred Kusch, Eugene Odum, and Ronal Larson.

Chapter 1
Piecemeal vs. Wholistic Planning

As far back as 1925, social critic Lewis Mumford said about cities, ``. . . as they grow, they fall behind in the barest decencies of housing; they become more expensive to operate, more difficult to police, more burdensome to work in, and much more impossible to escape from even in the hours of leisure that we achieve.''[1] Time has certainly proven Mumford to be correct!

In fact, the the concentric growth pattern of our cities since the 1920s has produced urbanization in the form of an incoherent sprawl of subdivisions, commercial strips, and industrial parks connected by congested freeways, rendering our cities even more problematic than they were in the 1920s. This has lead to the deterioration of much of the inner city and has created new living environments lacking in many of the basic elements necessary for a wholesome human environment. Unfortunately, what happened is that planners and decision makers did not, and for the most part still do not, consider the subtle sociopsychological needs of the individual. Their concern is primarily for institutions, organizations, physical systems. Rene Dubos makes a similar point:

Planners are primarily concerned with the technological efficiency of the urban system with regard to industrial, economic, and political activities. They pay less attention to the psychological and emotional needs of city dwellers or to the relation between city life and civilization. While the technological aspects of the urban system are fairly well understood and can be manipulated, little is actually known about the influence that cities have exerted on the development of human potentialities and therefore on the emergence of civilized life. Civilizations have flourished in cities for more than 5,000 years, but they have difficulty in surviving the huge urban agglomerations of the contemporary world.[2]

Besides a basic lack of consideration of sociopsychological needs, a great deal of what we have been doing wrong can be summed up in the term *piecemeal planning*. Piecemeal planning is the result of our tendency to try to deal with each goal or problem as if it existed in a vacuum, as if our attempts to deal with it had no impact on other values and problems. Our suburban neighbor-

[1]Carl Sussman, ed., *Planning the Fourth Migration: The Neglected Vision of the Regional Planning Association of America* (Cambridge, Mass.: MIT Press, 1976), p. 89 (hereafter cited as *Planning the Fourth Migration*).

[2]Rene Dubos, *Beast or Angel: Choices That Make Us Human* (New York: Charles Scribner's Sons, 1974), p. 92 (hereafter cited as *Beast or Angel*).

hoods provide an instructively appalling example. They are generally laid out with no more than two or three goals in mind: to provide every family its own house and yard, connected to water, sewer, gas, and electricity; to allow every resident to drive speedily through the neighborhood to his or her own front door; and to exclude even the most innocuous commercial enterprise.

Having achieved the original three goals, we suddenly discover a host of new problems. There is no local community because there are no local shops or public areas where we meet our immediate neighbors — only private houses and private yards, and the inhospitable streets. Children rarely see adults at work. Any errand means using a car and then it is difficult to find a parking place. In many communities, children cannot get anywhere safely without being chauffuered. The cars pollute the air. The storm runoff from streets and roofs produces erosion and flooding, and destroys aquatic life downstream. Sewage disposal becomes a problem even though fertilizer for agriculture is increasingly costly.

Unenlightened and undaunted, we tackle these problems in the same piecemeal fashion, and create a whole new set of problems. We install antipollution devices on cars, but that decreases gas mileage, and suddenly gas seems to be getting scarce. We build suburban shopping centers with huge parking lots, and huge ponds to contain storm runoff, and suddenly we notice that agricultural land is getting scarce. We provide neighborhood parks, and the alienated young people vandalize the facilities. And so on, indefinitely.

There is a pattern here: at each step, we neglect to look at the whole picture. We assume that our wealth, technology, and "problem-solving ability" can bail us out of any new problem we create. Often they seem to, but at what cost?

The resulting social problems, health problems, pollution, and depletion of nonrenewable resources are making more and more people ask what has gone wrong and what can be done. It is from this growing concern that we are gaining significant support for better urban planning, aiming to solve our problems and satisfy our needs in ways that are harmonious, rather than conflicting. We are beginning to look for ways to supply food, clothing, shelter, health care, and meaningful livelihoods, while also maintaining an environment conducive to physical and mental health, preserving the natural ecosystem, conserving natural resources and nonrenewable energy sources, providing human settlements that will survive more comfortably during severe environmental fluctuations, and developing a culture that encourages human fulfillment and happiness.

This is not a new concern but one which has been expressed by others over the past century. In 1898, Ebenezer Howard promulgated a scheme to build new towns rather than

adding population to the already large cities. Called the *garden city*, Howard's plan would have incorporated a unified system of community land ownership, greenbelts and a balance of land uses, including industry and housing for workers, industrial and residential balance, self government, and an intimate relationship between city and country. As Howard pictured it, "each inhabitant of the whole group, though in one sense living in a town of small size, would be in reality living in, and would enjoy all the advantages of a great and most beautiful city; and yet all the fresh delights of the country."[3] A series of small, self-sufficient towns was to be connected to the others through a rapid transit system, with a cultural center located at the core.

Two garden cities were built in England as a result of Howard's writings and influence. Both Detchworth, begun in 1903, and Welwyn, begun in 1919, stand today as living proof of the value of the garden city as a means of providing people with better living environments.[4]

During the early twenties, a group of about 25 friends and colleagues joined together to further Howard's concept. The group held a common belief that the existing centralized, profit-oriented metropolitan society should be replaced with a decentralized one made up of environmentally balanced regions. Called the Regional Planning Association of America, the organization had a membership which included people like Lewis Mumford and Clarence Stein, who was chief architect of Radburn, New Jersey, the only substantial attempt at garden city development in the United States. The group dissolved in the early thirties, after having been involved in the development of Sunnyside, a neighborhood community composed of houses grouped around open space owned by a community association, and Radburn. Radburn continued the Sunnyside theme on a larger scale, bringing together a series of Sunnyside-like neighborhoods, each of which evolved around an elementary school and shopping center. The automobile was de-emphasized in both of these plans, which used dead-end cul-de-sacs as the only access to the homes.

Long before the problems in our cities came to a head, the visionary members of the Regional Planning Association of America sought to locate people outside the city, arguing for "a dedication to a new social order where people have decent homes, a stable community life, a healthy and varied environment, and a genuinely urban culture."[5] Unfortunately, political and economic forces prevented realization of the vision.

The principles of Radburn were not forgotten, and they did serve as a model for subsequent *new-town* developments. A few have been built in the United States—notably Columbia, Maryland, and Reston, Virginia—and many more in Europe. Although each represents a noble attempt and a step forward, none has succeeded in completely achieving the original vision. All lack adequate decentralization and diversity.

While the memory of Ebenezer Howard and his garden city concept has faded, a number of new revelations have served not only to reinforce the validity of Howard's ideas but, if viewed as a whole, form the basis for a new broader vision of planning that I think can best be called *appropriate planning* or *wholistic community design.*

Individuals from various pursuits have contributed insight. One is E. F. Schumacher, who, in his book, *Small Is Beautiful,* succinctly expresses in the subtitle his philosophy: "Economics as if People Mattered."[6] Another is Howard Odum, whose work has played a major role in the development of the field of ecology.[7] Edward T. Hall's *The Hidden Dimension*[8] and Robert Sommer's *Personal Space*[9] explore the relationships of the physical environment, and especially the man-made environment, with the individual and society and, they brought about the emergence of a new field of environmental psychology. The combination of econom-

[5]Sussman, *Planning the Fourth Migration,* p. 45.

[6]E. F. Schumacher, *Small Is Beautiful: Economics as if People Mattered* (New York: Harper & Row, 1973) (hereafter cited as *Small Is Beautiful*).

[7]Howard T. Odum, *Environment, Power, and Society* (New York: Wiley-Interscience, 1971).

[8]Edward T. Hall, *The Hidden Dimension* (New York: Doubleday & Co., 1966).

[9]Robert Sommer, *Personal Space* (Englewood Cliffs, N.J.: Prentice-Hall, Inc., 1969).

[3]Ebenezer Howard, *Garden Cities of Tomorrow* (Cambridge, Mass.: MIT Press, 1965), p. 192.

[4]Ibid.

ics, ecology, and psychology has become the backbone of a new body of knowledge of the human-environmental relationship. The students of this new interdisciplinary field are a strong force in bringing a new awareness of the earth, people, and their interrelatedness. Whole Earth Day, started in 1970 by Denis Hayes and others, symbolizes and reinforces this awareness.

Evidence of the new awareness can be seen in both process and product. Though unsophisticated and many times misused, the *environmental impact statement* (EIS) or *environmental impact report* (EIR) required by some governmental agencies before approval of many projects is an example of a significant change in process aimed at examining the potential effects of an environmental manipulation. As for products, two of the most visible examples are the movement toward environmentally benign sources of energy such as solar, for which Amory Lovins argued eloquently in his book *Soft Energy Paths*,[10] and the development and adoption of different forms of organic agriculture as advocated years ago by J. I. Rodale and described in *Organic Gardening* magazine and many of the books published by Rodale Press. Another is the grass-roots movement toward ecologically planned communities, such as Cerro Gordo, near Shelter Cove, Oregon; the proposed Solar Village planned by California architect Sim Van der Ryn;[11] and the Village Homes neighborhood in Davis, California, which I developed as a commercial subdivision after years of discussion with my wife and many concerned and imaginative friends.[12] These projects, which are based on an integrated approach protecting human beings and the environment, are the inspiration for *A Better Place to Live*.

My major motivation for writing this book comes from a frightening awareness that we will be making some crucial choices in the near future. Are we going to place inevitable new growth in urban infill areas, increasing already too-dense populations, or will the new growth occur in garden cities? Will we realize the inadequacies of our cities and begin to retrofit them to make them more livable, or will we continue to make more severe the social and economic consequences of their inappropriate design? Will we go to war in order to increase our access to fossil fuels; will we rely on nuclear technologies and coal for our future energy needs; or will we turn to renewable energy resources and conservation?

There is a danger that if we wait until the problems become severe enough to create panic, we will succumb to seemingly quick and easy solutions, ignoring their long-term dire consequences. The nuclear industry, for one, is depending on this and confidently expects to recapture its large investment in nuclear research and development. According to author Richard Barnet, "The industry has predicted that if the choice is between blackouts and brownouts, which are now said to be inevitable for the nineteen-eighties, and nuclear power, the public will choose the latter, along with all the risks." Barnet continues, "A poll that was taken a few days after the crises at Three Mile Island put that choice to the very people who days earlier had feared they would die in a nuclear accident, and the results showed that only twenty-five percent of the respondents favored shutting down all nuclear plants."[13]

We must immediately proceed to produce and demonstrate the alternatives to the existing high energy, high technology society which concentrates masses of people and requires more centralized political and economic control. We must choose the best of the current technologies and the best of the planning tools and use them to build new communities and to rehabilitate old ones to create a more humane and ecologically healthy living environment.

The terms appropriate planning and wholistic design will suggest different things to different people. Therefore in the next

---

[10]Amory T. Lovins, *Soft Energy Paths: Toward a Durable Peace* (Cambridge, Mass.: Ballinger Publishing Co., 1977) (hereafter cited as *Soft Energy Paths*).

[11]Cerro Gordo and Solar Village will be discussed in more detail in Chapter 8.

[12]Village Homes is a 70-acre neighborhood community that I designed and developed in 1972 and completed in 1980. The neighborhood design includes a number of important innovations that will be referred to in different parts of this book. The neighborhood community as an entity, should not be confused with a garden city which would be composed of a number of neighborhood communities.

[13]Richard J. Barnet, "The World's Resources, Part I— The Lean Years," *New Yorker*, 17 March 1980, p. 77.

chapter I make explicit those assumptions, goals, and procedures that I think form the basis for appropriate planning. I discuss in the several chapters following a number of schemes to handle various technical and social problems of urban[14] living in humane, ecologically sound ways. The combination of these schemes should present a picture of how to achieve a harmonious, wholistic community design that offers an attainable alternative to the high-technology, high-energy consumption world that exists today.

In the last chapters, I explore methods and tactics — political, economic, and social — for implementation of appropriate planning, giving a number of examples of how to build garden cities and how to rehabilitate existing cities.

I realize that some of what I present here will be controversial even to some individuals highly supportive of humane and ecologically sound planning, but I see that as healthy. It is out of argument and discussion and trial and error that many new and different concepts are tested so that a truly appropriate pattern of growth can emerge. I think it is time to seriously begin that dialogue. This book is my contribution to it.

---

[14]When I use the term "urban," I am referring to towns with a population of 7,000 and more.

Chapter 2
The Basis of Community Design

After participating in community design as a planner, developer, and citizen advocate, I have come to the conclusion that the design process is influenced by the interaction of three main elements. In the forefront are the two most obvious elements: our goals and our procedures. Goals are what we individually or collectively want to achieve with our design. Procedures help us integrate our individual goals into collectively held goals (many times a difficult task) and also assist us in our design processes.

Underlying this is the third element, our assumptions. Failure to deal adequately with our assumptions in the past has probably been a large factor in the irrationality of our planning process. Our assumptions are often unstated, implicit in our understanding of the world around us. They are drawn from science, religion, philosophy, art, and literature—our entire culture—and shaped by the collective intuition of our generation. It is these underlying assumptions that influence our goals and the procedures we use. They help us make predictions about the outcome of our designs, and they generally direct much of our behavior.

Because these assumptions are so often unstated, they tend to go unchallenged and unexamined, even though they influence the design of our communities in ways that profoundly affect all of our lives. For this reason I think it is crucial that we take the trouble to make explicit the assumptions from which we work, in order to see whether or not they make sense, to show others our perspective, and to lay the groundwork for good communication and logical discussion.

It is the purpose of this chapter, then, to discuss goals and procedures, and to present a number of carefully selected assumptions that seem to form the basis of a wholistic approach to community planning. They include some abstract notions that overlap in complicated ways, but I think if you take the time to consider them now, you will better understand the importance of the concepts and design solutions presented later in this book.

Assumptions

Of the 12 assumptions I present here, the first 5 are based on modern ecological principles. They also reflect, in a subtle way, a general view of man's relationship to the earth that is embodied in a number of centuries-old philosophies—intuitive wisdom that is now being borne out by modern science. I find this expressed well by the modern Native American activist, Lame Deer, who said, "We must all see ourselves as part of this earth, not as an

enemy from the outside who tries to impose his will on it. We who know the meaning of the pipe also know that, being a living part of the earth, we cannot harm any part of her without hurting ourselves."[1]

The sixth assumption provides the main link between humanity's relationship to the ecosystem and its relationship to the human-made physical and social environment. The last six deal more with the human-made environment.

In reading these assumptions, keep in mind that this is not intended to be a complete list of assumptions for wholistic planning, but rather a set of selected assumptions that I think are especially important in view of the social and environmental changes of the past century.

ASSUMPTION ONE: Every living thing survives by numerous and subtle relationships with all living things and with the inanimate environment. When all living things are considered together, these relationships appear as complex, interdependent, and self-regulating structures or ecosystems, in which any one form of life depends on the rest of the system to provide the conditions

[1]Lame Deer, "Seeker of Visions," poster.

necessary for its existence. Human beings are as much a part of this ecosystem as any other form of life, and depend on the rest of the ecosystem for food, a breathable atmosphere, drinkable water, and a survivable climate. The earth has not always provided a suitable environment for humans, but was made hospitable over the millennia by functioning ecosystems.

I believe this assumption, drawn from the writings of a number of ecologists, forms the basis for understanding the relationship between humans and the natural environment.[2,3]

ASSUMPTION TWO: Human technology permits powerful manipulations of the elements of the ecosystem. These are intended to improve human life and comfort by satisfying immediate needs and desires, but they can and sometimes do have side effects that change or destroy parts of an ecosystem, if not an entire ecosystem, and are harmful to humans in the long run.

Human manipulation of the ecosystem has within a few lifetimes destroyed vast amounts of farmland and killed off the fish in hundreds of lakes, to mention only two examples. Ecologists can envision larger-scale changes, possibly already under way, that could have devastating effects on humans.

For example, burning fossil fuels releases huge amounts of carbon dioxide into the atmosphere. At the same time, other pollutants gradually migrate to the upper atmosphere where they may reduce the concentration of ozone. Changes in either carbon dioxide or ozone levels can be expected to alter the way the atmosphere transmits, reflects, absorbs, and reradiates the sun's heat, and this would gradually change the average temperature of the earth.

A few degrees' change either way could be devastating, scientists say. An increase could melt the polar ice caps, raising the sea level perhaps 250 feet, which would flood all seaboard cities and inundate vast areas of fertile land. A decrease could bring on another ice age. We used to suppose that ice ages took many

thousands of years to come and go, but now scientists are beginning to think they may come on very swiftly once the average temperature drops to some critical level. Either of these two alternatives would bring famine on a scale that would make the early- and mid-nineteenth-century famines look like mild discomforts.

Another possible result of human manipulation is that the various chemical compounds that never existed on earth until we created them and began to spray them on our crops and forests will, when they find their way to the ocean in sufficient quantity, kill off all the plankton—microscopic plants that account for 70 percent of the oxygen liberated by plants to replace what we animals consume by breathing and by the combustion and decomposition of organic substances. This would lead to a very gradual decrease in the amount of oxygen in the atmosphere, subjecting us to a stress which we now normally experience only at high altitudes.

ASSUMPTION THREE: Ecosystems and parts of ecosystems composed of a wide variety of species tend to adapt better to environmental changes or human tampering than those involving fewer species.

According to Ashby's law of the requisite variety in cybernetic systems, a system formed by more elements with greater diversity is less subject to fluctuations.[4]

This is an argument for maintaining a wide variety of crop and livestock species and diverse agricultural systems. For example, potato blight caused devastating famine in Ireland in 1848 partly because of the inhabitants' widespread reliance on that single crop.

It appears that a similar principle applies to human communities. Those communities with the greatest diversity in energy sources, in forms of economic enterprise, and in food sources will tend to be more stable and to adapt most successfully and painlessly to severe changes, be they environmental, political, economic, or social.

[2]Ramon Margalef, *Perspectives in Ecological Theory* (Chicago: University of Chicago Press, 1970).
[3]Odum, *Environment, Power, and Society.*

[4]Margalef, *Perspectives in Ecological Theory,* p. 21.

ASSUMPTION FOUR: Part of the ecosystem is a complex system of energy transfers that depends, ultimately, on energy input. Until relatively recent times, the sun provided the only significant energy input, and consequently, the ecosystem is best adapted to this source of energy. Nuclear fuels, and to some extent natural fossil fuels, introduce significant energy inputs to which the ecosystem is not adapted, and they yield by-products that change the chemical balance and radiation levels in the environment.

Like any human technological tampering, the use of nuclear and fossil fuels involves a risk of serious effects on the

ecosystem and the human beings who depend on it. Since all energy we generate turns to heat, one possibility is that it will contribute to a rise in the earth's temperature sufficient to melt the polar ice caps as suggested in Assumption Two. We also know that acid rain produced by the gases from burning coal can damage or kill agricultural crops and natural vegetation, and has killed the fish in many lakes and rivers. Smog has the same effect. Various forms of air pollution demonstrably reduce human health and mental capacity, contributing to a long list of disease conditions. Increased radiation can cause cancer, leukemia, and genetic changes.

ASSUMPTION FIVE: In the long run, every one of humanity's physical needs must be satisfied in one of two ways: (1) by consumption of "renewable resources" like lumber, that are continually generated by the ecosystem, and can be consumed no faster than they are generated by the ecosystem; or (2) by the recovery and reuse (*recycling*) of *nonrenewable resources* that, like metals, are not generated by the ecosystem, or, like petroleum products, are generated so slowly by the ecosystem as to be nonrenewable for all practical purposes. This recycling can be either planned, as in the recovery of used bottles and cans, or unplanned, as by mining the trash heaps of preceding generations.

There are two dangers in planning predicated on using a renewable resource faster than it is generated, or on using a nonrenewable resource without recycling. First, such use cannot be sustained, and second, it allows us to specialize in the use of that resource instead of meeting our needs in a diversity of ways. Lacking diversity, we are more likely to find ourselves in serious trouble (according to Assumption Three) when the inevitable shortage occurs.

This is precisely the situation in which we industrial nations now find ourselves as a result of the last century's specialization in fossil fuels. Fossil fuels are nonrenewable resources, and we have depended on them so heavily for our energy needs that we face, as they become scarcer, a difficult transition to renewable energy sources such as solar, wind, hydro, geothermal, and biomass conversion. Most of us cannot even imagine making this transition. If we had relied partly on these other energy sources all along, it would be much simpler to imagine and to carry out such a transition now.

ASSUMPTION SIX: Though humans seem to be the most adaptable of living things, they still have certain basic inherent physical and psychological needs that must be met by the ecosystem, the human-made physical environment, and the social environment.

Abraham Maslow proposes that these needs can be arranged in a hierarchy according to their urgency. He rates physiological needs such as food, water, and warmth as most urgent, followed by the needs for security, social interaction, esteem, and self-actualization, in that order. All of these needs are real and important, however. Providing for an individual's more urgent needs allows him or her to devote attention to less urgent needs, and thus reach higher levels of satisfaction and fulfillment of his or her total human potential—or, to use Maslow's term, "self-actualization."[5]

[5]I offer the following definition of Maslow's term. Self-actualization is that state of being in which a person is happy, productive, self-respecting, self-accepting, loving, and in the process of fulfilling his or her highest potentialities. The self-actualizing person, being happy and content with himself or herself, is therefore also generous in spirit, sensitive, and respectful of the needs of others.

It follows from this that some environments potentially allow their inhabitants to reach higher levels of fulfillment and well-being than do other environments. In designing our environment we must be aware of our responsibilities to optimize that potential. In doing so, we must give as much attention to the social environment as to the physical environment, if not more. For example, if the social environment is such that people are encouraged to seek their self-esteem through expensive possessions and conspicuous consumption, they will find it harder to reach fulfillment than if they were encouraged to find it through participation in a community of friends and neighbors that would simultaneously satisfy their social needs.

ASSUMPTION SEVEN: Humans are for the most part genetically adapted to the environment that existed from about 200 to 20,000 years ago.[6] This adaptation involves not just our physical makeup, but also our modes of perception and behavior, and relates to the social environment as well as to the physical environment.

In other words, we as a species are genetically better equipped to live and thrive in some social settings than in others,

just as we are obviously better equipped for some physical environments than for others. The human race is not genetically adapted to mass society or to the social effects of technological innovations like the telephone, any more than we are to synthetic chemicals, high radiation levels, noise, or a chaotic visual environment.

Rene Dubos states that:

Social contacts may have been more satisfying by the fire in a Stone Age cave or on a village bench than they are now through the convenience of telephone conversations and of other means of mass communication. Dancing to the sound of drums in the savanna or to a fiddler on the village green could be as exciting as dancing to electronic music. Throwing a rock at an enemy was a more satisfying way to express anger or hatred than killing him at long range with a gun or a bomb. The fundamental satisfactions and passions of humankind are thus still much as they were before the advent of the automobile, of the airplane, and of the television set; before the era of steam and electric power; and even before our ancestors had abandoned hunting for agriculture and for industry and had moved from the cave to the village or the city. In many cases, furthermore, modern life has rather impoverished the methods by which fundamental urges can be expressed. Modern societies can escape from boredom only by direct sensory experiences of primitive life; the need for these experiences persists in the modern world for the simple reason that it is indelibly inscribed in the genetic code of the human species.[7]

This suggests that village life or "tribal" life in groups of 50 to a few thousand persons, in buildings showing a common architectural style and blending harmoniously into the natural setting, may provide the most hospitable environment for human life, and that typical modern environments are much more stressful. I personally believe that one of the most serious sources of stress in our modern environment is people's confrontation with

---

[6]These times are of course very rough estimates. The period could extend back much further than 20,000 years; I chose that figure simply because we are fairly sure the human species existed in pretty much its present form for at least that long. The Native American Indians are thought to have separated from the Asian population 20,000 to 30,000 years ago, but the genetic differences between the two are slight, suggesting little evolutionary change in that period. Rene Dubos speculates that natural selection for characteristics already in the gene pool takes a minimum of 5 to 10 generations. If this is true, then it follows that humanity has adapted genetically little in the last 200 years. The great changes in human life-style have all occurred in that period. Until 200 years ago, the vast majority of humanity still lived in the countryside, in tiny villages, or in towns of a few thousand people. Travel or migration farther than a few miles was rare, except among nomadic tribes that moved as a group. Either way, most humans probably spent their entire lives among the same united group of people, in close contact with nature. Noise and air pollution simply did not exist except for the few people living in cities.

[7]Dubos, *Beast or Angel,* p. 157.

automobiles, moving or parked, or with streets designed for automobiles, even when no automobiles are present.[8]

ASSUMPTION EIGHT: The relationship between people and their environment goes both ways: humanity both shapes, and is shaped by, its environment.

This is a critical point for us to realize if we are to break away from those social patterns that are detrimental to our well-being. Take the example of the typical suburban neighborhood I described in Chapter 1. Because we are a society of mobile individuals with only weak community ties, we design our new neighborhoods with more concern for mobility than for commu-

nity life, and the neighborhoods then frustrate whatever inclinations toward community we still have, and keep us from learning how to get along with each other. Murray Bookchin describes this process well:

> Historically, the basis for a vital urban entity consisted not primarily of its design elements but of the nuclear relations between people that produced these elements. Human scale was more than a design on a drawing board; it emerged from the intimate association provided by the clan, the guild, and the civic union of free, independent farmers and craftsmen. Knitted together at the base of a civic entity, people created a city that formally and structurally sheltered their most essential and meaningful social relations. If these relations were balanced and harmonious, so too were the design elements of the city. If, on the other hand, they were distorted and antagonistic, the design elements of the city revealed this in its monumentalism and extravagant growth. Hierarchical social relations produced hierarchical space; egalitarian relations, egalitarian space. Until city planning addresses itself to the need for a radical critique of the prevailing transformation of existing social relations, it will remain mere ideology — the servant of the very society that is producing the urban crises of our time.[9]

ASSUMPTION NINE: Humans can adapt to a wide range of environmental conditions, but the cost of adaptation to inhospitable conditions is temporary or chronic stress. Victims can reduce this stress by becoming insensitive to the stimuli that cause it, but this produces a general deadening, a lack of awareness and responsiveness, that is equally harmful. Stress in its various forms, and insensitivity in response to stress, contribute to a wide variety of pathological human afflictions: heart disease, mental illness, and a general lowering of resistance to disease; destructive use of drugs and alcohol, apathy and cynicism, crime, and loss of sensitivity and compassion, to name only a few.

[8]The list of ways in which automobiles generate stress is a long one. The noise, fumes, and visual and tactile harshness of autos and roadways affect both drivers and pedestrians. Streets and parking areas form barriers and obstacle courses to pedestrian traffic in both commercial and residential areas, demanding constant alertness for moving vehicles, and constant attention from parents to their children's safety. Auto accidents involving pedestrians are one of the biggest killers in the United States, also maiming or injuring thousands of people every year.

Autos stress people in even more ways. They isolate them from all but visual contact with their surroundings, and carry them through the surroundings so rapidly that even the experience of visual impressions is vague and superficial, and chances for social contact are nil. It deprives people of the healthy and invigorating mild exercise they could get by walking — a great loss in our increasingly sedentary world.

In some ways, the auto is actually a burden to its owner. Its purely financial costs are a significant burden. For short distances it is more trouble than it is worth; the need to constantly return to the auto, move it and park it, often gives the driver the feeling that he or she is carrying the car around rather than vice versa. Shoppers using a good public transit system for the first time often experience an exhilarating feeling of freedom, of traveling light.

There is a wholistic health retreat at the northern end of California's Capay Valley where the guests are asked to park their cars in a field well up the road from the hotel and hot baths because the psychotherapist who runs the place believes that the mere sight of automobiles has become an anxiety stimulus for most people.

I suggest that the reader try observing his or her own feelings in the presence, and in the absence, of autos.

[9]Murray Bookchin, *The Limits of the City* (New York: Harper & Row, 1974), p. 124.

Our encounter with the unnatural stimulation in the modern environment is a constant burden on our capacity to function well. It wears down each individual differently. It is like ocean waves constantly pounding against a cliff. Sooner or later they will break it down; the length of time it takes depends on the strength of the particular formation. Long before the formation falls, however, there will be erosion.

To understand what causes stress and to avoid designing it into our environment is a responsibility that cannot be ignored as it has been in the past. Stress caused by noise provides a good example.

Recent literature abounds with references to noise as a contributory or aggravating factor in human disease. Noise has been implicated in such disorders as loss of hearing, hypertension, ulcers, migraine headaches, insomnia, gastric malfunction, colitis, and mental illness.[10] But perhaps of greatest concern is the effect of noise on the cardiovascular system.

It has now been well documented that exposure to noise (both loud sudden noise, and lower-level continuous noise such as city traffic noise) can cause such reactions as vasoconstriction, higher cholesterol levels, high blood pressure, and irregular heart-beat.[11] And while it has not been proven that noise has been a direct cause of death due to coronary attack, it has been well established that the risk of coronary attack is higher when one or more of the above-mentioned symptoms of noise exposure is present. Therefore, the connection between noise and risk of heart attack may be inferred. Indeed, the evidence was adequate to convince former U.S. Surgeon General William H. Stewart, who said in a keynote address to the nation's first conference on noise as a health hazard:

Donora [noise-induced] incidents occur daily in communities across the U.S. Not in terms of specific numbers of deaths attributable to excessive noise exposure, but in terms of many more than 20 cardiovascular problems . . . for which the noises of twentieth-century living are a major contributory factor.[12]

We cannot even consider the noises we think we are used to as anything less than sources of constant irritation. Furnaces, refrigerators, and air conditioners; the neighbors' radios, televisions and phonographs, all prevent people from experiencing the peace and quiet they need for real physical and mental health.

We manage to ignore these stimuli as we do all unavoidable irritating stimuli. But when we shut out a stressful stimulus we are also likely to reduce our sensitivity to other stimuli coming through the same sensory channel. Wilderness campers often notice that their hearing becomes keener after a day or two away from civilization, suggesting that in the city their hearing had become less sensitive in order to shut out the stressful noise.

Visual incongruity most likely has a similar effect. It may be more subtle, but nevertheless still reduces our sensitivities and possibly contributes to some physiological degradation.

The same thing can occur in response to social stimuli. When we are locked into social environments that conflict with our human nature, or that simply provide more social stimulation than we are capable of handling (as in overcrowding), we react by reducing our general level of sensitivity to social stimuli and become more or less callous and indifferent to others. This callousness and indifference carries over even to good social settings, and even to those we care for.

This is all part of a process of retarding or destroying human sensitivity to the natural and human environment. It must be considered to be a major problem of society.

ASSUMPTION TEN: Increasing the economic self-sufficiency of towns and regions would increase economic stability and security, both for towns and regions, and for the nation.

Towns and regions today are part of an extensive system of specialized production and distribution in which each town or

[10]Clifford R. Bragdon, *Noise Pollution: The Unquiet Crisis* (Philadelphia: University of Pennsylvania Press, 1970), pp. 68–72.
[11]Robert Alex Baron, *The Tyranny of Noise* (New York: St. Martin's Press, 1970), pp. 55–56.
[12]Ibid., p. 54.

region produces largely for export to the rest of the country.[13] Of course that network should not be scrapped entirely because it alone allows manufacture of items for which total demand is small (for example, commercial pizza ovens), and because it permits outside relief for regions suffering natural or human-made disasters. However, we have carried specialization further than is necessary or reasonable, particularly in food production. We have become so dependent on our system of distribution that we are alarmingly vulnerable to such disruptions of that system as war or natural disaster might cause, or to transportation cost increases resulting from fuel scarcity. It is frightening to think, for example, what would become of the inhabitants of New York or Tokyo if the food supply to either city were blocked for a few weeks or a few months.

ASSUMPTION ELEVEN: In order to improve the political stability of the world, the well-being of all the people on the earth should be of equal concern when decisions are being made that will affect their lives. This can only be accomplished if they share equally in the decision-making process. Every advance in this direction increases stability and the likelihood of the continuation of the human species.

Richard Barnet states that:

The choice is more democracy or much less. The effective participation of people in making the decisions that most directly affect them is the precondition for economic, political, and spiritual liberation. Until people can play a direct role in shaping their own physical and economic environment, they are not fully alive.[14]

The strongest argument for a political and economic democracy is that it is the noblest of all choices, recognizing a spiritual oneness of humankind.

A second issue is also important. The survival of humankind is at stake, and the failure to recognize the right for all people today to have the same opportunities to provide good lives for themselves will lead to unrest, increasing the chance of some sort of holocaust. Adlai Stevenson states:

We travel together, passengers on a little spaceship, dependent upon its vulnerable reserves of air and soil; all committed for our safety to its security and peace; preserved from annihilation only by the care, the work and, I will say, the love we give our fragile craft. We cannot maintain it half fortunate, half miserable, half confident, half despairing, half slave to the ancient enemies of man, half free in a liberation of resources undreamed of until this day. No craft, no crew can travel safely with such vast contradictions. On their resolution depends the survival of us all.[15]

As we begin to see that our own well-being is connected to the well-being of the larger body of humanity, our self-preservation instincts will work much differently. And if simultaneously we realize that because of the way we live, the resources we use, the way we use our technologies, and the way we build our cities, we are partially responsible for much of the human suffering in the world, then maybe we will change and restructure our communities so we can live with a more equitable portion of the world's resources.

ASSUMPTION TWELVE: The concentration of human populations into huge cities necessitates an economic system characterized by complex technology, high levels of energy use, a high degree of specialization, technical and economic interdependency, highly organized large-scale enterprise, and heavy capital

---

[13]Bedroom communities for commuters are no exception; they ''produce'' and export labor.
[14]Richard J. Barnet, ''The World's Resources, Part III—Human Energy,'' *New Yorker,* 7 April 1980, pp. 111–12.

[15]Adlai Stevenson, ''International Development—The Hope of the World'' (Speech delivered before the 39th Session of the Economic and Social Council, Palais des Nations, Geneva, Switzerland, 1965).

investment. Such an economic system in turn requires a high degree of social control over individuals in the society.

Social control can take a number of forms. It can be achieved through increasingly numerous and restrictive laws, rules, regulations, and administrative procedures. It can be achieved less overtly, through advertising, propaganda and news management, or by education that trains people early in life to think in certain ways. It can also be achieved through architectural design of the spaces people use. High population density is in itself a means of social control, since it makes people less able to provide for themselves and more dependent on the system. All of these methods of social control are very much in evidence in economically developed countries today.

As Amory Lovins points out, social control is necessary in a complex, highly interdependent economic and technical system because such a system demands very dependable, very predictable people to make it run smoothly. They must work when and where they are expected to work; they must buy when and what they are expected to buy. They must not often abandon their assigned roles to pursue some personal vision.[16] Security and safety are also more crucial in complex technical systems, and this demands increasingly thorough policing of people's activities and attitudes.

One of the tactics of social control is to persuade people that they are free. In our culture, this is done by encouraging the myth that today's mobility, anonymity, and lack of roots in community and family constitute personal freedom. A closer look shows that this "freedom" consists less of freedom to direct one's own life than of freedom to respond to the demands of the economic and technological system. When I speak of "personal freedom," I mean one's freedom to structure one's own life in response to one's own visions and priorities.

J. Andre, professor of psychology at California State University, Sacramento, argues that politics revolve basically around three fundamental psychosocial issues, each involving a conflict between two real and important psychosocial needs. One of these is the conflict I am discussing here, the conflict between the need for personal freedom and the need for social structure. Andre argues that in each conflict we must achieve some resolution that ignores neither of the two conflicting needs.[17]

Now, I believe that in our present resolution of this conflict we have given up too much individual freedom and accepted too much social control. More important, I believe we have done this because we mistakenly took the present structure of our densely populated urban areas and highly centralized technological system as a given. According to the assumption above, the present structure demands a high degree of social control. But the present structure is not the only possible structure. We have the option of developing a system that is more decentralized, less specialized, and based on a simpler technology that requires less energy and capital — a system that does not demand such heavy sacrifices of personal freedom.

I think that in the last 15 years we have already seen significant numbers of people moving in these directions as individuals — fleeing anonymity and regimentation by leaving cities and lucrative jobs in large organizations for small towns, for rural

---

[16]*Energy and Morality*. A film produced and directed by Swain Wolfe (distributed by Persistent Image, San Francisco, 1979).

[17]J. Andre, "Toward a Psychological Theory of Politics," California State University, Syllabus for Psychology 156/256. (Sacramento, 1975); M. A. Hudak, J. Andre, and R. O. Allen, "Delinquency and Social Values," *Youth & Society* II:3 (March 1980):353–68. Andre's system ("psychopolitics") begins with the assumption that human beings are primarily social animals (the "social metaphysic") who seek both solidarity with others (love) and status (power). This conflict between concern for the self and concern for the other is seen to be made up of three independent, bipolar components: self vs. the immediate other (love), self vs. all others (society), and self vs. the products of social thought (rationality). These three components taken together create the "social cube" which, at the level of values and political philosophies, is called the "psychopolitical cube" with the three dimensions of power-love, freedom-security, and emotionality-rationality. During the last five years, Andre and his students have amassed a considerable body of empirical evidence (18 studies with a total of over 2,000 subjects) which strongly supports his theory and relates it to such practical matters as socialization, delinquency, moral development, mental illness, social values, voting behavior, and interpersonal perception.

homesteads, or for self-employment or jobs in small local businesses. To do so they have had to depart from the mainstream of American society, and their willingness to leave the mainstream shows, I think, the beginning of a change in the mainstream itself.

Even if we had no concern for individual freedom, the mere cost of social control would give us reason to consider such a change. As writer-director Swain Wolfe puts it in his film *Energy and Morality*:

> At some point in the growth of an industrial society, the cost of maintaining social order will increase faster than the other areas of the economy ... The business and bureaucracy of social control is already a major industry in the U.S.[18]

Goals

From these assumptions we can extract a statement of an overall goal for planning human settlements. Human settlements should be designed:

- to meet basic material human needs, largely from within the settlement, but partly by participation in a larger economic system, in a diversity of ways all consistent with the preservation of a stable and healthy ecosystem
- to promote and support a way of life that permits satisfaction of psychological needs and simplifies the task of satisfying material needs
- to provide a physical and social environment harmonious with human nature

Listed below are some of the main features I would expect to see in any such settlement, which may be viewed as subsidiary goals. In reading them you will notice that there seems to be a great deal of overlap; I have not been able to come up with a neat classification of goals and solutions. I draw your attention to this because I think it is an inherent characteristic of a wholistic design approach. The aim of wholistic design is to allow everything to work together harmoniously, and you know you are on the right track when you notice that your solution for one problem has accidentally solved several other problems. You decide to minimize the use of automobiles in order to conserve fossil fuels, for example, and you realize that this will also reduce air pollution, encourage healthful exercise, reduce noise, conserve land by minimizing streets and parking, multiply opportunities for social contact, beautify the neighborhood and make it safer for children. Solutions like this do not lend themselves to neat categorical analysis.

Here, then, is a list of objectives I consider basic for a wholistically designed settlement:

- to approach self-sufficiency in energy through conservation and through maximum use of solar energy, wind power, and renewable sources such as woodlots and agricultural waste
- to manage water resources efficiently. In arid regions, for example, this means to minimize the demand for well water by reducing fresh water use, recycling *greywater*, and landscaping for absorption of storm drainage rather than for runoff
- to include diverse organic agricultural production for local consumption, in order to provide high-quality food free of dangerous chemicals, and to make use, through land application, of such wastes as sewage and greywater
- to maximize land use by including fruit and nut trees, vines, and vegetable gardens in landscaping of residential areas
- to reduce dependence on the automobile by encouraging foot and bicycle traffic, by providing all possible consumer services, jobs, recreation, education, and cultural opportunities within walking and cycling distance, and by general compactness of community layout
- to further reduce people's confrontation with automobiles by reducing streets designed expressly for cars and minimizing parking spaces

[18]Wolfe, *Energy and Morality*, p. 28.

- to produce as many consumer goods in the community as possible, with emphasis on goods and methods requiring little input of energy and scarce resources
- to provide useful, satisfying employment within the community for most of the residents, preferably in personalized small businesses locally owned and managed, with opportunities wherever possible for useful and educational participation by children and youth

- to provide opportunities for significant numbers of people from low-income groups to get job training if necessary, to buy housing, to find permanent jobs, and to become part of the community
- to provide the usual educational and governmental services as efficiently as possible
- to provide a physical environment and to foster a social environment that allows inhabitants to satisfy such basic psychological needs as security, community,

identity, and self-esteem, in diverse ways that do not involve excessive consumption

- to provide an overall planning process that: (1) is flexible and sensitive to the diverse needs of individuals and groups, (2) permits and encourages the inhabitants to become involved in design and development of the whole settlement and their own neighborhoods, and creates occasions for interaction and cooperation among them, and (3) incorporates at each stage of development the lessons learned from evaluation of previous stages.

- to provide a process for design review of proposed homes and other individual projects that is strong enough to maintain a harmonious visual environment in the neighborhood, and protect other valuable neighborhood qualities, yet sensitive and flexible enough to respond to individual needs and preferences

Again, this list represents only one way we might state what we consider the important goals of appropriate design.

When the goals for a project are complete and well defined, there is a much better chance of producing a good solution. A good solution also depends, however, on the procedures we used in planning, both in selecting goals and in creating plans and designs that are true to these goals. Thus planning procedures are crucial, and deserve serious consideration in their own right.

Procedures

We can talk about procedures for appropriate planning in two different senses. In the more literal and restricted sense, we would consider the procedures a designer or community might use, and what background they need to develop a coherent plan like those we have been discussing — a plan that deals simultaneously and harmoniously with all the various goals set for it. I will begin by discussing procedures in this limited sense.

In any such discussion, however, one inevitably begins to ask why such procedures are not in use already, why coherent plans are seldom made and almost never followed, and what it would take to change that. Once we ask these questions, our attention turns to politics, government, law, finance, sociology, education, and our national culture, and we find ourselves discussing procedures in the broader — very much broader — sense.

But first let us look at some design procedures; procedures in the limited sense.

Any plan for a human settlement intended to relate harmoniously to existing ecological systems must take detailed account of the particular characteristics of the site. It will not be possible to simply grade the site flat and superimpose a predetermined street plan. A detailed and sensitive process of site selection and site analysis will be required. Ian McHarg offers an inspiring view of how this might take place in his book, *Design with Nature*.[19] McHarg shows that careful consideration must be given to such diverse factors as topography, plant life, sun, wind, drainage, agricultural value of land, and so on. He also shows how systematic approaches, such as the use of overlay maps, can be of great value in finding a solution that reconciles these diverse factors. Planners trying to apply McHarg's ideas, however, must resist the temptation to use a system so slavishly as to blind themselves to problems or possibilities not included in the system. This is a particular danger with computer models, not because there is anything inherently wrong with the method, but because computers and computer printouts seem so formidably exact that people tend to forget the limitations of the model.[20]

---

[19]Ian McHarg, *Design with Nature* (Philadelphia: Falcon Press, 1969).

[20]Kern County, California, provides a good example. The planning staff there used a computer to inventory all land in the county in blocks of 10 square miles, and rate their desirability for various uses — urban growth, agriculture, and open space — according to 15 different factors. One of these is proximity to existing urban areas; land close to existing urban areas is rated more desirable for development than land farther away. This is a value judgment, and a highly debatable one; I would rather rate the land the other way around, for reasons I will explain in the next chapter. The point I want to make here is that the elected officials who make development decisions tend not to examine this assumption because they are hardly aware of it; it is hidden behind the computer model. All the officials see is the final numerical rating, and it seems so clear and simple that they are probably influenced by it somewhat no matter what verbal argument anyone may present against it.

Probably the greatest difficulty in site analysis and planning is that of making choices or trade-offs between conflicting goals — for example, what if the best building location for aesthetics and summer breeze happens to be a very inconvenient spot for sewage disposal, or if it happens to be on the best agricultural land. My own feeling is that problems like these can be complex, and so involved with subjective values that they have to be solved intuitively rather than exclusively through our skills as technicians. Computer models and other systematic approaches can help greatly in clarifying the problem, but the final solution must be a matter of skilled human judgment.

In much the same way as McHarg draws our attention to the many physical and ecological factors involved in good planning, a small group of social scientists has begun in recent decades to illuminate the social and psychological factors — the many ways in which design affects human behavior and mental health. Interest in such problems originally arose primarily from the need to explain the failures in the fifties of many large-scale public housing projects which had been designed to meet people's physical needs without much thought for their social needs. The most dramatic of these failures was the Pruitt-Igoe high-rise housing complex in Saint Louis, Missouri, which proved so nearly uninhabitable that it had to be dynamited.[21]

The work of these social scientists, however, has also done a great deal to explain the less dramatic shortcomings of our cities and suburbs as places to live — not uninhabitable, yet suffering from a definite malaise. It is becoming more and more apparent that cities and towns must be designed with social values in mind: designed to allow people to interact and cooperate with their neighbors; to give them a sense of belonging and being known; to allow them to change, improve, personalize, and otherwise affect their immediate surroundings; to provide safety and security in their homes and neighborhoods; to nurture the development of closer human relationships — friendship, intimacy, and family; to allow children to better see, understand, and participate in the society they are expected to grow up into.

Planning for a good social environment can be even more difficult than planning for a good physical environment, simply because human behavior is even more complex and unpredictable. Because of this, Robert Sommer,[22] one of the leaders in the field of environmental psychology, warns against planning based more on theories than on empirical observation. He feels it is essential to observe people in existing environments and listen to what they have to say about them. Interviews, questionnaires, and observations are among the useful tools for such evaluations. The information gained allows the planner to design what he or she hopes will be improvements. When these changes are incorporated in an actual project, social scientists must again listen and observe to see how people really react to them, so that planners can use what they learn in still another design. Sommer feels that planning aimed at improving the social environment proceeds best through such cycles of design, construction, and evaluation.

Appropriate planning, then, must occur through some sort of integrative process that takes into account a multitude of factors, both natural and social, and produces solutions that reconcile them as well as possible. Such planning is difficult to imagine because in our present society it is virtually nonexistent. For real examples, we have to look at settlements established before the Industrial Revolution.

In general, the earliest human settlements evolved naturally from small groups that shared the same basic assumptions and goals. Having limited technology and resources, their choices were fewer. Moreover, technological change took place much more slowly, so that the parameters of the design problem remained relatively constant, and this allowed a tradition of good design and successful solutions to develop. It was like Sommer's process of trial and improvement, carried out in a much more informal and leisurely manner. The results were strikingly functional and aesthetic.

The process was somewhat more complicated in the planning of ancient cities, but was unified by the central power of rulers who could commission architects and planners to weld the

[21]Marian Lies and Howard Palley, *Urban America and Public Policies* (Lexington, Mass.: D. C. Heath & Co., 1977), p. 172.

[22]Robert Sommer, *Design Awareness* (San Francisco: Rinehart Press, 1972).

needs of various groups into a coherent design, and execute it. Planning in Europe and the United States became more difficult as power was decentralized and interest groups became more divergent in their goals, and as technological change occurred at a faster rate. Inevitably, the results were more chaotic and less coherent.

In the past century, many planners, architects, and social critics have proposed use of a more comprehensive design process. Even the more cautious or less inspired new towns that have been built, like Columbia, Maryland, and Reston, Virginia, have created environments that were well organized as far as they went, and hint at the possibilities of planned development. But none of them has challenged the basic vision of suburbia, or addressed the problems of ecology and community. The best plans that have been put forward, like the garden city concepts of Ebenezer Howard, were never executed to their full extent because they never gathered enough backing.

I believe the basic problem is the fragmentation of power and authority over the planning process. There is no unified planning authority demanding designs that integrate a variety of needs and goals. The power over planning is divided among many individuals, officials, and institutions, each concerned only with some small part of the total picture — bankers concerned only with profit and financial security, public engineers concerned only with efficient sewage and traffic flow, and fire departments concerned only with providing adequate fire protection.

None of these problems is unimportant, but the official concerned with only one of them usually prefers to solve it in the easiest and most direct way. He or she has no responsibility for the overall plan, and therefore no incentive to be creative or flexible in solving his or her own problem. The fire fighter will want wide streets instead of considering smaller, more maneuverable fire engines; the banker will want to stick with plans that have been financially successful in the past. Any designer who wishes to see a comprehensive design adopted and executed today is likely to be forced into the role of educator, conducting special presentations or seminars for those in positions of authority, trying to make them see beyond their individual areas of concern. These efforts are likely to be met with some impatience or annoyance at first.

("Why are you telling me all this? All I need to see is the sewer plan.") They may eventually be rewarded with interest or even support, but it will be an uphill fight.

Still worse, the official with no responsibility for the overall plan may be more likely to use his or her authority to support personal prejudices in areas having nothing to do with his or her legitimate concern. For example, an officer of one bank I approached for development financing for my Village Homes project told me that the bank turned down my application not because the management doubted the financial feasibility of the project, but simply because it did not like what I was trying to do.

I think the only real hope for wholistic design is to create planning entities with enough authority of their own to develop comprehensive designs and carry them out in the face of a certain amount of opposition from special interest groups. At the same time, planning entities must have authority over large enough regions to allow them to develop integrated, coherent plans. What is "large enough" depends on what sort of planning we are talking about. To develop a coherent watershed plan for the Tennessee Valley required a planning entity covering parts of several states.

A regional planning approach, therefore, requires a hierarchy of planning entities. A regional planning agency would locate growth sites, both for new urban development and for redevelopment within existing cities, and would coordinate the planning for energy, water, and transportation within the region. Local planning agencies would handle the planning of garden cities or redevelopment areas under their jurisdiction. And within each of these local areas, there would be a community planning agency with jurisdiction over its own planning.

I think we should even go so far as to break these areas down into neighborhoods with their own planning entities. As an example, there are the design review boards in many recently planned neighborhood housing developments.

The reason for this hierarchy is to allow more of the decision making to take place as close to the place that is being affected as possible by having public hearings conducted before major decisions are made and by giving more access to those who make the final decision. This seems to be the most democratic way to approach planning. The planning process offers the greatest potential if the overall layout is designed in advance, including basic systems such as circulation, energy management, waste management, and major social services. Then, as the settlement is developed, the more detailed design of individual buildings and neighborhoods is left to smaller planning groups including residents and potential residents, under guidelines laid down by the overall planning entity. Approached this way, design could be an incredibly rich and satisfying process for everybody involved, and could restore our feeling that our neighborhoods are truly our own. It would also permit enough diversity and experimentation in neighborhood design to teach us what works and what doesn't.

Strong comprehensive planning will be politically feasible only where the general public understands the goals and assumptions of good planning and where individuals are ready to speak out and take action to see that such planning is implemented. Therefore, the role of education, both formal and informal, cannot be overlooked. The human-environmental relationship should be stressed in the earliest grades, and such education should be continued throughout a child's formal schooling. Films, books, and class curricula need to be expanded to include more in this area. Education of the general public must also take place. Again, films, books, courses, and seminars should be developed to broaden the public's knowledge.

The city of Davis has become nationally recognized recently for its environmentally sound planning policies. It is no coincidence that the University of California at Davis is the site of one of the first graduate programs in ecology in the nation. The citizens' group which was responsible for the city's innovations in energy planning was made up primarily of ecology graduate students. They so inspired and impressed the rest of the town with the urgency of responding to the energy crisis that constructive change became a possibility. Participating firsthand in the Davis experience taught me the value of education. Educated citizens can have an enormously beneficial impact on society.

Chapter 3
From Disorder to Order

To evaluate our urban structure and to consider new solutions we will have to consider what would be an appropriate distribution of the human population. We must ask:

- What is the most appropriate size for a community?
- What is an appropriate location for a community?
- What is the most appropriate population density within a residential neighborhood? Within a town as a whole? Within a group of towns, or a whole region?

I think these questions have some fairly specific answers. As you read, it will become apparent that I am not merely advocating "good planning" as a general thing, but arguing that good planning for America, for today, calls for a particular pattern of urban development that is quite different from the one we have seen. I am proposing a modular approach to both urban development and urban redevelopment. The module is a fairly self-sufficient moderate-density town with population between 7,000 and 30,000, and a certain general layout. The bulk of our future development, I feel, should be in the form of such modular towns, located singly or in clusters as appropriate to the site and region. Redevelopment of existing cities should aim at dividing them into clusters of modular towns.

This is an unusual approach because planners do not usually look at questions about size, location, and density as having any single correct answers. If you asked them about the appropriate size or density for a town, they would say, "It depends." Behind that answer is the belief that size and density in themselves do not matter a great deal; that there are no strong inherent advantages or drawbacks associated with particular size or density ranges.

I think this is incorrect, and a very serious error. This has not been apparent, however, until recently, for two main reasons. One is time lag. Our patterns of human settlement have changed drastically in the last century. The resulting social and environmental changes have been cumulative, and were not immediately noticed or understood by most individuals.

The second is our technology. Because of our technology, we have been able to tell families and businesses, in effect, "Locate wherever you chose. If it happens to be in the desert, we will bring you water — not just enough to drink and bathe in, but enough to grow a lawn and roses. If there is not enough space there for growing your food and disposing of your wastes, we will bring your food from somewhere else and carry your wastes away. If it is so crowded that social behavior is deteriorating, we will saturate the area with well-equipped police to protect you and keep people in line. If you want to live many miles from your job, we will sell you a cheap car and cheap gasoline to burn in it. If the area between your home and your job is already congested with millions of other people and their cars, we will build you a freeway to get you through quickly. Whatever problem you encounter there can be overcome by technology."

When we think of technology, we tend to think of it as ingenuity, as "American know-how." But technology, and especially today's technology, is also resources — steel, aluminum, concrete, petroleum and its myriad products, and above all, energy. The amount of energy our technology uses is not immediately apparent because a great deal of it is used indirectly. For example, in shipping food back and forth across the country, the energy used directly is fairly obvious; it powers the truck that transports the food, runs the refrigeration equipment that keeps it fresh, and so on. But making the truck also requires energy to dig the ore, transport it, refine it into steel, and machine it into parts; to heat or cool the factory, and transport the workers to and from their jobs. An economist would say this energy is "embodied" in the truck. But this is not all; also embodied in the truck is part of the energy required to build the truck plant and produce the materials for the plant; to make the machines that dug the ore, the mills and furnaces that refined it, and the cars that brought the workers to work: to locate and extract the oil and refine the gasoline that the workers' cars used.

There is a branch of economic statistics called *input-output analysis* that gives us estimates of the total amount of any resource embodied directly or indirectly in a particular type of good or service. These figures show that there is a great deal of energy embodied in almost all the goods and services we consume today. If energy gets scarcer and more expensive, everything gets scarcer and more expensive. Even recycling of nonrenewable resources gets more expensive, because it, too, requires energy.

We can already see this happening in our economy, and it is only beginning.

This is why I try to give specific answers to the questions concerning town siting, size, and density. It seems clear to me that some sites, sizes, and densities require more physical technology to make them work than others require — more nonrenewable resources, and more energy. So far we have pretty much ignored this fact in our planning decisions. As resources and energy become scarcer and more expensive, however, it will become harder and harder to do so. In order to maintain our standard of living, we will have to use energy and nonrenewable resources more and more frugally, and we will be led more and more toward those town sites, sizes, and densities that require the least energy and resources to make them work. We will also be led toward certain ways of laying out towns, certain ways of organizing production, and certain life-styles.

At the same time, as we become more aware of the ecological, social, and psychological consequences of various planning decisions, we will be led toward those sites, sizes, densities, layouts, life-styles, and so on, that allow us to live most harmoniously with our natural environment, with each other, and with ourselves.

It is my belief that these forces will all tend to lead us in the same general direction. In this chapter and the following ones, I describe what I think that direction will be. It will not be backward, but sideways, toward the kind of society our science and ingenuity might have produced if energy and resources had been scarcer all along, and if we had better understood the social and ecological consequences of the changes we were considering.

Location

In this century, the location of new development has been determined almost totally by politics and short-term economics with little consideration for long-term planning or for the ecological implications. There are some exceptions. Building on flood-plains has almost stopped. Sometimes open space is preserved for its own sake if it has some special quality, and at times, prime agricultural land is avoided. None of this has much affected growth patterns, however, except by reducing leapfrog development, because the most immediately desirable location for the next bit of development is always on the outskirts of an existing town, convenient to existing services and activities. The political and economic power of landowners on the outskirts, who stand to make huge speculative gains if their land is developed, also supports concentric growth. If there happens to be nothing but prime agricultural land on the outskirts, planners will talk gravely about the undesirability of building there, but in the end, development will proceed. Many times more serious problems are not even addressed, such as the folly of further building in areas such as the Los Angeles basin, where air quality is already abominable and water must be imported from hundreds of miles away. The burgeoning population that destroyed a once-beautiful city and scenic agricultural valley is already suffering from the past lack of planning, yet building continues.

Thus planning for new towns goes hand in hand with restricting the concentric growth of existing towns. Fortunately, there seems to be a willingness, especially in towns of moderate size, to restrict growth. Petaluma, California, where the growth restriction was unsuccessfully contested in court, is probably the best known example. Davis, California, and Boulder, Colorado, are others.

Where further growth is desirable, new towns located close to an existing city can substitute for amorphous concentric growth of the existing city. There should be a buffer zone of open space around each new town to give it a distinct identity and keep overall density low. The buffer zone need not be wide so long as there is strict control to keep it from being eaten up by later concentric growth of old or new towns.

In the near future, it may be necessary to locate much of the new development away from existing urban areas in locations that provide more of the attributes necessary to sustain a population in ecologically sound ways. This could lead to clusters of new towns or linear strings of towns in what are now rural areas. I believe that this could be done without destroying the rural setting if the towns are sited in the way that many European towns and villages are — small and with definite boundaries.

Locating sites for these new towns will be a difficult job. There are no perfect sites for new towns; some sites are merely preferable to others. It seems to me, however, that there are three factors of primary importance:

- availability of water without nonsustainable demands on groundwater
- potential for local production of a variety of wholesome food
- potential for meeting energy needs locally

Without these, it is impossible to talk of local self-sufficiency in any meaningful sense. They are also primary factors in energy demand. Transporting water and food to areas where they cannot be produced requires tremendous amounts of energy and resources. The same is true of transporting energy, though this is not immediately obvious because we are used to the idea of transmitting electricity great distances via high-voltage lines. But do do this, we must first convert energy in some other form into electricity, which is generally inefficient, and very wasteful compared to using the energy where it is produced, in its original form — heat, for example. Even when we generate electricity directly from wind or by hydro, the longer the distance it must travel the more we lose due to resistance in the transmission lines.

Here are some of the other factors that I think are important in selecting a site:

- absence of high air pollution and radioactivity; climatic conditions that will sufficiently dissipate additional air pollutants produced by the new town
- absence of agriculture using toxic chemicals, unless a buffer zone can be provided
- potential for development of an economic base; sites permitting development of some natural resource, as through agriculture, forestry, fishing or mining, or sites

near existing industrial centers are preferable
- proximity to existing transportation corridors such as freeways, railroads, and waterways
- low risk from natural hazards such as earthquake and floods
- proximity to a major cultural center
- scenic beauty, quietness, and pleasant climate

Once we have listed all the features of an ideal site, we must rank them according to importance. This is a very subjective job, and is heavily influenced by one's assumptions and goals. I favor giving precedence to ecological soundness, social values, and long-term stability, rather than to immediate convenience and economy. This often leads me to decisions that may appear uneconomical by traditional standards, including selection of sites that may have been considered unthinkable for development. I want to emphasize that such sites may appear uneconomical only because of the perverted popular idea of economy that ignores hidden costs and benefits, and future costs and benefits. Decisions favoring a healthy ecological system, and a humane and sustainable life-style for humans, will also appear economical whenever we look at the whole picture.

In many cases, intelligent public policy could bring out this underlying economy and take advantage of it. For example, building a new town may initially appear more inconvenient and costly than enlarging an existing one, for a number of reasons. But it also turns cheap rural land — perhaps even land with no agricultural value — into valuable urban lots whose worth increases as the town develops. In a growing old town, this increase in value normally accrues to speculators and other property owners as speculative income. But new town development could be administered so that if approached in the right way, the increase in value would be captured by the developing entity and used to offset the costs of establishing the town.

Locating new towns in rural areas may then be one of the best ways to deal with the scarcity of funds for building the basic service structure of the community as a result of decreased tax revenues.

Size and Density

Since the development of the automobile, urban sprawl has become our dominant pattern of development. It has created vast cities and megacities of uniform medium density, having neither the advantages of the true compact city nor those of the country.

The pattern I think we should work toward is one of small, relatively moderate-density towns with enough distance between them to give lower density overall. Moderate density within the town would have the advantage of providing stimulating social contact and eliminating most of the need for automobiles. Low regional density would reduce air pollution, allow local agricultural production for each town's needs, permit easier waste management and recycling, and put the countryside within easy walking distance of every home. This is essential if we are going to live within the limits of renewable energy supplies, maintain a healthy environment and ensure sustainable food production.

The ideal population for such a town would be between 7,000 and 30,000. This is a compromise, because both large and small populations have their advantages. A town with a larger population can support a greater variety of commercial services and job opportunities, and might be able to provide some city services (both utilities and social services) at a lower cost per person. The League of California Cities holds that 7,000 to 8,000 is the minimum population necessary to support adequate municipal services. I think this would also be the bare minimum for the degree of self-sufficiency I would hope to see in a new town, and larger would be better.

A small population, on the other hand, would give the town as a whole a stronger sense of community and would allow each resident a greater voice in government. Also, since the town's land area would be limited by the need to keep everything within easy walking and bicycling distance (two to six square miles), a smaller population would mean less crowding, which would make it easier to generate enough energy, recycle wastes, and disperse air pollution. On these grounds, I think 20,000 to 30,000 would be the maximum feasible population for a new town of this pattern. It is interesting to note that Ebenezer Howard projected 30,000 as ideal.

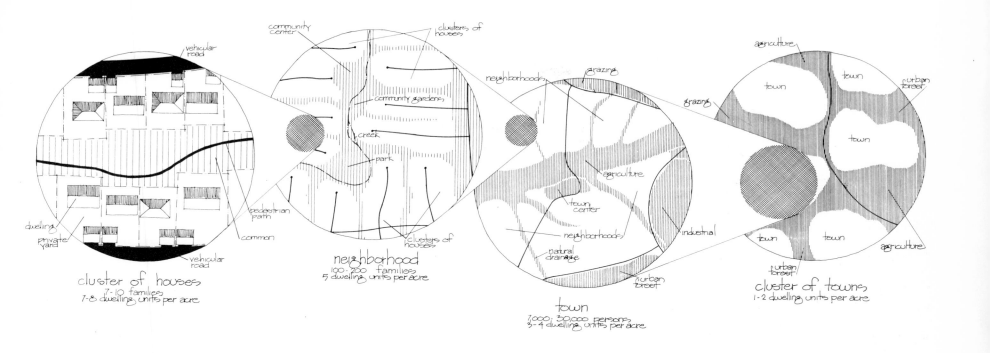

cluster of houses
7-10 families
7-8 dwelling units per acre

vehicular road

dwelling

private yard

vehicular road

pedestrian path

common

neighborhood
100-200 families
5 dwelling units per acre

community center

clusters of houses

community gardens

creek

park

clusters of houses

town
7,000; 30,000 persons
3-4 dwelling units per acre

neighborhoods

grazing

grazing

town center

agriculture

neighborhoods

natural drainage

urban forest

industrial

cluster of towns
1-2 dwelling units per acre

agriculture

town

town

urban forest

town

town

town

urban forest

agriculture

Let us see what this implies in terms of density. Taking a town with an area of three square miles and a population of 20,000, and assuming an average of 2.7 people per housing unit, we get an overall density of about 3.9 units per acre. If we assume that residential lots would take about half of the land, we get a maximum density of 8 units per acre within clusters of houses. These densities should fall in a range that avoids a feeling of overcrowding. Neighborhoods should have enough open space to reduce the density to about 5 units per acre. Commercial and civic areas, parks, and strips of intensive agriculture between neighborhoods would bring the town's overall density down to 3 or 4 units per acre. Finally, even the closest clusters of towns should have enough buffer space between towns to keep the overall town-cluster density below 1 or 2 units per acre.

A residential density of seven to eight units per acre is rather high even by present development standards; even duplexes on today's small lots average around six units per acre. However, I do not feel it represents overcrowding, for several reasons. First, de-emphasizing the automobile will save a great deal of space that is presently devoted to streets and parking. Second, the sense of overcrowding depends to some extent on design as well as density, and during the reign of the automobile, we have lost much of our sense of how to design comfortable compact housing. There is much improvement we can make, much of it merely by relearning traditional design solutions used before the auto, such as the court-garden style of house that appears in various forms all over the world, in a wide range of climates and cultures.

Some planning critics today would feel that the densities I propose are far too low. They favor extremely high urban densities, achieved mainly by using multi-unit structures and by eliminating the private yard. The extreme of this school of thought is represented by the massive, many-storied single-structure cities proposed by Paolo Soleri. A more moderate example is a cluster of housing complexes of two to six stories, separated by public open spaces, as in the Le Corbusier Marseilles Block Project in France. Proponents of very high population densities generally feel they are necessary in order to conserve agricultural land and to preserve areas of wilderness and sparsely populated countryside. They also argue that multi-unit dwellings save building materials, and that they conserve energy by minimizing heat loss through exterior walls.

That they require somewhat less building material is true, but their energy savings are probably very small if they are located in a large urban area. Any energy savings in multi-unit buildings may well be offset by the energy required to transport food into a densely populated area and transport waste out of it. Air pollution and noise also become more concentrated in densely populated areas.[1]

I have noticed that I consume less energy at home in Davis than when I visit Los Angeles or San Francisco. In Davis when it gets warm in the car, I roll down the window. In Los Angeles, I join the masses of humanity who roll up the window and turn on the air conditioner. I feel guilty about this, but I simply cannot tolerate breathing the smog–laden air on the freeways. Similarly, at home in Davis I open the windows at night when it's hot, but in the city I

[1] As used here, "air pollution" refers to such contaminants as carbon monoxide, hydrocarbons, nitrogen oxides, sulfur dioxide, and particulate matter. It does not refer to photochemical smog, formed by the action of sunlight on complex hydrocarbons in auto exhaust, which poses a different sort of problem. Unlike other pollutants, which are most concentrated near their sources, smog tends to spread evenly over an entire air basin; therefore, dispersing the sources within an air basin helps very little. The only solution to a smog problem is to reduce the total amount generated within the basin. This is one important reason for limiting population in enclosed air basins like the one behind Los Angeles.

succumb to keeping the window closed and turning on the air conditioner so that I am not kept awake by the noise from outside.

I think that the ideal urban densities are those that allow most of the needed energy to be produced on or near the site, as well as most of the food; that allow waste to be recycled on or near the site; and provide enough space to disperse smoke and other air pollutants. In effect, we are looking for densities that do not exceed the holding capacity of the land.

Conservation of agricultural land is a stronger argument for high urban densities, but I think it is not as strong as it appears at first. If population growth must occur in locations where only good agricultural land is available for development, high densities may be justified. But I think it would be more to the point to ask why population growth should take place in such locations at all. Because we are used to urbanization and concentric growth, we tend to assume that growth must take place around existing population centers, and that we have little choice in the matter. But with the kind of self-sufficient modular towns I am proposing, we do have a choice; we can locate them pretty much where we want. Even in our richest farming areas, we can find potential sites of little or no agricultural value. These same sites often have special aesthetic appeal. So far they have not been much used because they are slightly more expensive to build on, and require more imaginative planning. But if we are seriously interested in preserving agricultural land, these are the sites we should be developing.

On a rocky or hilly site, development could actually increase agricultural productivity, simply because of the detailed attention the home gardener is willing to give to terracing, erosion control, and soil improvement. In many cases, homeowners could produce food on land that would normally be rejected for farming.

My major objection to very high population densities, however, is simply that they create an inhumane environment for people to live in. It makes little sense to me to talk of preserving the beauties of the wilderness and the open country, which most people will experience only now and then, if the price is forcing

people to spend the other 98 percent of their lives in a stifling environment.

Studies of large communities of animals in the laboratory and in natural settings have shown that there are severe behavioral consequences when overcrowding occurs. John B. Calhoun has found that overcrowded rats exhibited deviate, increasingly bizarre social behavior until the animals were unable even to reproduce.[2] This suggests that evolution has equipped these animals with orderly ways of relating to each other which depend on the possibility of a certain amount of space between individuals, and which break down when that space is not available. It is not unreasonable to suspect that the same may be true of human beings, and we do not have to look far for *prima facie* evidence that it is. Crime, drug and alcohol addiction, poverty, prostitution, anonymity, broken families, gang warfare, and other maladies traceable to breakdowns of human social interaction are all more prevalent where population density is high.

I do not dispute the fact that humans are very adaptable, but I believe that adaptation often costs us a great deal. We are not tied absolutely to instinctive behaviors as animals are, but I believe we are better equipped by evolution for the sorts of behavior we used for tens of thousands of years before the recent development of cities. When those behaviors no longer suffice due to crowding, we lead impoverished lives because we are not constitutionally suited to the new behaviors we are forced to invent. These unnatural behaviors, I suspect, interrupt the normal flow of emotions and perceptions, and this limits the individual's capacity for self-actualization. The individual experiences this primarily as a feeling of emotional deadness and secondarily as an actual physical malaise.

High population density has its most obvious effects on the poorest and least mobile individuals living in the inner cities, but the effects also reach the upper economic levels. The more affluent tend to lose their sensitivity to the value of life and their capacity for helping and caring about others. They are forced to

[2]John B. Calhoun, "Population Density and Social Pathology," 206 *Scientific American* (February 1962):139–46.

suppress their natural compassion for the less fortunate individuals they see all around them because their numbers make the problem so overwhelming, or because they fear for their own safety if they get involved directly. This suppression carries over into the rest of their lives, where it translates into a general coarseness, cynicism, and lack of sensitivity and humor.

Also, I think that human lives tend to be impoverished by a lack of private or semiprivate open space. Public open spaces and natural areas within a city are better than none at all, of course. But if we assume that humans are by evolution most at home in a natural environment, it follows that each of us needs a bit of the natural at home; a piece of earth where we can enjoy sun, wind, rain, and growing things in privacy; and where we can fully interact with nature—not merely observe and experience, but dig, plant, prune, and harvest. This is especially true for those of us (the majority) who do not work on the land for our living. Public green spaces between multistory housing complexes are no substitute for the private or semiprivate yard.

It is significant that people seeking a high state of awareness or a high spiritual level have traditionally gravitated to natural settings with limited populations, such as mountains or deserts. I am sure many of us have personally experienced the soothing effect of retreating into the countryside or wilderness. Social scientists H. H. Iltes, P. Andrews, and O. L. Loucks have stated:

Unique as we may think we are, we are nevertheless as likely to be genetically programmed to a natural habitat of clean air and varied green landscape as any other mammal.

To be relaxed and feel healthy usually means simply allowing our bodies to react in the way which one hundred millions of years of evolution has equipped us. Physically and genetically, we appear best adapted to a tropical savanna, but as a cultural animal we utilize learned adaptations to cities and towns. For thousands of years we have tried in our houses to imitate not only the climate, but setting of our evolutionary past: warm, humid air, green plants, and even animal companions. Today, if we can afford it, we may even build a greenhouse or swimming pool next to our living room, buy a place in the country, or at least take our children vacationing on the seashore. The specific physiological reactions to natural beauty and diversity, to the shapes and colors of nature (especially to green), to the motions and sounds of other animals, such as birds, we as yet do not comprehend. But it is evident that nature in our daily life should be thought of as a part of the biological need. It cannot be neglected in the discussions of resource policy for man.[3]

Critics of the ideas I have presented here on density and crowding may argue that my conclusions are highly speculative. Admittedly, they are. Nevertheless, planners are required to make decisions every day regarding densities and access to open space. Until we have evidence to the contrary, I think it is wise to proceed with the following two assumptions: (1) humans have limits on the kind of environmental conditions to which they can adapt, and (2) the kind of environment we evolved in is the best guide to what we are physically and socially comfortable with.

[3]H. H. Iltes, P. Andrews, and O. L. Loucks, "Criteria for an Optimum Human Environment," manuscript 1967 (Quoted in Paul Erlich, *The Population Bomb* [New York: Ballantine Books, 1968], pp. 55–56).

Chapter 4
Security and Choice

As we prepare for the design of our communities, for both new development and the rehabilitation of existing cities, we must consider carefully how we will satisfy our basic needs. How will we get our water, our food, and the energy we will need to be comfortable and to pursue the activities which contribute to our well-being? Will we have adequate shelter? How can we be sure we will have the resources we need to sustain ourselves and how can we use them efficiently?

The key to a community's long-range security and stability lies in its ability to meet these basic needs locally. Failure to do this leaves a community subject to the hardships caused by disruptions like the 1978 truckers' strike that created temporary shortages of goods in many parts of the country, economic downturns such as the Great Depression of the 1930s, or even by some unforeseen natural catastrophe.

While I advocate a high degree of self-sufficiency for communities, I wish to make clear that I am not proposing total self-sufficiency, or the economic insularity of communities in existence before the advent of the railroad and highway. I am merely saying that there is no need to organize our economy so that virtually all goods have to be shipped from place to place using large amounts of energy as they are today.

Food is an outstanding example; only the smallest fraction of the food consumed in the average town today is produced in or around that town. The rest is shipped in, often from great distances. There is no inherent reason why this must be so. Today's towns have to import virtually all their food primarily because they were planned with no thought for food production.

This situation exists because, over the years, we have changed from a system of local production and consumption to a system of highly specialized, centralized production and distribution for consumption all over the country, indeed the world. So today, virtually all planning for satisfaction of our basic needs takes this high-technology, high-energy economic system as given.

I think it makes a lot of sense for each community to have its own dependable supplies of water, power, and other resources, and to be producing enough food and other essential items to be able to sustain itself at a subsistence level in an emergency. It should also be producing enough other goods and services for export to equal what it imports. There is a definite advantage, however, in keeping exports and imports to a minimum. Otherwise the community will be more economically vulnerable, because it depends on the outside not only to produce the goods it imports, but also to buy the goods it hopes to export to pay for those imports. It is vulnerable to changes in both supply and demand that are entirely outside its control.

There are benefits in being part of the larger economic system; that is, in having access to a much wider variety of goods and services. But this is only an advantage up to a certain point.

One example of what can happen to a region that exports what it produces and imports what it consumes is the situation that exists in some of the coal-mining communities in Appalachia. The local resource that the community has is coal. It is owned by outside interests, so the profits are spent outside of the community. It is true that the workers' salaries bring money into the community, but they do not represent the value of what the community is producing. A large percentage of the people work in the mines, so very few of the products the community consumes are produced in the community. Therefore, most of the money that people earn working at the mine must be spent for importing goods and services.

This leaves the community in an extremely weak position, because anything that stops coal production also stops the community's major source of income, bringing the already weak local economy to a grinding halt. This is not a hypothetical situation; it has happened over and over in the lives of many people living in local communities dependent mainly on one form of industry, especially when owned by outside interests.

In any of these localities the situation would be totally different if the community were more diversified in its industry and production, and if the profits from the industry were retained in the community. Many of the Appalachian communities, rich in resources, water, and energy, and with reasonably good growing seasons, could be prosperous and economically stable communities if those changes were made.

I believe that building more self-sufficiency into our local economies is not only of value to the people who would live in them, but it is also an important step in achieving a high degree of national security.

With a productive system that is decentralized in the sense that local communities are able to produce a high percentage of their basic needs, and centralized in the sense that the overall economy produces a variety of more specialized goods and services that are exchanged throughout the system, the nation could maintain a reasonable amount of stability during a major disruption. Our present centralized system can handle an emergency like a localized disaster by providing relief from outside. But the more decentralized system would have an advantage in a major disruption such as a nationwide energy shortage. In this case, each locality would still be able to produce the essentials and maintain a reasonable livelihood even if the problem was of fairly long duration.

Another very important advantage in having more self-sufficient communities is that more of the decisions that affect people's lives can be made locally, giving people more choices that represent real freedom. People will be more free to choose how their resources are used, what kinds of working conditions are acceptable, what energy supplies are used, and what environmental consequences are acceptable. When there is more local control, the votes and voices have much more significance, and when we can personally speak with the owner of a business we have more ability to persuade.

Our present form of commerce has effectively funneled the control of much of the local economic wealth — land, minerals, capital, and energy — into the hands of a few giant businesses. Richard Barnet cites numerous examples, frightening in their implications, of ways in which the world economy is increasingly falling into the hands of huge multinational corporations, or into the hands of international groups of national corporations that operate in concert with the cooperation of the national governments.[1]

Richard Strout, a veteran political correspondent for the *Christian Science Monitor*, also discusses this concentration of wealth:

> Concentration of American business is extraordinary. In 1977 the top 50 banks, for example, held assets of $600 billion. A Library of Congress report last year noted "that oil companies now own almost 50 percent of the known U.S. reserve of uranium ore." They have bought coal mines, too. The oil companies have (also) been scouting around for

[1]Richard J. Barnet, "The World's Resources, Parts I, II, III," *New Yorker*, February, March, April 1980.

non-oil investments; Atlantic Richfield owns the London Observer. Tenneco owns Holiday Inns . . . Mobil was the $11 billion company that absorbed Montgomery Ward.[2]

To say that *control* over wealth is concentrated is not the same as saying wealth itself is concentrated. The final owners of a corporation's wealth are the shareholders, but control over that wealth is mainly concentrated in a few hands. Wealth itself is distributed very unequally in our society, but even if wealth were equally distributed, concentration of control would be a cause for concern.

The larger an enterprise becomes, and the more power its managers have, the further they are removed from contact with workers and customers, and from the human needs the enterprise supposedly serves. Their only measure of success in operating the enterprise is often monetary profit, and it does not matter whether they make that profit by serving people or by harming them. It is acceptable to pollute the environment in order to keep costs down. It is acceptable to create artificial wants through psychological advertising, rather than meeting people's real needs. It is acceptable to treat workers like machines. It is possible and acceptable to buy political influence to evade laws intended to protect the public, or to get laws passed that discriminate in the corporation's favor. In a local business, managers have less power, and have too much contact with individuals and the community to feel comfortable with such practices because the community has more access to the local businessperson.

At the same time, control of a large portion of the nation's real, tangible wealth — particularly land and natural resources — puts large corporations at an economic advantage. As population increases and resources become scarcer, the prices of these resources rise, and they increase tremendously in value, as evidenced by current rates of inflation. Shareholders of large corporations benefit from this increase in value, at the expense of the majority of the population who lose more and more to inflation. This tends to increase the existing economic inequality.

The same process also increases the political power of corporations. Because these businesses control scarce commodities, they realize tremendous capital gains on the sales of their products and are able to use part of their profits in lobbying efforts designed to influence legislation. Recently, to get around legislation intended to limit campaign contributions, they have set up what are known as PAC's:

Big business is increasingly political. The rise of the corporate Political Action Committees (PAC's) is one of the changes transforming politics. Corporations and unions are forbidden to give directly to candidates but can set up special committees to raise and distribute money. There are around 800 corporate PAC's now (six times the figure of four years ago). There are more all the time.[3]

I do not think that there is some grand conspiracy on the part of these companies; it is rather part of a process that has gotten out of control because there is no proper preventive legislation.

I liken this process to a larger, more complex game of Monopoly. In Parker Brothers' Monopoly game, one player eventually gains enough wealth to squeeze everyone else out. In the real world, there are a number of winners — a select group of large national and multinational corporations. These businesses control virtually all of our natural resources, thereby exerting considerable control over all the other players. There are also a number of individuals in the game who are for the time being doing pretty well. But time is on the side of those who hold the strategic properties (in the Monopoly game Boardwalk and Park Place; in real life the resources, land, and energy supplies).

But what about the losers? Obviously, the elderly and disabled, the poor, and others living on a fixed income are struggling just to remain in the game. Wage laborers also lose, though not so heavily. Another group that has received attention lately as being hard hit by this game is the small farmer. Just as the

[2]*Sacramento Bee,* 27 April 1980.

[3]*Sacramento Bee,* 27 April 1980.

small lumber holdings were gobbled up by large corporations in the sixties, small farms are being gobbled up today. Jack Anderson recently discussed this problem in his column, "Washington Merry-Go-Round":

> For 60 years, the Curtises have been part of the American family farm tradition, the backbone of America's food supply. In 1975, Pete Curtis bought the family farm from his father. He wants to pass it on to one of his five children — if he doesn't lose it to his creditors. They have triumphed over hail, drought, disease, and other natural enemies. But today, economic forces more devastating than any natural pestilence may wipe them out. Small family farms, although they still make up 80 percent of America's 2 million farms, are in jeopardy. If small farmers like Curtis go under, they will be replaced by great agribusinesses . . . some owned by investment companies more interested in tax shelters than in working the soil. . . . With the decline of the family farm, a part of America will die. The loss would be more than nostalgic. There is evidence that small farms, in which the families work the land and care for it because they own it, produce higher quality agriculture than do the agribusiness monsters.[4]

Richard Harwood, Ph.D., director of Rodale's Organic Gardening and Farming Research Center, agrees:

> Generally, I see the major problem as large-scale, centralized agribusiness replacing small-scale, regionalized farming in this country. Such agribusiness is dependent on complex interactions in our economy and the availability of cheap energy — much more so than small local farms. Today we see single-owner farms disappearing across the country.[5]

It appears to me that the phenomena of economic expansion, high technology, high energy use, and centralization of power are the results of oversight and bad planning — of bad game rules, in terms of the Monopoly analogy. The basic rules of the Constitution of this country are excellent. But important rules have not been legislated or bad rules have crept in as times have changed too quickly, and as unforeseen circumstances required expedient, rather than carefully considered, action.

Changing the rules is always hard because the people who are winning like the rules. Today we see that the resources that keep the lights shining on this game are running out. But the winners, caught up in what I call the *fascination syndrome*,[6] lustful for more and more power, wealth, and victories, will go to any extreme to keep the game going. They will perpetuate this unhealthy system by influencing politics through lobbying, influencing people's views of the world through advertising, selling unnecessary items and welcoming any new sources of energy (even potentially dangerous ones) with open arms and a blind disregard for their possible consequences. For these people, anything goes to keep the game going.

If you are having trouble understanding my analogy of the Monopoly game, play a number of games with some friends. Pay attention to your emotions as you play, and see if you don't start to understand the syndrome.

Meanwhile, the game goes on; dangerous industrial wastes are polluting our land, air, and water, and people are

---

[4]*Sacramento Bee*, 29 April 1980.
[5]Carol Keough, "The Coming Food Crunch," *Organic Gardening*, May 1980, p. 90.

[6]The "fascination syndrome" is a state of being in which an individual is fascinated with one or more of the gamelike qualities of society that deal with power, money, manipulation, technologies, and organization. People become so intent on playing the game that they lose an overall perspective of any deeper meaning of life — who they are, where they are going, and their connectedness with the rest of the world. This fascination with intrigue and strategy can affect all portions of the population and is most likely an out-of-control expression of a normal response to the environment that has helped humans adapt to a wide variety of situations. It is an aggressive response to the environment, both social and physical, controlling and manipulating it in order to assure self-preservation.

suffering large-scale unemployment or menial employment which undermines their self-respect. Mahatma Ghandi was well aware of the threat of overmechanization:

> Every machine that helps every individual has a place. But there should be no place for machines that concentrate power in a few hands and turn the masses into mere machine-minders, if indeed they do not make them unemployed.[7]

It appears that Ghandi's concern was well founded; many of us have become machine-minders, some on the automated production line and others behind desks from eight to five; in both cases making a salary, but also helping concentrate the wealth. Others have become unemployed and have little hope, under current circumstances, of finding employment.

We can begin to solve the problems of menial jobs, unemployment, pollution, and lack of security for our communities and the nation, by redesigning our communities to include features that make them more self-sufficient. Richard J. Barnet suggests that:

> In the United States, we could start by redefining "national security" to make the security of local communities a prime national goal. Locally raised tax money should be used to develop community-based energy systems, development banks, and other institutions to revitalize local economies. Our national policy should be designed to enable communities to undertake a variety of such initiatives.[8]

Individuals and communities can begin to take responsibility for themselves by providing their own basic needs of water, food, shelter, goods and services, energy resources, and by recycling wherever and whatever they can.

[7]Schumacher, *Small Is Beautiful,* pp. 34–35.
[8]Richard J. Barnet, "The World's Resources, Part III — Human Energy" *New Yorker,* 7 April 1980, p. 109.

Water

On the scale of physical priorities for human existence, water ranks above the needs for food, clothing, and shelter. Second only to air as a necessity for survival, water plays a role in every aspect of our lives. Our bodies are about 65 percent water by weight, and in plants the percentage can be much higher.

We are inextricably bound up with the cycling and recycling of water through the ecosystem. The same water that we are carrying today as body weight may have come fairly recently from the sea. Having evaporated from and subsequently returned to earth as rain or snow, it was drawn from rivers or from wells, and we absorbed it by drinking and eating. After leaving our bodies, this same water will return to the atmosphere eventually to rain down again over land or sea, and the cycle continues without end.

While each of us needs a regular supply of drinking water to sustain ourselves, that amount is small in comparison with what we use every day around our house, and the amount we use in agriculture and industry.

Because water is essential to human life and the functioning of society, people have always tended to settle mostly in areas with good, natural water supplies. In days before the development of modern well-drilling technology, the location of communities was more limited to areas with sufficient surface-water resources. More recently, thanks to technological development and cheap fossil fuel energy, we have brought water from deep underground aquifers or from areas with an abundance of water via aqueducts to meet the needs of growing cities situated in areas of scant rainfall and very limited surface water. Today we are being forced to consider the high energy costs of pumping water through aqueducts or out of deep wells to be used in the drier parts of the country. We are faced with the fact that overdevelopment has been allowed to occur in areas that should be supporting much lower densities of population, based on water resources that are available at reasonable cost and can be relied on from year to year. The future quality of life in these areas will depend on a willingness to set limits on growth, and to reduce water consumption to a level compatible with economical and

reliable supplies. Failure to address these issues could lead to water shortages and bitter struggles, problems potentially more severe than the energy crises that began in the 1970s.

Besides keeping the volume of our fresh-water demands in line with the natural supply, we need to safeguard our supply for future years by controlling pollution. Contamination of underground and surface waters by toxic chemicals, heavy metals, and other dangerous residues has become so widespread that people in some areas of the country now drink water that is not even up to minimum official standards of safety.

In 1979 and 1980, tests conducted by the California State Department of Health showed that well over half of the groundwater wells in the San Joaquin Valley are contaminated with the agricultural chemical DBCP (1,2 dibromo-3 chloropropane). There was also evidence of localized industrial chemical contamination of groundwater wells near the Aerojet Company (by TCE, trichloroethylene) in Sacramento, and the Occidental Chemical Company in Lathrop (by DBCP). Further, tests have shown groundwater wells in the entire Los Angeles Basin area to be contaminated with TCE. According to the supervising sanitary engineer for the California State Department of Health, these agricultural and chemical pollutants have rendered the water unsafe for human consumption to the point where even showering with the water would be dangerous.[9] A recent study conducted jointly by the Environmental Defense Fund and the New York Public Interest Group found that some of the most potent cancer-causing toxins, and chemicals known to cause birth defects, were found in the water that served the people in and around Poughkeepsie, New York. Unfortunately, these two are not isolated examples. In 1975 the Environmental Protection Agency did a check of 79 cities across the United States and found that all samples contained cancer-causing chemicals.[10]

To reverse the trend and clean up our water along with other parts of the environment will require a serious and sustained effort from all of us. We are now beginning to hold industries responsible for cleaning up some of the pollution they have caused and to make them devise means of cleaner production for the future. Industries that produce by-products which pollute surface and underground water should be halted. Likewise, as consumers we need to consider the environmental impact of products we buy and try to choose those whose production, use, and disposal pose the least danger to the earth and its inhabitants in the long run. Communities can help to insure that they have

[9]California State Department of Health, Sanitary Engineering Section, Fresno, California, Gunter Redlin, Supervising Sanitary Engineer, personal communication.
[10]Carol Keough, *Water Fit to Drink* (Emmaus, Pa.: Rodale Press, 1980), p. 19.

adequate water supplies of a high quality by getting control of those supplies and using them wisely.

In many situations new supplies will be sought after. Instead of relying on contaminated rivers and wells, we may have to rely more on the collection of rainwater and storage of it in cisterns as has been done in many places in the past. In many areas, community water supplies can be improved by starting reforestation projects. At present, forests are disappearing from the earth at an alarming rate, and the results will be far more serious than most of us realize. Besides producing oxygen and preventing erosion of topsoil, forests help the earth to hold a reserve of fresh water accumulated during rainy seasons, to be released gradually throughout the year. Communities that invest the time and effort to replant the surrounding countryside where deforestation has occurred will be rewarded with a more dependable and abundant supply of water, as well as a healthier, more diverse ecosystem and a more pleasant environment. In developing areas, natural drainage that retains the natural creeks, swales, and native plants can be used to offer these same benefits.

Water conservation practices can be carried out by individuals and by industry and agriculture just by taking the time to find out where water is being wasted, and to devise means of using it more efficiently. Since our habit, acquired during the cheap energy era, is to waste water indiscriminately, we can reduce consumption dramatically just by taking simple precautions against waste. In homes, people can be careful not to run the water while brushing teeth, shaving, or hand washing dishes. Washing machines and dishwashers can be run only when full. Low-volume shower heads, water faucets, and flush toilets are simple devices that save water and energy. Gardens can be watered during cool hours of the day to minimize water loss by evaporation. In many cases, food-producing plants and trees can double as ornamental plantings, making more efficient use of both space and water. Drought-tolerant shrubs, trees, and ground covers can also be attractive, and require less care than plants with high water requirements. Industries, including agriculture, can maximize their use of recycled water, rather than fresh water, wherever possible. The economic incentive exists, as energy prices rise and reserve water supplies diminish, for both businesses and individuals to become more efficient water users.[11]

Low rainfall areas are not the only places where people need to conserve water. Even in areas where actual rainfall totals are high, the supplies of fresh water are still limited, and the water demands of industry and individuals should be kept at levels that allow a safe margin for yearly weather fluctuations. We must also remember that the more water we use, the more energy we will have to use for pumping and, if necessary, treatment.

The details of each community's water system design will depend on the unique characteristics of each local environment and the resources available. But whatever type of system is adopted, it should meet three basic requirements: efficient use of energy, high quality, and long-term sustainability without contamination. To the degree that our water systems pass these tests, we will be on our way to sound management of this essential resource.

In the final analysis, conserving our water supplies, keeping them pure, and using them wisely, will depend on each community acting on its own behalf. Richard Barnet states, "The most persuasive students of water politics seem to be those who urge the return to local communities of the responsibility for providing a safe and ample water supply." He further states that communities may well find that they have no alternative but to take three essential steps:

One is to raise the price of water to more nearly reflect its precious nature. A second is to take public control of crucial water supplies. Private ownership of the rainfall is beyond reason. A third is for communities to get together and resolve water conflicts themselves. Such regional planning is more likely to emerge from the bottom up than by an elaborate mechanism of ukases and bribes from Washington.[12]

[11]See Murray Milne's excellent book, *Residential Water Conservation*, California Water Resources Center, University of California, Davis, 1976, for water-saving ideas and equipment.
[12]Richard J. Barnet, "The World's Resources, Part II — Minerals, Food, and Water," *New Yorker*, 31 March 1980, p. 91.

Food Production

Food is next on the list of basic human needs. Because of the quantity we eat and because it must be consumed on a regular basis, food gathering and production has been one of the major activities of humans from the early hunter-gatherers to today's farmers, food processors, and grocery shoppers.

Of all the changes that humanity has undergone, the adoption of cultivation techniques, which brought about changes in the way we secure our food supplies, may be the most significant. It allowed humans for the first time to augment the production of the natural environment and to settle down and form the first permanent communities. As agricultural techniques were improved, largely through the use of plows and draft animals, production efficiency increased, enabling larger and larger concentrations of people to live far from their source of food.

Today less than 5 percent of American workers are involved in farming. It is large-scale, highly mechanized, fossil-fuel and chemical-dependent agriculture which has made this situation possible.

Unfortunately, just as we have made mistakes with other technologies, modern industrialized agriculture has brought with it many social and environmental problems. The most severe is that we have produced a system that leaves people highly vulnerable to disruption in the food supply system. Most people have little more than a few days' to a few weeks' food supply at home and no means to produce their own. While food in the United States seems relatively inexpensive, we pay a higher price for it than most of us realize. Low prices result partly from the exploitation of farm laborers being paid extremely low wages for the value of their work; many of them, in addition to their wages, require social welfare payments, which means that we pay even more for food when we pay our taxes. Low prices are also maintained by the presence of a few corporate farming operations whose objectives are less to profit from the sale of agricultural products than to take advantage of tax write-offs, and who thus can afford to sell their products at lower prices. Thousands of small farmers are being forced out of business annually due to competition from such tax-subsidized large farm operations. Food prices are also low because energy used in production is underpriced relative to other forms of energy and subsidized through tax incentives to oil companies. So again we end up paying the extra cost when we pay our federal taxes.

Also, there are costs which result from environmental problems created by chemical pollution from pesticides and fertilizers, costs that are generally not added to food prices. These are what economists call external costs, or *externalities*. The producer who creates the external costs does not have to pay the cost of the damage done by, for example, pollution of water; instead it is absorbed by the entire society through increased health care costs and government cleanup expenses. Since the producer does not have to pay the cost created by his action, the cost is not reflected in the price of the product being sold. But the consumer still pays indirectly, at some later time, so what appears to be a very economical system is really not so economical at all. It is difficult to determine exactly how much our food does cost us. Certainly it is more than it appears.

There is a growing scarcity of energy that the industry so heavily relies on. Producing chemical fertilizers and insecticides consumes a major portion of our energy supplies. Also, mechanization has changed agricultural field-production methods from labor intensive to energy intensive. It takes lots of energy to manufacture tractors, combines, and other large agricultural equipment, and still more to keep them running.

Soil erosion from current farming methods is causing the loss of critical amounts of topsoil from our farmlands. A report from Rodale Press states that 1 inch of topsoil is lost every four years, and this is from a base of only 5 to 20 inches of topsoil in most parts of the country. The report says:

To make matters even more appalling, these soil loss statistics do not end here. In addition . . . there is serious erosion caused by snow melt and improper irrigation techniques that does not figure into U.S. Soil Conservation Service soil loss analysis. On top of this must be added the cylical wind-caused erosion which varies from 3.2 tons per hectare in Nebraska to 36.8 tons per hectare in Texas. The 10 Great

Plains state's average soil loss to wind erosion is over 13 tons per hectare. According to General Accounting Office statistics, losses are higher per hectare today than in the Dust Bowl years of the thirties.[13]

The hazards to human and animal health from exposure to pesticides through their application is becoming a serious problem. David Pimentel and John H. Perkins estimate that, "The direct damages that pesticides do to the environment and to society add up to an annual cost of $839 million."[14] In addition to these costs we must address the question of how much human suffering from disease is caused by eating the pesticide residue in our food.

Another problem that one cannot really put a price on, but real nonetheless, is the deteriorating quality of our food. Today's tomatoes are bred not for taste but for ease of mechanical harvesting and convenience in packing. Thanksgiving turkeys that come more often frozen than fresh and that contain added fat, sodium, sugar, artificial color and flavor and other chemicals, and that are pumped up with water are just not going to taste as good as freshly killed, unadultered ones. And the added fat, sugar, and chemicals certainly can't make them any better, nutritionally, for you.[15]

Most of these problems are summed up in a U.S. Department of Agriculture report on organic farming. The report, in reference to a survey, states:

It has been most apparent in conducting this study that there is increasing concern about the adverse effects of our U.S. agricultural production system, particularly in regard to the intensive and continuous production of cash grains and the extensive and sometimes excessive use of agricultural chemicals. Among the concerns most often expressed are:

(1) Sharply increasing costs and uncertain availability of energy and chemical fertilizers and our heavy reliance on these inputs,

(2) Steady decline in soil productivity and tilth from excessive soil erosion and loss of soil organic matter.

(3) Degradation of the environment from erosion and sedimentation, and from pollution of natural waters by agricultural chemicals,

(4) Hazards to human and animal health and to food safety from heavy use of pesticides,

(5) Demise of the family farm and localized marketing systems.

I believe that to begin to solve these problems we will have to take three steps. Number one is to move in the direction of organic farming. Quoting again from the Department of Agriculture's report on organic farming:

The increasing cost of chemical fertilizers, pesticides, and energy inputs and/or their uncertain availability may lead to increased organic farming in the future. As input price relationships change, some farmers, especially the mixed crop/livestock farmers, or those operating small farms, may find organic farming just as economical or even more so than chemical-intensive farming. Much can be learned from organic farming about reducing soil erosion and nonpoint source pollution. Small farms, many of the mixed crop/livestock farms, and farms with access to ample quantities of organic wastes, could be shifted to organic farming methods in the future without having a large impact on total agricultural production.[16]

[13]Medard Gabel, *The Cornucopia Plan: Organic Paths to Food Security* (Emmaus, Pa.: Rodale Press).

[14]David Pimentel and John H. Perkins, *Pest Control: Cultural and Environmental Aspects* (Boulder, Colo.: Westview Press, 1980).

[15]For more about the food industry's role in the production and processing of our daily fare, see Jim Hightower, *Eat Your Heart Out* (New York: Crown Publishers, 1975).

[16]U.S. Department of Agriculture, "Report and Recommendation on Organic Farming Science and Education Administration," annual report (1980).

The second step is to encourage and support the smaller agricultural operations and family farms. This means almost total reversal of the trend that is occurring today. It will take government support of laws like an acreage limitation on water available for farmers from government water programs. We will have to insure that farmers receive a reasonable return for their produce in terms of the time, labor, and money required to grow the food. It is a mistake to insure minimum wages and other benefits to other sectors of the economy but not to farmers, as this results in all but the large corporate farms gradually going out of business — exactly the direction farming is going today. And the huge factory farms that are left cannot produce the same quality food that the small family farmer takes pride in growing. The workers on these huge farms are there only for the sake of wages, often under miserable conditions; the owner is often not a farmer at all, and not a resident on or near the land. Under such conditions, where is the motivation for quality? Just about the only sector that benefits from this situation is the huge petrochemical industry. As farmland is allowed to deteriorate, more chemical fertilizer is required to keep plants growing. Also, the plants grown on depleted soil need more pesticides, fungicides, and other agricultural chemicals every year because they have lost much of the natural resistance that plants grown in organically enriched soil possess. The increased use of chemical poisons deteriorates and contaminates the soil still further, and a vicious cycle is set up.

How can this destructive cycle be broken and avoided in the future? It can be accomplished by recognizing that a thriving small-farm industry is vital to a healthy, stable economy, and by guaranteeing, as in other sectors of the economy, that a fair return can be earned by the farmer, commensurate with the time, effort, and expense he incurs in the production of quality food. It is also vital that there be established strict guidelines as to which farming methods are acceptable in terms of their long-range environmental and health ramifications.

Small farms are best suited to organic agriculture, but there is a tremendous need for education of the farmers and would-be farmers in the skills and theory required to make this kind of farming a success.

Fortunately, there are already many individuals and organi-

zations working hard to see that these skills and knowledge are available for those interested in organic gardening and farming. Alan Chadwick, master horticulturist with deep insight into the workings of nature, has influenced the lives of countless young people and others who have seen or read about the awesomely beautiful gardens he has created, all without the use of chemical fertilizers or pesticides. His garden at the Santa Cruz campus of the University of California has brought worldwide admiration, and the lectures he has conducted in that setting have transformed the

lives and ideas of many of his listeners. He deals with the attitudes of humans, their mismanagement of the natural environment, and the unhappy consequences of modern man's lack of wisdom.

Chadwick's lectures are taken from his own life's experience and not from any book. Perhaps this is the main reason why they tend to affect his listeners so deeply as to change their lives. One of those listeners, John Jeavons by name, took on the task of researching the production possibilities of Chadwick's method of gardening. Over the past eight years, John and his staff of research gardeners and apprentices have conducted experiments to find out how Alan Chadwick's method can be utilized to produce the highest yields possible. They hope to provide the basic scientific information which will enable a farmer using these techniques to make a good living from a tiny piece of land. The result could be a tremendous increase in per-acre productivity of farmable land. John and his associates are continuing both research and educational work through Ecology Action in Palo Alto, California, and an excellent primer on Alan Chadwick's method of gardening is now available from them.[17]

On a larger scale, research and educational work is being done on all facets of organic farming and gardening by the Rodale organization based in Emmaus, Pennsylvania. Ever since the late J. I. Rodale began advocating the basic principles of organic farming, Rodale Press has been making people aware that organic methods do work and that the results of organic gardening and farming benefit everyone on many levels. At their Organic Gardening and Farming Research Center in Maxatawny, Pennsylvania, important research is being conducted which will add greatly to the knowledge of how best to make organic agriculture work for humankind.

Charles Walters, with his monthly publication, *Acres, U.S.A.*, is taking another approach — working to expose the American people to the dangers and grim consequences we can expect from toxic technology, and how this system is perpetuated and propagandized by certain huge financial interests. *Acres, U.S.A.* publishes case reports of successful farmers who use ecologically sound methods, and descriptions of the latest products and technologies for nonchemical farming.

The list of people and organizations working to promote a

[17]John Jeavons, *How to Grow More Vegetables Than You Ever Thought Possible on Less Land Than You Can Imagine* (Berkeley, Calif.: Ten-Speed Press, 1979). Publications on the technique may be obtained from Ecology Action of the Mid-peninsula (2225 El Camino Real, Palo Alto, CA 94306).

nontoxic, environmentally sound system of agriculture is long and growing. The educational task before them, however, is monumental, especially with certain industries, whose self-interests lie in preserving the present situation, pouring huge amounts of money into perpetuating the myth that petrochemical farming is the only way to feed the world.

The ''educational'' materials put out by the chemical companies, the land-grant colleges and extension services, and the various departments of agriculture, have almost universally ridiculed the idea that petrochemical farming could be replaced by a viable system more in harmony with nature. Present economic policies, if continued, may indeed prevent a successful transition to better farming practices, but it is not true that natural farming itself is untenable. If the agricultural colleges of today are not aware of how to make natural farming work, it will be up to the communities themselves to find those whose knowledge and experience can be passed on to farmers, and to set up their own local farming schools. Classes could be offered for home gardeners, community gardeners, and larger-scale farmers. The curricula in all these classes could consist of the same basic principles, applied in different ways, suitable to the scale of production.

Consumers, too, could benefit from classes dealing with the basics of an environmentally sound agriculture, and how their choice to buy one product instead of another directly influences which type of farming can succeed. For example, produce grown by natural methods should look attractive and fresh, but it need not be exactly uniform in size or color, and if there are a few small holes in a leaf of lettuce, this is not a matter of any consequence at all compared to whether or not the growing plant has been dosed several times with a deadly poison, whose residue could affect the health of the consumer. Such a readjustment of consumer attitudes could be a great step toward making small-scale natural farming an economically viable enterprise for growing numbers of people who would like to become small farmers if the chances of economic success were good.

The third step in stopping the adverse effects of our modern agricultural system is for people to grow more of their own food. There is already a substantial trend in this direction. A 1978 Gallup poll revealed that 42 percent of the nation's households raised at least a portion of their own food—a greater proportion than at any time since World War II.

How can we bring all three of these steps about? We can design our communities so that food production can take place at a number of levels: the individual household or group of households, the neighborhood community, the town as a whole, and the small neighboring farm.

Production at the household level is the most ecologically sound in terms of saving energy, and also in terms of using space efficiently. Vegetable gardens, herbs, fruit and nut trees, and grapevines can be integrated into private yards and small common areas to serve many of the same purposes as purely ornamental landscaping. Even a household with little interest in agricultural projects can enjoy the benefits of low-maintenance fruit trees and grapevines. Chickens or rabbits can be raised in a small space and fed partly with kitchen scraps and lawn trimmings. Their manure, together with garden waste, yields compost that is of great value as a mulch and fertilizer. Most households that make a serious effort at food production can supply a significant percentage of their food needs on residential lots of average size.

Even in the northern and high-altitude climates, making use of a well-designed solar greenhouse can provide good cool-weather fresh vegetables all winter long. This is the time of year when grocery store produce is likely to be high priced and low in quality, due partly to the extra transportation and handling required to import it from warmer regions still in production. And in cases where the greenhouse is attached to the home, it can reduce heating bills by donating some of its solar-heated air to the rest of the house, especially on cold but sunny days.

A number of households can arrange to plant trees and vines with varied ripening dates, within their individual yards or in a common area, and share the produce, so that they will all have a constant supply of ripe fruit in season and some left over to preserve for the rest of the year. Chickens or rabbits can also be raised as a group project; cooperative efforts many times can save time and space.

Either way, this smallest-scale agriculture provides an opportunity for community interaction. As a group project, it requires consultation and cooperation among households. And as an individual household project, there will often be surpluses to share with the neighbors, and this, too, provides occasions for social contact.

Agriculture at the neighborhood community level offers a different set of advantages. Like private yards, the neighborhood open spaces, whose function is to reduce density and give visual variety, can be landscaped with plants that produce food. Such varieties as *Rosa rugosa,* blueberry, and pineapple guava can be used as ornamental shrubs; nut trees can be used for their shade and ornamental value.[18] Orchard, vineyard, and vegetable crops can be planted as border barriers or landscape relief. Other plants

[18]Mark Podems and Brenda Bortz, *Ornamentals for Eating* (Emmaus, Pa.: Rodale Press, 1975).

usually considered purely ornamental provide forage for bees.

Beekeeping has two very important functions in the community. The first is to pollinate the crops. Without an adequate population of bees, production of many fruits and vegetables is lowered drastically. The second function is the production of honey, which is slightly more nutritional, and can be used in place of sugar.

Food processing, such as drying fruit, shelling nuts, and food storage can often be done more conveniently or economically at the neighborhood level, since it involves equipment and facilities that a household or group of households could neither afford nor fully use. The neighborhood in many instances could maintain community root and fruit cellars, frozen storage, and dry storage at a much lower cost per household than if each household provided its own.

Agriculture at the neighborhood level can provide jobs for a few agricultural workers that would give them a visible and respected place in the community. It would also create opportunities for children to become involved in the food production process either informally or through their schools; this would not only be educational for them, but would also give them a healthy sense of self-esteem by allowing them to make a real contribution to their families and their neighborhood.

Agriculture at the town level should aim to fill the gaps left by household and neighborhood food production. Seeds and grains, for example, would probably not be grown by households and neighborhoods because they are produced for feed and for storage rather than consumed fresh, and because they could be grown much more efficiently on a larger scale, in fields of five acres or more. The same would be true for hay, and for certain types of produce for drying, canning, and juicing. Town-level agriculture would also supply fresh produce for the town's markets and restaurants, and through the markets, for the down-town community. Finally, town-level agriculture might grow regional specialty crops for export, or for use by a town business such as a winery or a soy sauce factory producing for export.

In order to ensure a priority on production for local use, and to prevent the use of dangerous chemicals or other practices not in the public's best interest, the town should retain ownership of farmland that is within its borders and lease it to individual farmers. The lease should be extended for as long as the land is properly cared for and its productivity maintained. Agricultural spaces within the residential neighborhoods, however, might be owned by the neighborhoods themselves through their neighborhood associations.

If possible, agriculture should extend beyond the circumference of the town. A mixture of forest, grain crops, dairies, poultry farms, and orchards and vineyards can create a beautiful setting for the perimeter of a town. Forests can supply grazing land, wood for energy and construction projects, and the natural setting necessary for human fulfillment. Grain crops can provide food for people and animals and can be used for alcohol fuel production. Dairies and poultry farms which would be more difficult to locate inside the town could still very efficiently supply the town with dairy and poultry products.

In general, the agricultural policy of the community should be formulated to help small, family-size farms remain profitable, rebuilding the traditional relationships between the town and the small-scale local farmer.

Goods and Services

We cannot speak of the goods and services necessary for a community without speaking of the nature of the occupations that produce them. The value to society of the goods and services, and quality of them, reflect almost directly the well-being of the laborers as a result of the working conditions. Products that rely less on mechanical energy and more on human energy usually are of higher quality and have a higher aesthetic value. Where this is not the case, a good argument can be made for using technology. However, whenever business is considering the introduction of new technologies and manufacturing techniques, all of the ramifications should be considered. Such things as the amount of energy that would be used by the new system, the effect of the system on employment (both quantity and quality), and functional and aesthetic factors must be taken into account if we are to make responsible decisions.

I think these principles are borne out by the changes I have seen in the home construction industry in the past 20 years. When I began working in construction, carpenters (to take one trade as an example) had a deep understanding of overall construction. They were highly skilled with their tools, and they produced quality work which reflected their pride. Their wages were not high, but were very close to those of a schoolteacher. But gradually their interest shifted toward higher wages, and away from the satisfaction of good work. Contractors, in order to pay carpenters higher wages and still compete, encouraged faster and sloppier work. The traditional hammer with a claw for pulling nails was replaced by the *rigging axe* — a hammer with a hatchet blade that enabled one to simply hack away at the wood if the lumber did not fit together well. Instead of showing neat, precise construction with straight, perpendicular walls, a wood-framed house is now often so irregular that workmen joke that it "looks like an earthquake hit it before it was finished." As a result of this shift from quality to quantity, carpenters have much less pride and satisfaction in their work, and seem to enjoy it much less than they did 20 years ago.

There is a vicious circle here. The worker, having accepted the idea that work is almost inevitably dull, unpleasant, unreward-ing, and destructive of his well-being and human dignity, feels that he deserves a high wage for enduring it. Employers respond to high wage demands by trying to use workers' time more efficiently, through organization or automation, which tends to make the work dull, unpleasant, unrewarding, and destructive of the workers' well-being and human dignity. It also reduces the number of person-hours of work needed, and therefore the number of available jobs, leading to unemployment. This unemployment is not limited to the obvious sort that appears in labor statistics: the number of people actually hunting for jobs. It also includes young people pursuing unnecessary schooling because they can't find work, housewives with grown children who would enjoy a challenging job but can't find one, and those holding marginally useful government jobs. Finally, the speeded-up work may become less-skilled work, so that eventually it commands a lower wage than before.

We tend to forget, more and more, that the value of work to human beings is not measured entirely by the product. Doing the work may in itself be valuable or worthless to the worker; stimulating or boring; or supportive or destructive of his health, happiness, and sense of self-worth.

When I was young, I learned patience and skills building model airplanes and trains. It would take hours to produce a model, and I found great satisfaction in having accomplished the job. But today, years after I started making models, I notice that kids can buy plastic models that can be assembled in a matter of minutes and look far more authentic than the ones I built. The product itself looks better, but I wonder what the kids learn from this, and how the experience helps them grow? This is a clear and simple example of how technologies have seduced us and helped to produce an unsatisfying society. Again, I notice that young people today use more drugs and alcohol than we did when I was a boy, and I suspect that they, like many adults, are drugging themselves in response to their boredom and dissatisfaction.

Companies and workplaces today tend to be designed almost solely for efficient production, with little regard for their impact on the happiness of the workers or their consistency with the rest of the workers' lives. Thus, it is common to see people spending dreary hours commuting to jobs far from their communities, where they work in a harsh, noisy environment, doing uninteresting tasks which permit no initiative or creativity, and whose ultimate purpose they often do not understand.

I believe that economic activity should be drastically reorganized so as to satisfy, or at least be consistent with satisfaction of people's social and psychological needs. Work should take place in a pleasant environment not too far away or too separate from the workers' community life. This does not necessarily mean less efficient production, but even if it does require some sacrifice in productivity, a result, for example, of a switch to smaller-scale production, it is worth it. Production is not an end in itself. Goods and services are valuable only because they satisfy human needs. It makes no sense to sacrifice human values in the workplace for a few more goods and services.

Two restaurants in my hometown exemplify, for me, the extreme ends of the spectrum of business style. One is the Blue Mango, which is owned and managed cooperatively by those who work there. The nucleus of the group that started the restaurant is composed of members of a local amateur dance company, who already knew each other as friends and had learned to work together. I feel very comfortable eating there. The physical arrangements and decor are pleasant and show a good deal of care and individuality. The cooks, waiters, and waitresses generally seem to be at ease on the job, and to enjoy what they do and do it well, possibly because they are working for themselves and not to please some supervisor. Many of them eat there themselves and hang out there in their leisure time, reading or chatting. Their attitude communicates itself to the customers, and makes for a pleasant ambience. It also leads them, I think, to provide very personal attentive service to customers, without any obsequiousness. I have a great deal of faith in the wholesomeness of the food they serve, because I know some of these people are concerned about good nutrition and would not want to serve bad food, especially to their friends who eat there.

Directly across the street is a branch of a national fast-food franchise chain. The decor is harsh and standardized, and it is designed more for durability and easy cleanup than for anyone's enjoyment or comfort. The workers are underpaid and closely supervised. They have to be closely supervised because they

have no reason, either financial or personal, to care whether the business succeeds or fails. The work they do is so simplified and standardized as to appear incredibly boring. What they say to customers is also standardized, and their smiles are mechanical. I have very little faith in the food they serve because it's all shipped in partially prepared by the franchiser; the workers have no knowledge of or control over the ingredients, or any interest in their wholesomeness.

Many other productive enterprises now carried out by large, centralized, impersonal businesses could just as well be handled by small, friendly local businesses. In France and other European countries, fresh and wholesome baked goods and cold meats are still produced by neighborhood bakeries and *charcuter-*

ies, instead of by a few large manufacturers. Clothing and furniture can also be produced efficiently on a fairly small scale.

At first thought, it might appear that small local businesses would not suffice for complex industries or mass production, because we assume that such operations have to be carried on in mammoth centralized plants. But Paul and Percival Goodman argue in *Communitas* that:

> . . . this universal and obvious assumption is probably false: it fails to consider the chief social expense in all large-scale production, labor time.
>
> It is almost always cheaper to transport material than it is men.
>
> If the plant is concentrated, the bulk of workers must live away and commute. If the plant were scattered the workers could live near their jobs, and it is the processed materials that would have to be collected for assembly from their several places of manufacture. (We are not here speaking of primary metallurgy and refining.) The living men must be transported twice daily; the material and mechanical parts at much longer intervals.
>
> Which transport is easier to schedule? The time of life of a piece of steel is not consumed while it waits for its truck: a piece of steel has no feelings. Supply trucks move at a convenient hour, but the fleet of trains and busses congests traffic at 8–9 A.M. and at 4–5 P.M. If the men travel by auto, there is mass parking, with one shift leaving while another is arriving, and the factory area must be still larger to allow for the parking space. After one gets to this area, he must walk to the work station: it is not unusual for this round trip to take three-quarters of an hour. During part of this shifting, the machinery stands still.[19]

If the Goodmans were writing today, they would probably emphasize that it also takes more *energy* to transport people than to transport materials.

A return to decentralization and smaller businesses paves the way for a return to direct marketing. This has its own advantages of creating more satisfying human interaction and reducing costs by eliminating the need for wholesalers and warehouses.

In his study of direct marketing, Rober Sommer has observed that in farmer's markets, the prices are lower and the food is fresher. But beyond that, there are social advantages:

> A farmer's market is a community event. It is a place where people congregate and exchange ideas and talk "neighborhood" and politics. By contrast, the supermarket is a sterile and desocializing environment.[20]

Sommer notes that direct marketing is beginning to enjoy a renaissance. Ten years ago, for example, Massachusetts did not have a single farmer's market; this summer there will be more than 30 of them in operation.

I believe as decentralization occurs and smaller businesses reappear, direct marketing will be a natural occurrence. Craftspeople who sell or deliver directly from their shops or homes, and farmers marketing their own produce, will become the most efficient and energy-conserving distributors.

I would like to remind you of the basic assumption presented in Chapter 1: increasing economic self-sufficiency will increase economic stability and security. It should be obvious that we have carried specialization too far, and are now so dependent on our system of distribution that we are in a highly vulnerable situation. If, for instance, our access to imported oil were eliminated, portions of the country might well be unable to obtain certain basic necessities such as food.

Our dwindling energy supplies demand that we find a new system for the supply of goods and services. A move in the direction of decentralization offers a very appealing solution, using less energy, offering more security, and increasing our personal choices of how we will satisfy our basic needs.

[19]Paul and Percival Goodman, *Communitas: Means of Livelihood and Ways of Life* (New York: Vantage Books, 1947), p. 83.

[20]Robert Sommer, "Direct Marketing, Point/Counterpoint," *Western Fruit Grower,* February 1980, pp. 10–11.

Housing

Shelter is another of the basic human needs. It provides protection from variable weather conditions for people and their belongings. It also offers protection from intruders, indicates territorial bounds, and provides a sense of security. The use of shelter has permitted humans to inhabit most of the earth's land surface, providing warmth in otherwise uninhabitable locations. For thousands of years the process of building and using shelters has been a basic part of the human living experience. Because of this it seems reasonable to believe that there is a basic predisposition that motivates humans to obtain shelter, satisfying both a physical necessity and psychological needs. This predisposition results in a pattern of housing preferences which manifests itself in most cultures.

Given a choice, most people want their own homes for their immediate families. They want privacy and they want their house to be connected to the earth, giving immediate access to the outside. It is also a desire that the outside surroundings be a part of the family's domain. As a society plans for the housing needs of its people, it would be very shortsighted not to recognize these desires and the importance of satisfying them. We must also recognize the need to provide for individuals who do not fall into the mainstream of society by assuring whatever alternatives, whether they be communal housing, high-rise apartments, or whatever.

Providing the type of housing desired by people is easier said than done, especially today with housing prices and the cost of construction increasing faster than wages. And providing good housing for low-income people is almost impossible. The solution to these problems lies in returning to the method by which people built their shelters for thousands of years, by building it themselves. It is only recently in time that the specialization of labor has created a situation where most people are not directly involved in the construction of their own houses.

For most people in our society, a lack of skills in design and construction is one of the main obstacles to building one's own house. Many people have overcome these obstacles by reading books on the subject, or just digging right in and starting the project and learning while building. We are now seeing the emergence of shelter schools which should make the problem of learning the required skills easier. Several of these practical owner-builder training centers are now in operation in various parts of the country.

For example, the Shelter Institute of Bath, Maine, was established in 1974 by Bowdoin College physics professor Charlie Wing, *Maine Times* editor John Cole, and Canadian lawyer Pat Hennin and his wife, Patsy. The Hennins continue to operate the school, which at this writing has taught more than 4,000 amateurs how to design and build their own homes (some 1,000 dwellings have been constructed), and Wing has now organized a similar school, Cornerstones, in Brunswick, Maine. Heartwood, in Washington, Massachusetts, and the newer Northern Owner-Builder, in Plainfield, Vermont, have followed the lead of these pioneers.[21]

Each of these schools offers amateurs the opportunity to combine theory and hands-on experience in a series of weekend and extended courses. Their goal is to help nonprofessionals overcome their ignorance and fear of what was once a most common endeavor. The courses are intensive and nurturing; no one is expected to know very much upon enrolling, and instruction is patient, personal, and comprehensive.

[21]For further information contact:

Shelter Institute
33 Center
Bath, ME 04530

Heartwood School
Johnson Road
Washington, MA 01235

Cornerstones
54 Cumberland Street
Brunswick, ME 04011

Northern Owner-Builder
RD1
Plainfield, VT 05567

A sampling of Cornerstones' course offerings illustrates the variety of experiences offered: Energy-Efficient House Building (the basic three-week course); Earth-Sheltered Housing; Energy-Efficient House Renovation; Passive Solar Greenhouses; Passive Solar Design for Professionals; and House Building for Women. Courses at the other schools explore the mysteries of finish carpentry and timber framing, "envelope" housing, and site selection and preparation.

On the West Coast, in Berkeley, California, a nonprofit organization called the Owner-Builder Center provides a range of classes, consultation, and other help for people who want to build their own homes. The center estimates that you can save 20 percent serving as your own general contractor; 44 percent by also doing the finishing work; 58 percent by doing all of the building; and 65 percent if you yourself build with labor-intensive recycled materials.[22]

The Owner-Builder Center suggests several steps to follow. Once the land is purchased, spend a lot of time on your property before you start to build. Plot the angles of the sun at different times of the year, note prevalent wind conditions, the view, privacy, and access. The biggest mistake in owner-builts is the lack of design. Often using an architect will prevent expensive changes once you start building and find the design was not right.

Next learn how. Not just the actual skills, but become familiar with the overall processes that are involved. Read books. Take classes either from groups such as Owner-Builder or university extensions, junior colleges, and free universities. If you can, practice on a small outbuilding first.

Next, get the tools you need and acquire the materials you will need. Now, you can start the hard physical work of building the home. The Owner-Builder Center reminds people that they will make mistakes but help can be obtained from people who have gone through the process before, from professionals, or from groups that provide consultations at the building site itself.

There is no question that owner-built houses require a

[22]*House Building – Volume I* (Berkeley, Calif.: Owner-Builder Center, 1979), p. 4. (The Owner-Builder Center, 1824 Fourth Street, Berkeley, CA 94710.)

large investment of time and energy, often greater than one imagines at the outset. Yet the benefits in terms of emotional satisfaction and the opportunity to build superior quality and special, personalized features into one's house are considered by many who have built their own homes to be well worth the effort. In cases where several people in a community have the opportunity to build their houses at the same time, cooperating on some of the work, the experience can be especially rewarding.

In many cases, even where the necessary skills can be acquired by a prospective owner-builder, there still remains a need for some help with finances to make the endeavor possible. Obviously, inflation, high interest rates, and other economic factors can put a lot of pressure on the owner-builder, even though costs are less than those involved in buying a finished home. However, certain small-scale projects now under way offer hope that more can be done to allow a greater number of people the satisfaction of becoming owner-builders.

For example, with money from the U.S. Farmers Home Administration, the Rural California Housing Corporation is combining subsidized mortgage interest rates with self-help to provide new homes for families with $7,000 to $15,000 annual incomes. According to the *Sacramento Bee* newspaper, since 1967, about 1,000 homes have been built by the corporation in central and northern California.

The corporation starts a subdivision by first purchasing the lots in rural areas or cities with fewer than 10,000 persons. Next, 8 to 10 qualified families are organized, loans negotiated, and a work schedule arranged.

Each group of families goes to work under a company team leader who supervises each phase of the construction and determines which jobs, such as wiring, should be done by professionals. Each family is required to work a minimum of 30 hours a week. In the early stages of construction, the entire group works on pouring concrete foundation slabs, placing framing, and nailing roof beams. Later, each family works on finishing their individual homes.

It generally takes 8 to 12 months to complete each set of homes. With no money down, a couple with one child under 18 and an income of less than $11,700 can move into one of the houses for a monthly mortgage payment of $150.

In the Village Homes neighborhood we have also been involved in a program geared to help low-income people build their own houses. Low-income families desiring to participate in the program were offered jobs working in construction, building houses and installing landscaping in the neighborhood. After they worked six months and had acquired a basic understanding of some of the aspects of home building they had the opportunity to start building their own houses, under the supervision of a job foreman. They performed enough work during evenings and weekends to earn the down payments for their houses. Construction took about seven months. By the end of this period the people in the program had acquired skills that allowed them to find jobs that were much better paying than what they had before entering the program. The seven families that have gone through the program have been extremely happy to move into a stable housing situation; they like the neighborhood and they seem to feel more secure with their new jobs. The children of several families who were migrant workers are now in a much better situation for getting the education necessary to break out of the low-income life-style that they seemed destined to live.

If developers of new communities or those in charge of rehabilitating old ones would undertake this type of self-help project, offering an opportunity to low-income people who are willing to work and learn new skills, there would be far more benefits to the people involved and society as a whole than can result from welfare programs. New home owners' participation in the construction of the neighborhood could also reduce the costs of the house by reducing the final price of building sites.

In Village Homes, residents have been involved in the cooperative construction of community buildings, a swimming pool, paths and foot bridges, fences, and such. There are other aspects of new communities that residents might also help build and/or install, including water-recycling facilities, utility systems, landscaping, local energy-generation systems, and even streets and paths running within the community. All these projects could cut costs, thus opening the neighborhood to people with less money but plenty of willingness to work, and at the same time build community spirit and encourage friendly relationships and mutual respect among residents of the new development.

Psychologist Eugene R. Streich, who conducted studies of

people who lived in houses designed by Frank Lloyd Wright, told me that a group of people for whom Wright had designed a rural subdivision near Kalamazoo, Michigan, spoke very highly of their experiences building their houses together. They ordered materials as a group to get lower prices and cooperated in the actual building process to make the job easier. There were picnics, recreational activities, and a generally friendly atmosphere. Several of the people, interviewed 20 years later, said that the time they spent building their homes together was one of the most enjoyable periods of their lives.[23]

Wherever possible the use of local materials for building, such as adobe, wood, and stone, would further cut materials costs and create an appearance more in harmony with the local environment. In many cases this would mean substituting labor to process the materials for more expensive ready-to-use materials. The use of poured adobe for internal walls is an example of how a local material can be used to reduce materials costs and add natural heating and cooling capacity to the house.

All of these things which reduce the cost of housing emulate the way that homes and communities have been created for most of the history of our society: local materials, owner-built dwellings, and neighborhood or community cooperation. And it may be that even though we initially may consider these options because of the financial pressure exerted by a deteriorating economic climate, we will come to see that the ideas presented have merit in themselves. In fact, the combination of new, environmentally sound, small-scale technologies with old-fashioned community spirit and local self-reliance could be the beginning of an invigorating and very rewarding experience for everyone involved.

[23]Eugene R. Streich, personal communication.

Energy

We are all aware that the Industrial Revolution of the last 200 years has done more to change human life and the face of the earth than all that occurred in the previous 20 centuries. We are so accustomed, however, to thinking of this revolution as a single phenomenon that we tend to overlook the fact that it consisted of a number of changes not inevitably related.

To understand our present energy crisis, it is important that we be able to see at least two of these changes as distinct from one another. The first change was the tremendous burgeoning of applied technology that allowed us to satisfy our wants and needs in ways that could hardly have been imagined before. The second change was the exponential increase in our use of energy, particularly from nonrenewable sources — coal, oil, and natural gas. Before the Industrial Revolution we had relied almost exclusively on inexhaustible and renewable sources of energy — sunlight, wind and water power, and the burning of wood and other nonfossil fuels.

Although the second change followed the first, one should not assume that the growth of applied technology *had* to result in the increased consumption of nonrenewable energy sources. The growth of applied technology resulted from the expansion of scientific knowledge which, if fossil fuels had not been available, would have shown us ways to do without them. Apart from high-temperature processes like steelmaking that depended on coal, the Industrial Revolution could have been fueled with renewable energy. Early factories did in fact use water power, and early steam engines burned wood. Hydroelectric generation once provided a great deal of our electricity. The shift to fossil fuels was a choice we made based on their temporary abundance and relative low cost, once our technology made it possible for us to drill and mine for them.

Similarly, our high per capita consumption of energy in general is not inextricably connected to our standard of living. It is the result of the technological choices we made. Because energy was temporarily cheap and plentiful, we had little incentive to choose the energy-conserving alternatives. No one choice was crucial, but taken together they have led to continually increasing consumption of fossil fuels, and have created our ominous and unnecessary dependence on them.

In recent years, individuals in our society have begun to realize that this dependence is a dead-end road. We are running out of the easily recoverable fossil fuels which have been the mainstay of our high-energy technology.[24] The United States already spends $80 billion yearly to import oil. Imported oil exacerbates inflation, weakens the economy, and sends prices for food, clothing, and shelter soaring as we must export more and more to pay for the imports. Every American family watches its standard of living slip as the dollar diminishes in value.

It has been obvious for years that we could not depend indefinitely on the dwindling supply of oil for energy. Until recently, however, we imagined that we could either switch to our vast reserves of coal or convert to nuclear energy before oil became scarce. In both instances, it appears we were wrong.

The increased use of our coal reserves would pose serious environmental problems. For example, according to a U.S. Department of Energy (DOE) memorandum, a current plan to convert more than 60 oil- and gas-fired utility power plants to coal would boost air pollution over the Northeast by more than 25 percent and would sharply increase the acidity of rainfall in Canada.[25] Acid rain has already killed the fish in many northeastern lakes and has reduced the crop yield on agricultural lands.[26] The higher the acid concentration becomes, the more severe the problem will be. If we increase coal burning in the years to come, we could also add significantly to the carbon dioxide in the atmosphere, which could warm the polar ice caps with the devastating effects mentioned in Chapter 2. In addition, air pollution from burning coal will increase health-care costs and work time lost, not to mention a great deal of less urgent sickness and

[24]John Fowler, *Energy Environment Source Book* (Washington, D.C.: National Science Teachers Assoc., 1975), p. 187.
[25]"The Acid Earth," *Harrowsmith* staff report, *Harrowsmith* 27 (April 1980) 4:7.
[26]Ibid.

discomfort—all "external costs" that eventually have to be accounted for.

The potential dangers from nuclear energy are even more frightening. We have failed to develop, and probably never can develop, a really safe nuclear fission plant, or a safe way of disposing of the radioactive wastes. The radioactive materials are simply too deadly for too long. Unfortunately, the cost of maintaining the wastes already accumulated will be a tremendous burden on society for thousands of years to come. And the near disaster at the Three Mile Island reactor in 1979 dramatized the risks that environmentalists and some scientists have been warning us about for years.

Even the mining of uranium poses serious dangers that we are just beginning to recognize. Radioactivity from uranium mines on the Navaho reservation in New Mexico, for example, has contaminated the water and land around people's homes, posing a threat of health problems for years to come.[27] Also, we have found that the lung cancer rate among uranium miners is four times the national average.[28]

Its dangers aside, nuclear fission also seems less and less practical because of the enormous cost of fission plants. Capital costs and operating costs for nuclear plants are increasing more rapidly than those of conventional plants. While reactor fuel costs 20 to 30 times what it did a few years ago, the primary reason for the increase is the expense of trying to make fission reactors safe. The increased costs have exceeded most utilities' financing capabilities, and have done more to block construction of fission plants than the protests of environmentalists.

A nuclear plant costs $1 billion or more, takes 10 to 14 years to build, and lasts for only 30 or 40 years before it must be decommissioned. Given the economic and political climate of the times, utilities aren't inclined to commit themselves to new nuclear projects. Now, in 1980, there are 67 reactors licensed for commercial power operation in the United States, 85 under construction, and 11 in the planning stages.[29] The ones that are still in the planning stages or are less than 25 percent constructed are likely to be simply written off by the utility companies because they cannot afford them.

An alternative process, nuclear fusion, has appeared until recently to offer a cleaner and safer source of atomic energy. Indeed, the largest single unknown factor in the future energy picture is whether or not a practical, safe, nuclear fusion process can be developed. Unlike fission, which produces energy by splitting atoms, fusion produces it by joining atoms, theoretically without creating any radioactive waste. However, preliminary experiments with fusion suggest that the process may not be as clean in practice as first supposed, raising the same questions of safety and economics that have made fission reactors impractical. And there is a very real possibility that fusion may just not be economically feasible.

Neither nuclear fission nor nuclear fusion should be used without taking into account the long-term effects and costs. The government has subsidized this industry from the beginning, and the industry has not had to pay for many of the problems it has created. The external costs could mount up for centuries as the effects of radiation take their toll and waste has to be continually guarded.

Not only nuclear fission, but our entire system of energy use in the world today has created many similar external costs that we are passing on to future generations. To continue the established approach in spite of overwhelming evidence of the costs represents more than a lack of understanding or consideration on our part; it represents gross negligence.

In the past few years the problems and limits of our energy habits have become more clearly defined. But what are the solutions? How can we lead a good life today without requiring future generations to pay for our luxuries?

There are different answers to this question depending

[27]Allan Richards, "Church Rock: The Continuing Story," unpublished paper (April 1980).
[28]*San Francisco Examiner,* 22 April 1980.

[29]Federal Nuclear Regulatory Commission, Office of Management and Program Analysis, "Status of Nuclear Power Reactors Under NRC Purview," 30 June 1980.

upon whom you ask, and the content of the answers seems to be highly influenced by the specific interest of those asked. In general, those in the energy business who have invested heavily in nuclear and fossil fuels tell us that increasing the use of coal and nuclear energy is the answer, and "business" in general seems to agree with them, probably because of a fear that any change in the energy production system might cause economic problems. There are other individuals who have nothing to gain financially from either increasing or decreasing the use of coal and nuclear power, who take the position that these sources pose serious health, environmental, and economic problems. They conclude that we must reduce energy use where possible and make a transition to solar energy.[30]

Amory Lovins feels it is crucial that we move in this direction as quickly as possible. He calls it the "soft path":

We stand at a crossroads; without decisive action our options will slip away. Delay in energy conservation lets wasteful use run on so far that the logistical problems of catching up become insuperable. Delay in widely deploying diverse soft technologies pushes them so far into the future that any credible fossil fuel bridge to them has been burned: they must be well underway before the worst part of the oil and gas decline. Delay in building the fossil fuel bridge makes it too tenuous: what the sophisticated coal technologies can give us, in particular, will no longer mesh with our pattern of transitional needs as oil and gas dwindle.[31]

He further states:

Indeed, one of the infinite variations on a soft path seems inevitable, either smoothly by choice now or disruptively by necessity later; and I fear that if we do not soon make the choice, growing tension between rich and poor countries may destroy the conditions that now make smooth attainment of a soft path possible.[32]

Denis Hayes, director of the Solar Energy Research Institute, also believes solar is the best answer to our energy problem, while he warns us of a new era of limits:

Renewable energy sources—wind, water, biomass, and direct sunlight—hold substantial advantages over the alternatives. They add no heat to the global environment and produce no radioactive or weapons-grade materials. The carbon dioxide emitted by biomass systems in equilibrium will make no net contribution to atmospheric concentrations, since green plants will capture CO_2 at the same rate that it is being produced. Renewable energy sources can provide energy as heat, liquid or gaseous fuels, or electricity. And they lend themselves well to production and use in decentralized, autonomous facilities. However, such sources are not the indefatigable genies sought by advocates of limitless energy growth. While renewable sources do expand the limits to energy growth, especially the physical limits, the fact that energy development has a ceiling cannot ultimately be denied.[33]

Hayes further states that:

About one-fifth of all energy used around the world now comes from solar resources: wind power, water power, biomass, and direct sunlight. By the year 2000, such renewable energy sources could provide 40 percent of the global energy budget; by 2025, humanity could obtain 75 percent of its energy from solar resources. Such a transition would not be cheap or easy, but its benefits would far outweigh the costs and difficulties. The proposed timetable would require an unprecedented worldwide commitment of resources and

[30]The term "solar energy" as used here, refers to direct solar energy and all of its derivatives—wind, photovoltaic, hydro, water currents, and biomass.
[31]Lovins, *Soft Energy Paths*, p. 59.

[32]Ibid.
[33]Denis Hayes, *Rays of Hope: The Transition to a Post-Petroleum World* (New York: W.W. Norton & Co., 1977), pp. 27–28.

talent, but the consequences of failure are similarly unprecedented. Every essential feature of the proposed solar transition has already proven technically viable; if the fifty-year timetable is not met, the roadblocks will have been political — not technical.[34]

There are three things we must do to accomplish this. First, we must develop renewable and environmentally acceptable sources of energy. Second, we must begin to use energy much more efficiently and frugally. Third, we must restructure our economy and our society to minimize the need for operations and activities that demand energy. In the remainder of this chapter, I will discuss what we can do in each of these areas.

As you read, keep in mind that a large part of the job will depend on the efforts of local communities. It cannot be expected that the industries that have traditionally made profits by selling energy will suddenly help communities become more energy self-sufficient. Each community must determine which alternative sources have the most potential for its situation and must pursue the development of those sources. Each community must also take the necessary steps to reduce energy consumption to a point within the limits of sustainable solar energy sources.

Environmentally Acceptable Renewable Energy Sources

Solar energy, including that embodied in wind, water current, and biomass, has been used for thousands of years. Denis Hayes points out that "direct solar and its various indirect forms fit well into a political system that emphasizes decentralization, pluralism, and local control."[35] There is no better example of this than in a solar home, where the owner can rely more on the sun for heating and water heating than on the utility company.

Solar space heating is beginning to take hold all over the country as a method of heating in housing and commercial

[34]Ibid., p. 155.
[35]Denis Hayes, "Worldwatch Paper II — Energy: The Solar Prospect," March 1977, p. 7.

buildings. Many of the early projects are reporting excellent results: up to 100 percent solar heating in many parts of the country, and depending on the design, up to 60 or 80 percent even in some of the coldest regions.

In the Village Homes project we have built over 14 different types of solar homes, demonstrating that a wide variety of systems and architectural styles can be effective. A study of

utility bills in the community shows that the simplest designs, which cost almost no more than a conventional home, are getting 40 to 50 percent solar heating, and many of the more sophisticated designs are getting as much as 85 percent.[36] The Village Homes recreation center gets almost all of its winter space heating from rooftop solar panels which are used during the spring and fall to heat water for the swimming pool. Homeowners plan to build a hot tub for summer parties to complete the year-round use of the

solar system. The 2,800-square-foot Village Homes office building gets about 85 percent of its space heating from the sun and is naturally cooled.

Elsewhere in the country, solar-powered commercial and industrial facilities are performing well, including a solar-heated airport in Aspen, Colorado, a solar dairy in Oakdale, California, and the Cary Arboretum building in New York.

Solar water-heating systems, popular in the 1920s and 1930s in California and Florida, are becoming popular again, there and in many other states. Solar water-heating systems are now commonly being installed in residential units, and are capable, in most parts of the country, of producing 50 to 100 percent of the domestic hot-water needs. Again, in the Villages Homes project, we have used three different systems and find that we get about

[36]David Bainbridge, Judy Corbett, and John Hofacre, *Village Homes' Solar House Designs* (Emmaus, Pa.: Rodale Press, 1979), p. 38.

75 percent of our hot water from the sun using 48 square feet of collector and an 80-gallon tank.

Solar Electricity

While still not competitive with conventional sources, solar electric generation is seen as having great potential both for large-scale power plants and for smaller units that would generate power for individual houses or housing developments. Several techniques are being developed.

Photovoltaic cells convert sunlight directly into electricity. Their cost is still high, but experts believe it will decrease rapidly over the next few years. Housing tracts with rooftop solar cells could become small, part-time solar power plants, selling their excess power during the day to the local utility, and buying it back again at night. Photovoltaic demonstration projects are providing electricity to a Papago Indian reservation near Tucson, Arizona, to a naval station in California, and to several schools and colleges across the nation.

A second type of solar generation uses mirrors to focus the sun's heat on a boiler. The U.S. Department of Energy is underwriting a 10-megawatt facility halfway between Los Angeles and Las Vegas that will have 1,800 concave mirrors, each 24 feet high and 20 feet wide, focusing the sun's rays on a central receiver. The steam produced will turn massive underground turbines to generate electricity. The same concept could be used on a smaller scale. The Israelis have developed the concept of *solar ponds,* which are pools 10 to 20 feet deep with a bottom layer of highly saline water. The sun's rays, penetrating the less salty upper layers, heat the bottom water to temperatures as high as 250 degrees. This heat is transferred to another fluid such as propane or ammonia which is vaporized and then activates turbines that turn generators to produce electricity.

Hydroelectric Generation

Hydroelectric power, once a significant energy source in America, is currently receiving a great deal of attention as a nonpolluting, environmentally benign source of electricity. In the last century, and in the first few decades of this century, water power made New England an industrial center. Across the nation, in fact, water power produced a substantial amount of our total electricity (40 percent in 1900,[37] as compared with 13 percent today[38]). Much of that power came from small hydroelectric generating plants (less than 15 megawatts capacity), erected at low-head dams (less than 65 feet high). Some 2,800 of these dams are still in existence (though many have deteriorated from neglect and the passage of time), and 200 of them are still used to produce cheap, dependable, clean electric power.[39] A recent study by the Army Corps of Engineers and the New England River Basins Commission estimated that the present hydroelectric output of the region (about 600 megawatts)[40] could be tripled by using the existing dams, some of which still have the necessary equipment to generate power.[41] Nationwide, an estimated 50,000 small dams suitable for hydroelectric generation are sitting idle waiting to be put to work.[42]

Monticello Dam, located near Winters, California, is one example. The 300-foot dam, impounding over 1.6 million acre-feet of water, was built in the early 1950s to hold irrigation water for California's Central Valley. At that time, fossil fuels were very cheap, and it was not worthwhile to add a hydroelectric plant to the dam. Fortunately, the designers had the foresight to install two outlet pipes on the dam to feed a power plant. There are now three different proposals before the Federal Power Regulatory Agency to fit the dam with power plants generating from 1,000 to 1,600 kilowatts.[43]

The Rollins Dam on the Bear River in California is an example of a high-head dam where a power plant was added.

[37]Greg Luft, "Small Hydro: Part of the Energy Answer," 65 *Reclamation Era* (1979)1:20.

[38]Michael Harris, "Reinventing the Waterwheel," *Environmental Action* 11:1 (June 1979):24.

[39]Bruce Palmer Smith, "Power from Yesterday's Dams," 20 *Environment* (November 1978):9:79.

[40]Federal Power Commission, "Hydroelectric Power Resources of the United States: Developed and Undeveloped," Washington, D.C., January 1976, p. 59.

[41]Thomas E. Klock, "Interim Report on Inventory of Existing Dams in New England," Boston: New England River Basins Commission, December 1978, Table 3.

[42]Michael Harris, "Reinventing the Waterwheel," p. 24.

[43]Federal Bureau of Reclamation, Water and Power Resources Division, Jim Conwace, personal communication.

The 220-foot rock-fill dam was originally built with a diversion tunnel through the bottom, which was plugged after completion of the dam. In 1978, work began to drain the dam, to unplug the diversion canal, and add a 13,700-kilowatt power plant at the base of the dam. The project, undertaken by the Nevada Irrigation District with Tudor Engineer Corporation as consultants, began producing power in 1980.[44]

Small-scale hydro power generation hit its low in the early 1970s and has been increasing ever since, though there have been problems. In particular, conflicting interests and priorities have tended to turn even small projects into nightmares of bureaucratic and legal wrangling.

Springfield, Vermont, is a notable case. Sitting astride the powerful Black River, this toolmaking town of 10,000 voted in 1975 to harness the energy at its doorstep — energy which had once powered its mills but had long been abandoned in favor of imported electricity from fossil-fuel generation. At this writing, the $57 million project, which would involve refurbishing five dams and building another, rebuilding generation plants, and taking over the local distribution system, has become hopelessly mired in regulatory and legal battles, waged largely by the existing electric utility which fears a sizable loss of revenue.[45] Other projects have met similar fates.

But the idea of small-scale, locally owned hydro power is just too enticing to be abandoned completely, as entrepreneur Ted Larter has proven to the citizens of Barlett, New Hampshire. Larter, a businessman from Lowell, Massachusetts, bought a dilapidated generating plant and dam at Goodrich Falls and refurbished it at a cost of about $35,000. Today it produces a steady flow of electricity — about 300 kilowatts, which is enough for 90 households. Encouraged by this success, Larter bought and restored another abandoned plant in Franklin Falls, New Hampshire. This low-head plant produces a steady 200 kilowatts. Here again, though, entrenched interests have fought back. Larter is forced to sell his surplus power to the reigning utility company at a low "nuisance" rate which keeps the project from making a profit.[46]

Fortunately, the Public Utilities Regulatory Policies Act (PURPA), enacted in 1978 by the federal government, aims to change this practice of "nuisance rate" payments. Under the act, any qualifying power producer would be guaranteed a fair price for excess energy sold to a large utility. A producer qualifies either by using a cogenerative system, or by being a small producer using a renewable resource. The fair price is determined relative to the short- and long-term marginal costs of power.

As Larter and others have shown, in spite of the legal and financial problems, small-scale hydro power works and its time will come again. Communities which can use such nearby resources are at an advantage in their quest for energy self-sufficiency.

Wind Generation

Wind-powered electric generators were common on United States farms before rural power lines were built, and in recent years, many of these old machines have been reconditioned and put back into operation. Larger capacity wind generators now on the market cost more per kilowatt of generating capacity than most systems using fossil fuels, but their cost is dropping rapidly. Recent studies by the U.S. Department of Energy (DOE) on large wind systems at several sites in the United States have shown that future designs will be economically competitive with present utility services.[47]

In windy areas, these turbines may provide the major

---

[44]U.S. Army Corps of Engineers; the Hydraulic Engineering Center and U.S.A.C.E.; Institute for Water Resources (1979); Feasibility Study for Small Hydropower Additions; U.S. Army Corps of Engineers, GPO 689-166/037.

[45]Glen J. Berger, "Low Head Hydroelectric Power in New England: The Black River Project," Solar Law Reporter, vol. 3, October 1979, pp. 569–74.

[46]Michael Harris, "Reinventing the Waterwheel," Environmental Action 11:1 (June 1979):27–28; and Bruce Palmer Smith, "Power from Yesterday's Dams," 20 Environment (November 1978):9:18–19.

[47]U.S. Department of Energy, ENERGY, Winter 1979, vol. IX, no. 1, pp. 11–20.

source of electricity for a community, though other sources must be available as a backup when there is no wind. A Massachusetts firm plans to erect at least 20 and perhaps as many as 2,000 windmills in Pacheco Pass, east of Gilroy, California.[48] The maximum power envisioned is 100 megawatts—enough to supply the needs of a city of 100,000. For this project, the state has agreed to buy the electricity produced at 3½¢ per kilowatt hour—about the going rate for electricity from coal-fired or nuclear plants.

Clayton, New Mexico, a remote town of 4,200, is the site of a wind-generation experiment sponsored by the DOE and the National Aeronautics and Space Administration (NASA).[49] Clayton produces its own electricity by means of seven diesel-powered generators. The number of generators operating at one time varies, depending upon fluctuating power needs. DOE and NASA erected a two-blade windmill on a 100-foot tower near the town and linked its generator to the diesel system. It became operable in January 1978, for a two-year test. After initial shakedown runs and some modifications, it performed admirably, feeding an average of 92 kilowatts into the Clayton power grid during the first six months of operation. The Clayton windmill can provide 15 percent of the town's off-peak hour requirements, and has saved the town a considerable amount of fuel. The windmill produces power at wind speeds between 9.5 and 40 miles per hour (mph) and reaches its maximum output of 200 kilowatts in 22.4 mph winds. Wind speed is within this range at Clayton about half of the time.

The biggest drawback of wind generation is its variability; varying wind produces varying amounts of power. In a controllable system like Clayton's, however, the windmill's power generating fluctuations are less troublesome. Like low-head hydro plants, wind-generating systems have a high initial cost (especially since the technology is still being perfected), but they pay for themselves rapidly since no fuel is needed to operate them.

Biomass

Biomass is a term used to describe renewable organic material—wood, agricultural waste, animal waste, garbage, and such—that can be used to generate energy. It is actually solar energy that has been stored through the process of photosynthesis. This energy can be converted to a variety of useful energy forms—hydrogen, charcoal, methane, and synthetic oils—with by-products usable as food, fertilizers, and chemicals.

In the mid 1800s, wood supplied over 90 percent of our energy needs. As late as 1940, 20 percent of the homes in the United States still used wood for space heating.[50] While the use of wood for heating has almost ceased in recent decades, airtight stoves, particularly those of Scandinavian design, have influenced change in American stove designs that has helped make wood heating popular once again. Burning wood in the home in an airtight stove is far more efficient, in terms of useful heat production, than any system that involves converting wood to gas, alcohol, steam, or electricity at some central heating plant, because there is less energy lost in conversion or transmission.

There are many stoves now on the market that burn wood very efficiently. A few kinds provide water heating as well as space heating. Woodstoves are very appropriate in areas of low population density with much open space, where they will not produce high concentrations of carbon monoxide and particulate matter. (This in itself is an argument for low-density, decentralized settlements.)

Wood can also be used on a larger scale to generate electricity for a community. Burlington, Vermont, a town of 40,000, has already taken steps in this direction. Before 1977, Burlington bought most of its electricity from outside sources

[48]"Wind Energy," *East/West Journal*, July 1980, vol. 10, no.7, p. 72.

[49]All references to the NASA project in Clayton, New Mexico, are from: Thomas W. Reddock and John W. Klein, "No Ill Winds for New Mexico Utility," *IEEE Spectrum*, March 1979, pp. 57–61; from personal communication with Robert Johnson, city manager, Clayton, New Mexico.

[50]U.S. Department of Commerce, *Residential Energy Uses*, pamphlet #003-024-01554-4 (Washington, D.C.: Government Printing Office, 1975).

which used oil, coal, natural gas, or nuclear power to generate electricity. In that year, it refurbished its municipally owned, 10-megawatt coal-fired generating plant and converted it to burn wood. The conversion has been a complete success.[51]

The Burlington wood burner consumes 1,000 tons of wood chips each week. Waste from nearby lumber, pulpwood, and firewood operations is hauled to the plant, chopped into small chips, and fed to a large furnace which heats water into steam to drive turbines. There's nothing unorthodox about the system; it merely burns wood instead of coal. In New England, wood is plentiful, and it is a renewable resource. Yet the Burlington wood-refurbished coal burner produces electricity at two-thirds of its former cost. Operating at 70 percent of capacity, the plant produces 10 percent of the electricity required by the town's 15,000 households and businesses. Burlington voters are so enthused about the project that they have approved construction of a 50-megawatt wood burner, as well as a 10-megawatt low-head hydroelectric plant, to be located on a nearby river.

Agricultural waste has also been used successfully in the production of energy. In Brazil, sugarcane waste is being used to produce alcohol to power cars, trucks, and buses. The cane waste is made into a mash which is fermented, producing alcohol that can be distilled off. Spoiled grain, fruit, and vegetables can also be used; so can wood chips. By 1985, alcohol should replace 20 percent of Brazil's oil consumption.[52] The alcohol can be used to power machines directly or may be combined with gasoline to make gasohol.

Garbage and sewage can be used to generate methane. In Palos Verdes, California, the Los Angeles County Sanitation District has drilled "methane wells" into its garbage landfills to tap the gas that naturally is produced there as the organic matter in the garbage decomposes. The city is selling 2 million cubic feet of gas a day to the local gas utility.[53] Similar processes are drawing off usable gas at almost a dozen other dumps in the nation. Some cities burn the gas to generate electricity. The city of Modesto, California, has gone one step further and intends to use the methane it taps to power municipal cars and trucks.[54]

Alcohol and methane from biomass conversion can be used for cooking and in automatic forced-air furnaces. Methane-powered forced-air furnaces will be more expensive to operate than wood-burning stoves, however, because of the cost and energy waste involved in producing these fuels.

Biomass can also be burned directly to produce heat and/or electricity. On the main island of Hawaii, the residues from sugarcane fields in 1979 provided almost 35.4 percent of the electrical power generated.[55] In Madera County, California, a plant that will generate 50,000 kilowatts (enough for a city of 50,000) will be powered by pelletized refined fuel made from wood and agricultural waste.[56] And in Eugene, Oregon, a 33.8-megawatt biomass steam plant provides steam heat for a business district, a large hospital, a large cannery, and a 20-acre greenhouse system. It is also used to provide electricity in cases of extreme emergency or for general use when abundant wood waste is available.[57]

Solid waste may also be used as biomass. Using solid waste can help solve two problems that most communities today face: the increasingly high cost of fuels and the scarcity of available sanitary landfill sites.

The first refuse-burning power system in the country was built in Ames, Iowa, in 1971 and has proven a success.[58] The plant employs huge machines which grind, shake, and ultimately separate recyclable materials — glass, aluminum, and ferrous metals — from the daily trash haul. Oil, wood, and paper are also separated, and the remainder of the solid waste — more than 80 percent of

[51]James Ridgeway, *Energy Efficient Community Planning* (Emmaus, Pa.: JG Press, 1979), pp. 157–60.

[52]Ibid.

[53]Los Angeles County Sanitation District, Refuse Department, Joe Edberg, personal communication.

[54]City of Modesto, Sewage Treatment Facility, John Amstutz, personal communication.

[55]Hawaii Electric Co., Jitsu Niwao, personal communication.

[56]Sierra Power & Light Co., Franz Schneider, personal communication.

[57]Eugene Water & Electric Board, Maynard Cotton, personal communication.

[58]Ridgeway, *Energy Efficient Community Planning*, p. 165.

the original weight—is burned with coal to produce steam. The Ames plant processes about 150 tons of solid waste a day, collected from the university town of 46,000 itself and from 12 smaller communities. Burning 80 percent coal and 20 percent refuse-derived fuel, the Ames generating plant produces electricity at a cost on a par with a coal-burning plant. And Ames' need for landfill area is much less than it used to be; only 7 percent of the refuse collected is buried.

The Ames system has had its problems, as any pioneering system will. The grinding and separating machinery was very expensive and did not always perform well; some parts of the plant were overdesigned (estimates of refuse amount and content were inaccurate). Then, too, there have been organizational problems within the 13-town area which the plant serves. Nevertheless, the Ames plant was successful enough to inspire several others which are either in operation, under construction, or being financed: at Hempstead, New York; Franklin, Ohio; Saugus, Massachusetts; and the aforementioned plant at Burlington, Vermont.[59]

We can learn several lessons from the Ames experiment. The first is that separation of trash at the source, rather than at the plant, is more desirable because it eliminates the need for mechanical separators. Had a functional trash-segregation system been devised in Ames, significant savings in operating costs would have been realized. Second, accurate estimates of the amount and kind of refuse must be made before the system is built. Third, attempting to coordinate the refuse policies of 13 separate municipalities virtually guarantees administrative problems.

On a small scale, with rigidly enforced separation of recyclable materials at the source and within a more administratively unified area, refuse-fueled electric generation should work well. Our real aim, however, should be to reduce the amount of refuse we produce in the first place. This will be more energy efficient in the long run.

Geothermal

Geothermal energy, not normally considered a solar derivative, is a site-specific resource that can be used to generate electricity as well as to provide heat and steam for low-temperature applications. Hot springs have been used for thousands of years for bathing, healing, and ritual purposes. More recently, geothermal energy has been used for heating over 11,000 homes in Reykjavik, Iceland.[60] Electrical generation from geothermal sources dates back to 1900 in Lardello, Italy, and has subsequently been used in New Zealand, Japan, and in parts of the United States.[61]

There are several basic types of geothermal energy, and the ways to harness them vary considerably. Some of the methods are currently being used, and others are still in the developmental stages. The most common system uses *dry steam* from the earth to power conventional generators. Wells are drilled to depths of 2,000 feet or more, tapping reservoirs of steam in the earth's crust. Dry steam, which is primarily water vapor with no liquid, is found in relatively few locations.

Geothermal dry-steam systems do have environmental impacts. First, the geothermal steam gives off hydrogen sulfide, a colorless toxic gas which has a characteristic odor of rotten eggs. Newer units are able to scrub up to 90 percent of the gas from the steam, although the resulting residue is corrosive and difficult to manage. Hydrogen sulfide emissions are approximately one-fourth that of comparable coal plants. Other emissions include ammonia, boron, carbon dioxide, bicarbonate, sulfur, and radon.

The largest geothermal-powered generating station in the world is located at The Geysers in Geyserville, California. The plant, run by Pacific Gas & Electric (PG & E), began operating in 1960, and has over 15 generators ranging from 11,000 to 135,000 kilowatts.[62]

[59]Ibid., p. 168.

[60]Linda Bazdur, ``Geothermal Energy for Space and Process Heating,'' in D. M. Considine, ed., *Energy Technology Handbook* (New York: McGraw-Hill, 1977), pp. 7-43.

[61]John M. Fowler, *Energy and the Environment* (New York: McGraw-Hill, 1975), pp. 319-20.

[62]R. J. Bowen and E. A. Grow, ``The Geysers Geothermal Field in California,'' in D. M. Considine, ed., *Energy Technology Handbook*, pp. 7-34.

Ocean Tides

The ocean can provide sizable amounts of energy for coastal communities in two different ways:

We can take advantage of the varying temperatures of the water at different depths. Warm ocean water from the surface can be used to vaporize a liquid with a low boiling point which then turns a generating turbine. Next, cold water from far below the surface is used to condense the vapor back to liquid form so the process can be repeated.

Japan and the United Kingdom are using the force of waves to operate experimental generators. The floating power plants could be various sizes, up to several miles wide, and could send electricity back to shore through underwater cables. In the United States, Washington, Oregon, Alaska, and Hawaii are states that hold the most promise for wave-power-generated, energy.

Reducing the Need for Energy

The new energy supplies in the future, with the exception of passive solar, are undoubtedly going to cost more than cheap fossil fuels of the middle decades of this century. This increased cost will affect not only the price of the energy we use ourselves, but also the prices of all the goods and services we use, because it takes energy to produce them. Rising energy prices have already caused staggering inflation that has reduced the living standard of most Americans, and we can expect even greater energy price increases in the near future.

Conversion to renewable energy sources will not entirely solve our energy problems. Unless we also learn to get along with less energy than we use today, we will find ourselves spending more and more of our income, directly and indirectly, for energy, and we will have less left for our other needs. If we hope to maintain our standard of living, we will have to find ways to use energy much more frugally and efficiently — ways to do the same jobs with less energy.

Unfortunately, very few economists in this country are facing this issue squarely. It is such an obvious point that surely they cannot have overlooked it; I can only assume that they do not want to think about it because they are so used to the idea that we can solve any economic problem by increasing produc-

tion. But that is no longer the case, as the present state of our economy proves.

I am sure part of this country's current economic problems would not exist today if, as a nation, we had prepared for rising energy costs by reducing our energy consumption years ago. Daniel Yergin estimates that through conservation efforts in this country, "the possible energy savings would be the equivalent of the elimination of all imported oil — and then some."[63]

Let us consider the variety of things we can do, or are already doing to move in the direction of reduced energy consumption.

In general, it is best to produce our energy at or near the point of consumption. Advantages include:

- reducing the equipment needed for transmission and converstion of energy
- reducing the energy lost in transmission lines and conversion
- increasing stability by using small independent units rather than interdependent systems susceptible to major failures
- localizing both the environmental impacts of energy production and the control over means of production — leading, we may hope, to wiser energy use

Decentralizing energy production by using many small facilities has an additional advantage: it increases flexibility and makes it easier to design systems specially tailored for high efficiency. Cogeneration systems are a good example. Cogeneration makes efficient use of energy by capturing what would normally be wasted and using that energy for an additional purpose.

For example, a sugar processing plant can burn its own wastes to produce electricity for machinery and steam for various heating processes. Excess electricity can be sold to the local utility. Until recently, local utilities have been unwilling to purchase this

[63]Robert Stobaugh and Daniel Yergin, eds., *Energy Future: Report of the Energy Project at the Harvard Business School* (New York: Random House, 1979), pp. 136–37.

spare electricity. But in California, the Public Utilities Commission has taken steps to reverse this situation. Pacific Gas & Electric now pays higher rates to power cogenerators than the utility now charges most of its customers for electricity. The higher payments reflect what the energy would cost PG & E if it had to build a new power plant to produce it.[64]

One common cogeneration system powers an electrical generating turbine and pipes the excess steam through the city or neighborhood for space heating. District heating systems using this technique are common in Western Europe where there are over 1,000 such systems currently in use. In New York City, Consolidated Edison delivers steam used by its electrical generators to over 2,000 apartment and office buildings in Manhattan.[65]

A great deal of energy could also be saved by designing electric appliances to operate with less power. Household appliances in particular are seldom designed to use electricity efficiently. Refrigerators now use as much as 200 kilowatt hours of electricity per month, but could be designed to operate on one-tenth of that amount by using more insulation, tighter door seals, and more efficient motors. The cost of these improvements would be trivial, but refrigerator manufacturers have ignored this fact because they feel (probably correctly) that buyers do not consider energy efficiency when choosing a refrigerator, even when the reduction in their electricity bills would more than offset the slight increase in the price of the appliance. Refrigerator motors today use twice as much electricity as they did 15 years ago, simply because it is cheaper to build the less efficient motors.

Rising electric rates will probably make some buyers more interested in appliance efficiency, but in order to seriously influence manufacturers, government intervention in the form of efficiency standards or taxes on less-efficient models will probably be required.

Nationally, the Federal Trade Commission now requires that refrigerators, freezers, dishwashers, hot water heaters, washing machines, room air conditioners, and furnaces offered for sale

carry an energy label that will tell the consumer what the costs in energy will be to run the appliance.

A number of cities and counties have taken dramatic steps toward reducing energy requirements of buildings. In California, for example, Davis, Livermore, and Santa Clara County have adopted energy audit and weatherization ordinances to cut down energy use in residential buildings. Similar steps are being taken by Fitchburg, Massachusetts, which hopes to reduce winter home fuel use by 30 percent. And in Portland, Oregon, the city government hopes to cut back total residential and commercial energy use by 30 percent by 1995.

The conservation measures required are quite simple but effective: insulating ceilings and hot water heaters, caulking and weather-stripping windows, installing energy-use meters, and replacing gas pilot lights with electric ignition devices.

In Philadelphia, 59 hospitals have saved nearly $5 million in two years by such conservation measures as improving boiler combustion efficiency, optimizing physical plant use, and reducing domestic hot water temperatures. Similar programs are under way in Michigan, Ohio, Illinois, New Hampshire, Vermont, New York, and New Jersey.

Even high-rise buildings are undergoing design changes to cut down on energy costs which have risen to account for nearly one-third of total building operating costs. By such techniques as limiting exterior wall area, reducing window area, and insulating and coating the glass that is used, savings of 30 percent have been achieved. Houses may also be oriented and designed to reduce or eliminate the need for conventional heating and cooling.

Alternatives to refrigerative air conditioning are numerous. Good shading (both from trees and landscape plants, and from the design of the building itself) and good insulation are basic and effective in any climate. Where nights are cool, masses of masonry or water inside the house can be cooled at night by natural ventilation and will retain their coolness during the day. In dry climates, water evaporation in passive systems like roof ponds can often provide sufficient cooling, or evaporative air conditioners such as "swamp coolers" can be used. Often simply keeping the air moving with fans is quite sufficient.

In hot, humid climates the problems are more difficult but

[64]State of California Public Utilities Commission, Ward Mefford, personal communication.
[65]Stobaugh and Yergin, *Energy Future,* p. 158.

ingenious solutions are possible, such as cooling air by circulating it through underground tunnels, or radiative cooling of large masses of water ("cool ponds") by exposure to the sky at night. If these methods do not suffice, a dehumidifier can be used, which will still consume less energy than an air conditioner.

Transportation is another area with much potential for energy savings. We know how to manufacture automobiles that are far more energy efficient than most of those on the road today. There are already diesel-powered cars available now that are capable of getting 50 miles per gallon.

Unfortunately, American automobile manufacturers have been slow in making the necessary conversion to smaller, lighter cars unencumbered by energy-consuming luxuries like power steering, power brakes, and automatic transmissions. These same automobile manufacturers are now having trouble staying in business as consumers exercise their preference for fuel-efficient, foreign-made models. This should inspire the production of more energy-efficient cars in the future.

In any car it is possible to get 20 percent further on a gallon of gas through more-efficient driving habits. The California Energy Extension Service is developing an extensive program to train thousands of drivers to get where they want to go while using less fuel.

All of these conservation measures are aimed at reducing our energy consumption without substantially changing the way we conduct our lives. At the same time, however, we should look at how we could change our life-styles to eliminate energy use altogether where it is not really necessary.

Energy has, in recent years, been so inexpensive that we have used it to do more and more of the work we used to do for ourselves. Technology has provided us with some outstanding labor-saving devices that greatly enhance our lives. But it has also given us a plethora of gadgets whose appeal is based more on their novelty than on any real usefulness.

Consider the contemporary bathroom. We no longer need to use our own muscles to shave ourselves, curl or dry our hair, brush our teeth, or rinse out our mouths. There are even electrical devices to help us wash our faces.

In the kitchen, there are electrical gadgets to beat the eggs, mix the cakes, chop the ice, blend the sauces, chop the vegetables, and open the cans. There are electric coffee grinders, coffee makers, and on and on. Each gadget individually may not consume much energy, but collectively, when used by large numbers of people, they consume a significant amount. As a society, we need to develop an ethical awareness of and opposition to such waste so that people will simply avoid buying or using unnecessary gadgets.

Such an awareness would also lead us to question the need for other less frivolous appliances. Garbage disposals, for example, can be eliminated and that good organic material which typically goes down the drain can be put to better use by composting and recycling it back into the garden. Clothes can be effectively dried outside on a clothesline, or inside on drying racks during bad weather. Since the advent of cheap electricity, we have learned to consider such clotheslines and drying racks unsightly, but when designed into a house or yard as standard elements, they can be quite unobtrusive.

With regard to transportation, we can all try to walk or ride bikes whenever possible rather than driving our cars. And we can organize our time and errands so that we accomplish many things with one trip by car when driving is necessary.

Simply dressing appropriately for the climate makes a great difference, too. We have to realize that, in hot weather, the business suit is a cause of energy waste, as are short skirts and sheer hose in cold weather. This is a good example of how broadly our life-styles affect energy demands.

Reducing mechanization and automation in our industrial production could also decrease overall energy use substantially while helping to solve the unemployment problems and relieving the frustrations born of conveyor-belt-type jobs. This will depend, of course, on whether or not energy becomes expensive enough to make labor costs competitive.

Restructuring for a Low-Energy Society

Given our existing built environment and economic

production and distribution system, we can only go so far with energy conservation; then there is no more we can do. At this point we will have cut our energy use 40 to 50 percent, but we will still be using a large amount of energy to transport people and freight. Currently, we are using approximately 50 percent of our energy for these purposes. Conservation can cut that in half, but even half of that is a lot of energy, and with a growing population it will increase.

In the future, energy for transportation could come from our dwindling oil supplies or from synthetic fuels. Neither solution addresses the long-range problem and both will be very expensive, in terms of money and environmental impact.

The solar alternative for running vehicles — photovoltaic- and wind-generated electricity, or alcohol from biomass — will also be very expensive, and their availability will be limited. The only realistic long-range answer will be to reduce the need for transportation through appropriate planning.

Unless we restructure our urban form and our centralized system of production, energy conservation will provide only temporary relief. This is because the current design of our built environment evolved without the constraints of limited and expensive energy. The present structure requires high energy input to function. We cannot solve the problem simply by making autos more efficient. For example, we must change the structure so that we do not need to use autos as much.

While we are conserving energy to keep things running, we must also be hastily restructuring it for the long run. John and Nancy Todd of the New Alchemy Institute put it this way:

If it is assumed that making adjustments with parts of the total system is only buying time, the vital support elements of our society must be totally redesigned. For a transition to take place, the new process being created must be allowed to coexist within the present structure.

It is perhaps the first time in history that people are being asked to create the landscape of the future. There will be little time for the slow adaptation of techniques that has characterized change in human experience until now. The central task now is to find an adaptive structure in which individual lives have a wide range of opportunities available to them, within environmental and social contexts that enhance the whole society.[66]

There are a number of ways we can begin to change our present high-energy structure:

To facilitate the use of renewable energy sources, we can locate new development in areas where those sources are most plentiful. To eliminate the need for much of the energy now consumed by automobiles and trucks, we can design our neighborhoods and cities (including our production and distribution systems) in such a way that the need for these kinds of transportation is minimized.

Neighborhoods should provide maximum convenience for pedestrian and bicycle traffic with paths that connect all parts of the neighborhood, but avoid unnecessary contact with auto routes. Automobile routes through the neighborhood should be minimized.

To further reduce the need for driving, commercial and public facilities should be centralized. Residential areas should be kept within ½ to 1¼ miles from the town center, which should be rich in entertainment and commercial variety. Schools should be kept within ½ mile of all neighborhood homes. Convenience stores and other services should be strategically located, close to all neighborhoods. Baskets and trailers on bicycles can be used for carrying children and packages, while very small, enclosed pedal or electric vehicles (with maximum speeds of 6 or 7 miles per hour) may prove workable for the elderly or for general use by everyone in severe climates.

In a town designed and built to include these features, the convenience normally associated only with the auto will cease to exist. The auto will not only lose importance as a means of transportation within the neighborhood and town, but it may actually become an inconvenient way to get around.

[66]John and Nancy Todd, *Tomorrow Is Our Permanent Address* (New York: Harper & Row, 1980), p. 52.

Regional transit could also be more efficiently organized if our urban sprawl were broken up into new towns and rehabilitated suburban areas. Buses or trains could link the centers of the towns, with trams or buses making local runs from town centers into the neighborhoods. The more convenient regional transit is, the more it will be used.

There are many other ways town planning can save energy in the non-residential sector. Low crime rates that may result from well-designed communities will reduce the amount of fuel used by patrolling police. As in Davis, bike path systems can allow bicycles to be used as part of the police patrol system. Centralized commercial areas can cut down on energy used by delivery trucks and vans. More food and other consumer goods can be produced locally, cutting down on long-haul transportation energy expense. Also, locating some businesses and industries in each neighborhood can provide employment that will make commuting less necessary.

In addition to the reduction of energy in buildings and transportation, there are many procedures in the production of food and other goods that can be changed to save energy.

In food production, energy use could be greatly reduced in several ways. Crops could be grown in and around the new town, which would cut down on transportation costs. Organic, labor-intensive methods of farming could cut down on machine use and artificial fertilizers and pesticides. Crop planting could be timed so that crops are harvested as they are needed, reducing the need to store surpluses in refrigerated warehouses.

In making the transition to environmentally sound renewable energy sources, conservation and appropriate planning must become priorities for every individual, for each community, and for the country as a whole. Barry Commoner states:

As a non-renewable energy source is depleted, it becomes progressively more costly to produce, so that continued reliance on it means an unending escalation in price. This process has a powerful inflationary impact: it increases the cost of living, especially of poor people; it aggravates unemployment; it reduces the availability of capital. No economic system can withstand such pressures indefi-

nitely; sooner or later the energy crisis *must* be solved. And this can be done only by replacing the present non-renewable sources — oil, natural gas, coal, and uranium — with renewable ones which are stable in cost. That is what a national energy policy must do if it is to solve the energy crisis, rather than delay it or make it worse.[67]

While the federal government, if it so chooses, can help the solar transition to occur in an orderly and expedient manner by providing helpful legislation, it will ultimately be up to the individual and the community to make the change. There are few incentives for the large energy corporations we have relied on in the past to assist us in becoming energy self-sufficient. In fact, most likely there will be an ongoing political and economic battle, with the government in the center, over whether we should have locally produced energy on a small scale, or coal and nuclear power produced by large industry.

Land and Resources

The land and its rich supply of resources are the physical foundation of our society. Our food comes from the land, and we use the earth's resources to build our houses and cities and to make the products that help us live from day to day.

In order for a population to survive it must have access to the land and its resources, and for it to flourish, the land and resources must be rich and plentiful. If the population is to sustain itself for more than a short duration, it must maintain the renewable resources in good condition, and it must not deplete the nonrenewable resources.

Land and resources are the basis of wealth. A modest accumulation by an individual, community, or country helps to ensure stability and survival. A large or disproportionate accumulation enables disproportionate power and control.

Throughout history, empires have been built by military

[67]Barry Commoner, *The Politics of Energy* (New York: Alfred A. Knopf, 1979), p. 49.

takeovers of people and their lands. Fortune after fortune has been amassed by the shrewd maneuvering of individuals as they gain control over other individuals, land, and resources. The struggle for control of the power that wealth provides has probably caused more human suffering than anything else, with the dislocation of people from their lands by either war or economic reasons causing the largest amount of suffering. Richard Barnet makes the point:

> The fact that people are hungry is due less to insufficient food production than maldistribution. Most people who are forced to stop eating do so not because there is insufficient food grown in the world but because they no longer grow it themselves and do not have the money to buy it.[68]

If a population does not starve from the lack of control over land and resources, their freedom is certainly diminished along with the quality of their lives. Following are several of the many instances where the lives of people are impoverished by being without land and resources:

Professor Walter Goldschmidt, in his 1946 study of the California farming towns of Dinuba and Arvin, indicated that where large agribusiness concerns had taken over most of the land around a community, buying it up from small farmers who could no longer afford to maintain it, the quality of life for most members of the community decreased.[69] These findings are further supported by a report of rural community life by Professor Dean MacCannell of the University of California, Davis. He states:

> In areas such as the Westlands and the Imperial Valley of California, where giant corporate operations are the norm,

we find poverty, inequality, ignorance, and a full range of related social pathologies.[70]

The report indicated that, as a result of a federal water project that was intended to help the family farm, large agribusiness has benefitted instead by purchasing large tracts of land and farming them. This has happened because a 1902 law which was designed to protect the small farmer by limiting the amount of water allowable from federal water projects to 160 acres per customer was not enforced.

Perhaps the most glaring example of what happens to a group of people when they are deprived of their resources is that of the Native American communities that live on reservations. They have had the right to their land and resources taken away from them, leading to severe problems. The land they live on and the resources on it are not theirs to use as they see fit. The federal government holds it in guardianship for them. If they want to do something with it, they must go through months of bureaucratic red tape, many times only to receive a denial of their request. This inability to have control over their lives has left many of them apathetic and most all of them dependent on the federal government. One wonders if this may be the reason why alcoholism and suicide are higher among Native Americans on the reservation than among any other segment of the population in the United States. Given control over their land and resources and some assistance made available upon their request, the Native American communities could probably become prosperous communities in the years to come.

Many minority communities in the ghettos of our cities are without land and resources and are largely dependent on the federal government. Their communities have no economic base, and again, severe social problems exist. For most people in the United States, these cases may seem unusual and of no direct concern. But I believe we should be concerned. The more our

[68]Richard Barnet, ``The World's Resources, Part II—Minerals, Food, and Water,'' New Yorker, 31 March 1980, p. 59.

[69]Walter Goldschmidt, ``Small Business and the Community: A Study in the Central Valley of California on the Effects of Scale of Farm Operations,'' a report of the Special Committee to Study the Problems of American Small Business, U.S. Senate, 79th Congress, 2nd sess., Pursuant to S. Res. 28, Dec. 23, 1946, U.S. Government Printing Office, Washington, D.C.

[70]Dean MacCannell, ``Report on Current Social Conditions in the Communities in and near the Westlands Water District,'' California Macrosocial Accounting Project, University of California at Davis, Applied Behavioral Sciences Department, working draft, 1980.

local land and resources are bought up by foreign interests or large multinational corporations, the more they are out of our control and the less choice we as individuals and communities will have over our lives.

We can begin to change the direction of this trend if we are careful in both the way we carry on our business and the way we structure our urban patterns and local economies. We can support local small businesses that are supplying materials from their own holdings, such as small timber companies or mills, cement producers, gravel quarries, small farmers, and tile manufacturing companies. Members of communities can form investment corporations to get a large enough amount of money together to buy holdings of resources, or several communities could jointly purchase resources that they need to sustain some of their local industry. New development can be planned out with a certain amount of land set aside for food production or energy supply from forests. And communities can be spaced far enough apart to allow for land and resources to be located around them, giving more chance for local business to operate at a smaller scale.

In this day and age, it will be impossible for a community to provide the full range of resources it needs. However, by obtaining ownership of a substantial amount of some important resources, a community can increase economic stability. The next best thing an individual or community can do is to build with materials that are as durable as possible so that they do not need to be replaced. Short-term savings that come from buying less-durable products do not add to a community's stability if the community is going to have to rely on outside sources to continually replace those products. Buildings and roads must last. Using concrete for paving is an example of this principle. In many cases, concrete may be expected to last for 100 years or more, whereas asphalt must be repaved every 10 to 15 years. Asphalt requires more sophisticated technology than cement and lends itself more to centralization. Durable building materials like tile floors are superior to material which has to be replaced periodically, and tile is something that can be produced locally by a small business operation.

Resources must be conserved in the community, soils maintained and improved, and forests reestablished. Where this has not been practiced, the resulting lack of resources and decline in the quality of land has, throughout history, led to the decline of civilizations.

It is clear that the ability for each community to have control over its own energy, food, shelter, and water is largely dependent on the community's ability to have control over a significant amount of land and resources. This can occur through small local business, community-based corporations, or public ownership of some of the lands which are then leased to private businesses. It is clearly up to the members of a community to assure that they have the resources and land necessary for a strong community base.

Recycling

Nature is an excellent teacher of waste management policy. "First," she says, "forget the term 'waste' and the mentality that goes with it. Second, take the by-products and end products that you used to call waste, and recycle them all."

We should try hard to bring our activities into line with the dictum of nature (and of simple logic): "waste not, recycle." If we are producing any actual wastes, that is, products which cannot be recycled in some way, the buildup of these wastes will eventually cause severe problems, threatening the environment, our health, and perhaps life itself. Waste products of this type should not be produced.

The tendency of our society to create unusable wastes and to neglect the recycling of materials that could be reused shows a basic, shortsighted irresponsibility, an attitude we must change if we want to maintain a reasonable quality of life and a livable environment. We are beginning to realize the importance of recycling, but our understanding needs to grow until we are fully aware that token or partial recycling will not suffice. All materials used by society must enter this continuous, circular path, in which they undergo changes of form, ultimately becoming useful again after the passage of an appropriate length of time. Further, to maintain the health of the ecosystem, including humans, we must not produce substances whose existence threatens our well-being, even though these materials eventually degrade to harmless by-products. I am speaking here of cancer-causing pesticides, highly radioactive substances, and any other materials that eventually break down, but whose intermediate by-products threaten the integrity of the ecosystem.

Life-support systems, including industries and their by-products, should be analyzed to see that the integrity of the ecosystem is maintained. Both processing of raw materials and disposal of end products should be done in ways that avoid environmental destruction, making maximum use of natural energy systems already operating in the environment. Besides solar and wind energy, these include tidal, geothermal, and magnetic energy forms, as well as biological systems like photosynthesis and bacterial transformations.

With these ideas in mind, let us now consider some specific waste problems, how they are presently being handled, and what might be done to deal with them more effectively in the future.

Sewage, commonly referred to as wastewater, is the used matter discharged into sewers and transported by water. Sewage contains not only human excrement but also the residuals from sinks, baths, and laundry, as well as industrial wastes and often street runoffs from storm sewers. The United States spends a great deal of money for the disposal of sewage. The cost is high because of the energy and resources required to safely treat the wastewater to acceptable standards set by local, state, and federal officials. Though these standards are necessary, the methods we now use to attain them are questionable. The conventional methods were adopted with the assumption that cheap energy and plentiful resources would continue to be available. As these conditions change, there is a need to look for new approaches, and to reevaluate the merits of more energy-efficient alternatives.

In the past, treatment facilities used digesters to anaerobically treat sludge. The solids settled out in the sewage treatment process, and methane gas was captured for heating and power generation. With the advent of the aerobic digester (where air is pumped into the sludge for treatment), methane gas recovery was lost. Conventional treatment methods have been designed to treat sewage in the shortest amount of time and on the smallest amount of land; disposal of sewage is by the most expedient means. This has resulted in a cost savings to the user. Unfortunately, this system requires large amounts of energy. With rising energy costs, the economics of sewage disposal are changing.

Many options do exist for a community to adequately treat its sewage, recover valuable by-products, and reclaim the final effluent without consuming large amounts of energy. The number of options depends on the type of sewage to be treated. Efficient systems require cooperation between the town, homeowner, and industry to assure that the sewage is nontoxic and free of heavy metals.

One option is disposal of sewage on the land, termed *land treatment*. Most soils have the capability to physically and biologically treat wastewater. Land treatment uses the soil ecosystem to remove pollutants and was a commonly used method of sewage disposal in the United States at the beginning of the century. With the pressure to develop land, the method lost popularity. In some places it is now making a comeback. Muskegon, Michigan is an example. In the late 1960s, Muskegon County needed a sewage treatment facility capable of removing 80 percent of the phosphorus in the wastewater. The county opted for land treatment because of the cost-effectiveness of the system and the county's desire to recycle nutrients. Wastewater is first pumped into aerated lagoons. The cleaner surface water is then pumped off and used to irrigate corn.[71]

Overland flow and marshes offer two additional options for centralized treatment. The overland flow system uses a sloped surface covered with vegetation, usually grasses. The sewage is applied to the vegetation where microbiological activity at the surface of the soil reduces the pollutant concentration and removes nutrients. Industries, notably Campbell Soup Company in Paris, Texas, and municipalities including Pauls Valley, Oklahoma,

[71]Y. A. Demirjian, *Land Treatment of Municipal Wastewater Effluents, Muskegon County Wastewater System* (Washington, D.C.: U.S. Environmental Protection Agency, Office of Technology Transfer, 1975).

make use of overland flow.[72] The system promises to be popular in the future because it requires less land than the land-treatment method and is low in energy use.

Marshes are another possibility for treating effluent. For years, natural marshes have treated runoff for removal of nutrients and pollutants. Now man is creating artificial marshes for the same purpose. Brookhaven National Laboratory in New York developed an artificial marsh of cattails and duckweed for treating wastewater.[73] The National Aeronautics and Space Administration laboratory in Bay Saint Louis, Mississippi, uses water hyacinths with algal lagoons to produce an effluent of exceptional quality.[74] The use of water hyacinths, as with land treatment, promises to be popular due to its ability to not only remove nutrients producing plant biomass for energy production or fertilizer, but also to reclaim the wastewater. The first full-scale facility with these options is located at Hercules, California. The plant began operation in May 1980.

For a new garden city with scattered greenbelts and food-producing areas, a centralized collection and treatment system may not be the best method for handling the sewage. Septic tanks, though usually found almost exclusively in rural areas, could be used. Septic tanks require large *leach fields,* areas of soil that absorb the sewage by means of perforated pipes. Therefore, part of the agricultural lands of the new town could provide leach-field areas for sewage disposal from the neighborhoods they surround. A series of three or more septic tanks could serve groups of 8 to 20 houses. The effluent from the final septic tank could be used for subsurface irrigation of fruit trees and biomass-producing crops. This system would require a septic-tank-mainte-

nance service district. If development were occurring on land with a slope, sewage lines could run a considerable distance where effluent could then be discharged into a leach field or, if the soils were not adaptable, then to marshes to decompose so that later it could be used for surface irrigation of biomass forests. The district's duties would be to maintain the pumps and periodically pump the sludge out of the tanks to be injected into the soil or further composted (capturing the methane gas by-product) and used for fertilizer.

The efficiency of sewage treatment and the potential for wastewater reclamation and sludge fertilizer are primarily dependent on the absence of toxic substances, heavy metals, and large quantities of salt in the sewage. On the household level, this is managed by not using products containing such substances. There is already an array of household products that are compatible with sewage reclamation. A new town could prohibit by ordinance the use of household products that are detrimental to sewage treatment. Homeowners wishing to use products that contaminate sewage — for instance, silver nitrate which is a waste by-product of the film-developing process — would be required to install equipment that could remove the harmful substances before the sewage enters the sewer system.

In addition to preventing discharge of harmful substances to sewers, efforts need to be made to reduce the quantity of household wastewater. These efforts will reduce the waste load to the treatment facilities and in most cases, improve treatment efficiency. Water-saving toilets and flow-limiting faucets for sinks and showers should be required in all houses. Homeowners should be encouraged to recycle washing machine rinse water for the wash cycle. Present evidence also indicates that water from showers and washing machines, called *greywater,* may be used for subsurface irrigation of flowers, shrubs, and trees. In my own home I have installed a second drain from the shower that feeds drip lines buried 6 inches under the soil in a small orchard, next to a berry patch, and in the compost pile. To encourage water conservation in rental properties, all units should have water meters that require residents to pay directly for their water use and allow them to monitor it.

Another possibility for sewage reduction is the waterless,

[72]Metcalf and Eddy, Inc., *Wastewater Engineering: Treatment, Disposal, Reuse.* 2d ed., rev. by George Tchobanoglous (New York: McGraw-Hill, 1972), p. 804.

[73]N. M. Small, *Meadow/Marsh Systems as Sewage Treatment Plants,* BNL 20757 (Upton, N.Y.: Brookhaven National Laboratory, November 1975).

[74]B. C. Wolverton and R. C. McDonald, ''Water Hyacinths for Upgrading Sewage Lagoons to Meet Advanced Wastewater Treatment Standards, Part I'' NASA Technical Memorandum TM-X-72729 (St. Louis, Mo., October 1975).

no-flush toilet which eliminates 35 to 40 percent of the household sewage and provides an option for recycling of nutrients. As the name implies, the toilet requires no water; human excrement is disposed of in a chamber where biological activity or a heating source renders the material suitable for composting and subsequent use as a fertilizer on plants.

To deal with the more varied problems arising from industrial by-products, the simplest approach is to require industry to supply its own treatment and disposal system. Present Environmental Protection Agency (EPA) regulations specify on-site treatment of selected industrial wastes. Shasta Paper Company uses on-site treatment and wastewater reclamation at its Shasta mill, near Anderson, California. The wastewater is treated and then used for crop irrigation; over 400 acres of oats, wheat, and corn are raised on reclaimed water.[75]

If industry does use the community's centralized sewage system it must be held responsible for the removal of harmful toxins. EPA now uses this ''pretreatment'' requirement for many industries. A community should require this from all industries using its system.

Communities may look to industry as a buyer of reclaimed wastewater. There are numerous cases of industry using reclaimed water treated by a municipality. An excellent example of this type of cooperation is that of the city of Burbank and Burbank Power and Light. The utility company uses over 7 million gallons a day of reclaimed wastewater from the city's treatment facility for circulating and evaporating in a cooling tower.[76]

How we handle the issue of recycling depends on our priorities, as individuals and as a society. If we set too high a value on immediate convenience and on short-term profits, problems are certain to multiply. It seems that the age-old desire to get something for nothing, to separate rewards from responsibilities and profit, is at the root of the problem.

There are bacterial species that tend to multiply in a restricted environment until they die of their own wastes. Unlimited growth of communities and nations accompanied by ever-increasing production of wastes, is a course which may lead human evolution down the same road. Once a community or a country reaches a certain density of population, a size which can be reasonably supported by the resources of the land, numerical growth should stop.

[75]''Industrial Water Recycling'' pamphlet, California State Water Resources Control Board, Office of Water Recycling, March 1979.

[76]Ibid.

Chapter 5
Design with Nature for People

By our very nature we are builders. In an attempt to create a comfortable and stable habitat we are constantly altering the environment. We have put acre after acre of land into cultivation, sometimes terracing steep hills and mountains with massive rock retaining walls. We have built reservoirs and aqueducts, huge cities, and extensive roadways. We have built levees to claim lands from the ocean and from floodplains. We have erected bridges over rivers and we have carved tunnels through mountains. Many times we have bestowed upon a setting physical changes that accomplish our intended purpose and at the same time add to the spirit and character of what nature had already provided. In other instances we have failed miserably at maintaining any semblances of natural beauty or ecological function.

We must realize that our insensitivity to the natural setting is part of an insensitivity to ourselves, reflecting a lack of understanding of our aesthetic needs, and of ourselves as an integral part of nature. When there is evidence in our designs of a lack of consideration for the physical environment, we will usually also find a lack of consideration for our own physical and social needs. It shows that we have forgotten who we are and what we need, and we have allowed our fascination with novelty and technology — fascination with what we are physically capable of doing — to carry us beyond what is really in our best interests. Communities and cities designed without sensitivity to the natural setting do not reflect our true nature and will fail, often dreadfully, at providing us with an environment in which we can live comfortably and fulfill our potential for happiness.

This chapter is devoted to urban design concepts which look beyond novelty and technology, toward a harmonious relationship between people and nature. It is about design with nature, and design for people — two aspects of that single harmonious relationship.

Drainage

The drainage of water from the land is an intricate process and an integral part of the ecosystem. It affects, and is affected by, the materials and contours of the ground, and the living things in and on the ground, particularly plant life.

At the same time, however, natural drainage and the ecological communities related to it are a rich and satisfying part of man's subjective environment — aesthetically, sensually, and psychologically. It is subtly stimulating and comforting to experience the movement and sound of water in its great variety, flowing through almost-level fields, making its way along tiny creeks or swales, rushing down steeply inclined streams, or over falls or river rapids; or flowing smoothly and silently in a deep winding channel. The animal and plant life in these waterways and along their banks is endlessly fascinating. I am sure every reader cherishes at least one memory of peaceful hours spent near naturally flowing water.

As we have built our towns and our cities, we have paid little or no attention to preserving natural drainage for either its aesthetic value or its ecological value. We have filled in existing waterways and have built so that runoff is collected immediately in street gutters and underground drainage pipes or sewers. As the waterways have been destroyed, so have the plants and animals that lived along them. The accelerated storm runoff creates enormous engineering problems, requiring huge holding ponds, oversize sewage plants (if sewers are used for storm drainage), and channel straightening downstream that destroys additional natural areas.

In Seattle, Washington, where I lived when I was 6 years old, there was a creek near my house. It had water in it all year long, though only a trickle in the summer. It was my favorite place to play. I could watch the small trout, or fish for them, or just sit on the grassy bank and daydream. I picked morel mushrooms there in the spring and blackberries in the summer. When I was 20, I went back to find that spot, but it was gone. The streambed had been filled and leveled, and the water diverted into a concrete pipe under a street.

When I was 14 and 15, I played and fished along the American River in Sacramento, California. The banks of the river provided a home for many varieties of wildlife, and the pools and undercut banks harbored a great variety of fish. A few years later, the Army Corps of Engineers straightened most of the river and graded the banks to a uniform slope, which they covered with large rocks to prevent erosion. The many miles of river that were altered this way look very harsh and unnatural, and there are now fewer varieties of fish, plants, and animals.

When I was 25 and living in San Anselmo, California, I decided to build a house for my family on a lot that had a small creek running across the back. After I had bought the lot, as I was getting my building permit, an engineer from the Public Works Department apologized to me for the fact that the creek had not yet been replaced with an underground concrete pipe. I told him that I preferred that it be left as it was, but he said the city had a right-of-way across my property, and would eliminate the stream sooner or later.

I lived in that house for a little over a year. During that time, I enjoyed the sound of the water and watched the deer that came to drink, the small trout in the pools in the summer, and the steelhead spawning in the winter. But all the while I wondered how long it would stay that way.

After all the trouble and expense of eliminating natural waterways and wildlife habitats, we go to further expense trying to build sterile substitutes back into our cities. We build fountains and fake pools and streams that use pumps to circulate the water. Some are bare concrete; others include plants and naturalistic landscaping, but since they are created by man rather than by a process of ecological balance, they usually require constant maintenance. Having destroyed the habitat of the deer, fox, and muskrat, we establish zoos and spend huge amounts of money in vain attempts to make the cages look like natural environments. The very best one can say about these efforts is that they are a little bit better than having no living things or running water at all.

Maintaining natural beauty and wildlife habitat are only two of the arguments in favor of natural drainage. It can also reduce costs, conserve water, and delay storm runoff so as to reduce flooding problems.

Storm drains are expensive to build, operate, and maintain, and great savings can be realized by relying instead on man-made surface drainage swales and any natural waterways existing on the site. In Village Homes, the construction cost savings alone amounted to about $800 per house—enough to cover most of the cost of landscaping the parks and greenbelts. Because the water is not dropped below ground level, no pumping stations or energy are required to pump it back up. Also, blockages in a surface drainage system merely raise the water level instead of stopping the flow, and they are easily spotted and removed, whereas in a subsurface system they can put a storm sewer completely out of action and be difficult to find and clear.

On large waterways a bulkhead or retaining wall is sometimes needed on a bend where the current is undercutting a bank and threatening property. But this is far less costly and less destructive than straightening the whole channel.

Natural drainage also provides opportunities for the ground to absorb and retain water, which is particularly beneficial in areas that have light annual rainfall. In California's Sacramento Valley, for example, the entire winter's rainfall can be absorbed by the ground without saturating it below a depth from which the roots of grass, shrubs, and trees can recover the water. Therefore, any rainwater that can be made to soak into the soil, instead

of running off, means an equivalent reduction in watering requirements during the dry spring and summer. Native plants can often survive with no additional water at all. In wetter regions, water absorbed into the ground surface or into streambeds may eventually find its way into underground aquifers that supply water to wells. This is important because in many areas the underground water level is becoming alarmingly low due to increased pumping from wells for irrigation and domestic uses.

Modern drainage systems, on the other hand, tend to maximize runoff and carry the water to rivers or large streams, or to evaporation ponds. Only in a few areas are recharge ponds being used to get water into the ground and replenish the water table, and these do nothing to directly satisfy watering needs in the neighborhoods where the rain originally fell.

In areas with greater rainfall, natural drainage is valuable in evening out downstream flow rates. The many small waterways that contain water only during rains and for a few days afterward keep the water moving slowly and allow it to soak into the banks where it is held and gradually released. Thus the rainfall reaches the larger streams gradually over many days. In neighborhoods where runoff is carried in street gutters and underground pipes, these natural delaying processes do not occur, and rainfall reaches streams and rivers in a matter of hours. Storms produce sudden heavy surges that can destroy small streams and create flooding problems in larger ones, requiring major artificial controls like holding ponds and straightened channels. In towns where storm drainage goes into the sewage system, these surges require sewage plants with absurdly large peak capacities, and unusually heavy storms may still force dumping of untreated sewage into streams, rivers, or bays.

In the typical subdivision, lots are graded to slope toward the street. In Village Homes, we graded lots away from the street so the rainwater trickling off roofs and lawns finds its way into shallow swales running through common areas behind the houses. These swales carry the water slowly to larger channels landscaped like seasonal streambeds, with rocks, bushes, and trees. Runoff from streets goes directly into these larger channels. Small check dams in these channels help to slow the flow of water and prevent surges downstream. Water generally flows over these check dams for a full 24 hours after rainfall has stopped. In light rains, the surface drainage system allows all the water that falls to be absorbed into the ground. In heavier rains, the system empties some water into the city's storm drains, but nowhere near the amount of runoff that a typical subdivision would.

The potential mosquito problem is easily managed. The creeks are either designed so that they will drain completely within two or three days or they are designed to retain water year-round and are stocked with mosquito fish — which happily feast on the mosquito larvae.

All of the surface drainage swales and channels in Village Homes were created artificially by grading, because the natural drainage channels on the site had been obliterated years ago when the land was leveled for irrigation. Therefore the new drainage channels we created conform to the street plan, rather than vice versa. During excavation and grading of the site for streets and utilities, we found signs of a seasonal creek bed that had been filled in when the site was leveled. It was, of course, too late to change the street plans, and I am not sure there would have been any advantage in restoring the channel in its original location, though we were able to create larger ponds in those areas so the water would be more easily absorbed into the sand. On undisturbed sites, however, I feel the natural drainage patterns should be respected as much as possible. Natural channels should be used where they exist, and where an artificial channel is created, it should begin from where the water naturally begins to accumulate.

It is interesting that natural drainage was one of the most difficult innovations to get approved for Village Homes. Despite the fact that such systems seemed so serviceable, the city's Planning Department and Public Works Department were adamantly against it, and the Federal Housing Authority (FHA) refused to approve it. They all said it wouldn't work; that it would require continual maintenance and wouldn't significantly reduce the amount of runoff. The planning director said it would harbor vermin—an engineering term for wildlife, I suppose. So far there have been no such problems. Each winter I get a pleasant feeling of warmth and righteousness around the Christmas season as storm drains back up and pumps fail in other parts of Davis, while Village Homes is beautiful with its multitude of little streams and its gentle waterfalls.

I think this is a good example of how planners and engineers have habitually tried to overcome nature instead of understanding her and collaborating with her, even when it is more costly and less practical to do so.

Village Homes is by no means the only place in the United States where natural drainage is being used successfully. I got the idea myself from Ashland, Oregon, where a small creek runs through the city park and adds a great deal to the beauty of pedestrian walks in the downtown area. Ian McHarg, author of *Design with Nature,*[1] has probably done the most extensive work with natural drainage, and has designed such a system for the Woodlands project now under construction in Houston, Texas.[2]

[1] Ian McHarg, *Design with Nature* (Philadelphia: Falcon Press, 1969).
[2] Reference in Ian McHarg's drainage study on the Woodlands.

Landscaping

Historically, human beings first exploited and then learned to manage the plants in their environment to meet important human needs. They used plants for food, fiber, and fuel, and for protection from sun and wind; to hedge cattle in and enemies out, and to define social spaces. They also learned to manage plants to delight the senses with color and fragrance, the sound and movement of windblown foliage, and the order and complexity of natural forms.[3] I believe these pleasures go deeper than mere stylish aesthetics; I believe they reflect the fact that our perceptions and responses are genetically tailored to the natural environment and to living things, so that such environments are good for us psychologically. Humans managed their landscape environment to meet all these needs simultaneously, in an integrated way.

The word *landscaping* has different connotations today. Both as generally practiced, and as taught in schools of landscape architecture, landscaping has little to do with protection from climate or with definition of spaces, and nothing at all to do with food, fuel, or fiber. Its aesthetics reflect stylish fads and status seeking more than any understanding of what is intrinsically delightful to the human spirit.

This kind of landscaping is a wasteful practice — wasteful of land, wasteful of energy, wasteful of human resources, indifferent to intangible human satisfactions, and in many ways destructive to the environment. It is a symptom of the illusions of inexhaustible wealth and resources, and our delusions of scientific omnipotence

[3]Rene Dubos, *The Wooing of Earth: New Perspectives on Man's Use of Nature* (New York: Charles Scribner's Sons, 1980).

Landscaping for Climate Control

Plants are invaluable for controlling sun and wind, and, in cold-winter climates, for controlling drifting snow. The most obvious example of wind control is the large-scale windbreak of tall trees which reduces wind speeds for long distances in its lee, and for many times the height of the trees. But smaller plantings are also useful for more detailed control, either by moderating the wind's force or controlling its direction. Relatively small plantings near a building can reduce wind speed next to the building by diverting wind around or over the building. Foliage against the wall of the building—tall shrubs or a trellis with vines—can further reduce wind speed to create a virtual dead-air space next to the wall, which significantly reduces heat loss through the wall in cold weather. Shrubs can also be used to protect outdoor living spaces or entrances to buildings from wind.

In hot climates proper landscaping can improve ventilation by locating near buildings plantings planned for detailed control of wind direction. Landscape architect Robert F. White's studies at the Texas Engineering Experiment Station, published in 1945 and often reproduced, show in detail how various combinations of trees, shrubs, and hedges planted beside or upwind of a building can increase or reduce the airflow through the building, change the patterns of circulation within the building, or even reverse the direction of flow.[4] This knowledge can be particularly valuable in locations where wind directions are fairly regular. Around Davis, for example, because of the north-south orientation of the Sacramento Valley and its relationship to the Carquinez Strait air corridor, the summer breeze blows predictably from the north in the morning and the south in the evening. In hilly areas, wind patterns may be more complex but still fairly predictable in any one spot, so landscaping for ventilation control calls for a familiarity with the patterns around each house available only to someone who lives there.

and mastery of nature. We have neglected the uses of plants for climate control partly because we imagined we would always have plenty of cheap energy for heating and air conditioning. In urban areas, we have landscaped our homes and towns with unproductive plants because we thought we had plenty of land to grow food elsewhere, plenty of water to irrigate it, plenty of energy for machine cultivation and long-distance hauling, and the ability to maintain ecologically unsound mechanized farming with large quantities of ecologically unsound pesticides and artificial fertilizers.

To make landscaping an element of appropriate planning, we must work to rediscover the art of landscaping to satisfy diverse human needs simultaneously, making it an expression both of thrift and of care for the ecosystem. I want to discuss in detail two aspects of this: landscaping for climate control and landscape productivity. I will relate both of these aspects to energy conservation and mention other elements of appropriate landscaping wherever they seem most relevant.

---

[4]Robert F. White, "Effects of Landscape Development on the Natural Ventilation of Buildings and Their Adjacent Area," Texas Engineering Experiment Station, Research Report, no. 45, College Station, Texas, March 1945.

Where summers are warm, shading is an important goal of landscape plantings. Good shading can keep temperatures comfortable both indoors and outdoors. It can also save energy by reducing or eliminating the need for artificial air conditioning. I want to discuss shading in some detail because it becomes particularly complicated around houses that use solar energy.

Everyone knows it is more comfortable in the shade on a hot day because one's body is directly heated by solar radiation when in the sun. What is not so obvious is that lack of overall shading raises temperatures throughout the neighborhood, even in the shady places. Unshaded pavement — streets, parking lots, patios, and walkways — is especially bad. Pavement is often dark-colored and absorbs more of the radiation that strikes it than lighter surfaces. It does not cool itself by water evaporation as vegetation does. And its mass stores heat during the day so that it remains hot well into the evening. A study in Davis by the University of California has shown that evening ambient temperatures are up to 10 degrees lower in neighborhoods where streets are well shaded than in those where street shading is poor.[5]

Streets and parking lots should not be designed without considering how they can be shaded. In Village Homes we made streets easier to shade by eliminating the parking lanes on either side, and substituting intermittent angled parking bays with four parking spaces each. Thus shade trees could be planted between bays, or between a bay and a private driveway, separated only by the two travel lanes with a total width of only 20 to 24 feet.

At the same time, trees used for shading must not substantially shade solar heat collectors on the roofs of houses, or south-facing windows that function as solar heat collectors in the winter. Deciduous trees can be used to provide shade in the summer, when solar space heating is not needed, since they lose their leaves in the fall and allow sunlight to reach the collectors or windows through the bare branches. But some deciduous trees do not lose their leaves early enough in some climates. Also, collectors used for domestic hot water work year-round so they

[5]Jonathan Hammond, Marshall Hunt, Richard Cramer, and Loren Neubauer, "A Strategy for Energy Conservation," City of Davis, California, Energy Conservation Ordinance Project (Davis, 1974).

the Codes, Covenants, and Restrictions (C, C, & R's) of the subdivision, or by local or state ordinance.[6]

It is particularly crucial to shade windows from direct sunlight during the summer, since any sunlight that falls on them enters the building and immediately turns into heat. Indoor curtains or blinds help very little unless they are light in color (to reflect solar radiation) and fitted to the walls (to prevent heat from sneaking into the room), because most of the light striking them turns into heat, just as it would if allowed to cross the room and strike the other wall. Once the sun's energy passes through the glass, it's in, and its heat will raise the temperature of the room.

With thoughtful planning, deciduous shrubs and vines can shade windows as effectively as artificial shading devices, like awnings, and can do it much more cheaply and attractively. They are particularly valuable for shading south-facing windows used for solar heating, because their foliage provides more shade in the fall than it does in the spring when leaves are just beginning to form. Therefore, they can be arranged to shade the windows in the fall when the sun is getting lower in the sky but the weather is still warm, and still admit the sunlight in the spring when the sun is at the same angle but the weather is cool. A fixed awning or overhead roof used for the same purpose would either give too much shade in the spring or too little in the fall.

Landscape Productivity: Food and Fuel

Landscaped spaces in our towns and suburbs today are almost entirely unproductive. This is a relatively recent development; a few centuries ago it was quite common for each house to have its own garden, fruit trees, and vines. Small fields, forests, orchards, and vineyards surrounded towns so closely as to be part of the immediate landscape. The pattern still exists in many small, old European towns.

This was a very efficient use of land. The same pieces of land provided both the space needed for growing food and fuel,

must never be shaded. Thus shade plantings require careful planning. The landscape designer must be familiar with leaf-fall dates and growth patterns of various species in the local climate, and must be able to use them creatively to provide shade or sunlight where and when it is needed.

In addition, advice by the neighborhood group as a whole concerning landscaping on private lots is necessary to make sure that plantings on one lot do not shade a neighbor's solar collectors. This can be accomplished with a provision for solar rights in

[6]Gail Boyer Hayes, *Social Access Law: Protecting Access to Sunlight for Solar Energy Systems* (Cambridge, Mass.: Ballinger Publishing Co., 1979).

and the pleasant public and private outdoor territories needed for human activity, interaction, and comfort. Productive trees, bushes, and vines performed the same functions as the unproductive ones now generally used for landscaping: providing shade, wind protection, and privacy; defining spaces; and creating a pleasing atmosphere by echoing the natural environment in which humans evolved.

Our present neglect of productive landscaping is wasteful in a number of ways. It not only wastes land, but also wastes energy and resources used in transporting and marketing agricultural produce. It wastes fertilizer (which requires additional energy, if chemically produced) and water where irrigation is required. It also wastes human labor. Unproductive landscaping requires about as much labor from the homeowner as productive landscaping, but it also requires others to work to produce the food elsewhere, and to process and distribute it.

Our tendency to imitate the wealthy, however, is also a factor contributing to the prevalence of unproductive landscaping. Just as our penchant for separating kitchens from dining and living rooms even in small houses imitates the design of larger houses designed for families with servants, the ornamental landscaping of small yards can be seen as an imitation of larger yards which, in turn, imitate the rolling lawns of the country estate. Thorsten Veblen, who developed the concept of *conspicuous consumption,* observed that lawns are considered tasteful not so much because they have the same aesthetic appeal as a well-kept pasture, but because they are kept manicured by expensive and wasteful means rather than by simple productive grazing.[7] Their appeal is the same today; the difference is that today even the humblest wage earner must establish his status with a tiny piece of wasted pasture which he keeps manicured by his own labor. Similarly, the lack of a vegetable garden and the use of unproductive trees, shrubs, and vines in landscaping once indicated that the owner was one of the wealthy few who could afford to have their food grown and brought to them by others. Today, all but

the very poorest have adopted that sign of status, and those who still have vegetable gardens hide them in the backyard.

Turf lawns are particularly wasteful in many situations, because they demand lots of water and fertilizer to keep them attractive and healthy. In Village Homes we tried to reduce the need for individual lawns by providing a large public turf playfield for field sports, in hopes that this will encourage homeowners to devote their own yards to food-producing or drought-tolerant plantings.

Suburbanites used to purely decorative landscaping tend to assume that vegetable gardens are unsightly. A sprawling, neglected garden can be an eyesore, but in a relatively dense residential area where lots are small and the garden space is at a premium, gardens are less likely to be neglected. With the garden right under the window and on public display, there is no reason to think that the homeowner will neglect its appearance any more than he or she would neglect the appearance of a purely decorative yard.

In Village Homes we reversed the typical neighborhood pattern by encouraging people to put their fenced private yards on the side of the house facing the street, and leave the yards on the other side open to a narrow common strip between the two rows of lots. The common strip is managed collectively by the homeowners on either side. People tend to do their gardening on the part of their lots facing this common strip, or, by mutual agreement, on the common strip itself. Some groups of homeowners have developed very creative ways of integrating vegetable gardens with individual or communal patios or children's play areas. Since this is the "public" side of the houses, owners tend to keep their gardens as well maintained as people in a standard subdivision keep their front yards. In fact, they experience a very similar social pressure from their neighbors to keep these publicly visible areas neat.

Nut trees, fruit trees, and fruiting shrubs and vines present no more neatness problems than unproductive landscape plants. With their diverse sizes and growth habits, one or another of them can be used for almost any landscaping situation. Apple, filbert, fig, and apricot trees, with their spreading growth pattern and different sizes, are suitable for shading patios of various sizes.

[7]Thorsten Veblen, *The Theory of the Leisure Class* (Boston: Houghton-Mifflin, 1973), pp. 98–99.

Trees with a more upright pattern — plums, cherries, and pears — are good for protection from the afternoon summer sun. In mild-winter climates, citrus trees, because they do not lose their leaves, can provide a year-round windbreak or visual barrier. All of these trees are available in dwarf and semidwarf varieties that can be used in landscaping like medium-size or large shrubs. Other species like blueberries and currants grow naturally as shrubs. The smaller fruit or nut trees can be planted in rows and pruned flat to form a unified hedge or tall barrier, or they can be trained in the very flat and formal espalier style, hugging a fence or shading an east or west wall. The bramble fruits — raspberry, blackberry, and boysenberry — can be trained on supports to make a high or low fence. There are also plants considered primarily ornamental, like crab apples and jujubes, that bear edible fruit.[8]

Grapevines are exceptionally versatile. In virtually any climate, some variety of grape can be grown and eaten fresh or made into raisins or juice. They can be trained on supports to make a low fence, or on a vertical or overhead horizontal trellis to provide shade just where it is needed. They are particularly suitable for summer shading above the south-facing windows of a passive solar house. Although I have no personal experience with them, I expect that the kiwi vines (``Chinese gooseberries'') that have recently been introduced to this country would be equally

[8]For more detailed information see Mark Podems and Brenda Bortz, *Ornamentals for Eating* (Emmaus, Pa.: Rodale Press, 1975).

useful in appropriate climates, and their egg-size sweet fruits are a special delicacy.

Public areas can also be landscaped with productive plants. In addition to the varieties already mentioned, the larger nut trees, like walnuts and pecans, can be used for large-scale shade. In Village Homes we have allowed wild cherries, *Rosa rugosa,* and blackberries to grow wild along some of the natural drainage channels and in other areas. Tiny orchards and vineyards here and there in residential areas provide a bit of openness and relief from the monotonous pattern of houses and lots.

It is important to realize that the urban landscape is capable of food production in economically significant quantities. In these days of large-scale mechanized agriculture, it is easy to write off as insignificant the yield of a peach tree here, two grapevines here, and a half-dozen tomato plants there. But 100 peach trees scattered through a neighborhood of 1,000 persons are as productive as 100 trees in 1 acre of orchard, and 1,000 such neighborhoods are equivalent in production to 1,000 acres of peach orchard. And those neighborhoods do not produce peaches alone; they have space for apples, pears, plums, apricots, and cherries; for nuts and berries and grapes, and a wide variety of fresh vegetables in season.

An important advantage of neighborhood agriculture is that it allows for a healthy ecological balance that cannot be maintained in large-scale, single-crop plantings. Since plantings of any one species are small and separate, they do not encourage pests of that species to build up a large population, and they make it harder for pests and diseases to spread. This makes it possible to avoid costly and environmentally destructive pesticides, and to use natural controls instead. In Village Homes, orchards and vineyards are no larger than half an acre, and are next to landscaping that harbors enemies of their pests. For example, blackberries planted near vineyards harbor the anagrus wasp, which preys on the grape leafhopper. Thickets are provided for birds that feed on insects, and small ponds allow insect-eating toads to complete their life cycles.

Firewood for heating and for electrical generation is likely to be an important part of our energy supply in coming years, and we could save additional energy by growing the trees near where the firewood will be needed, instead of hauling it long distances. This makes it reasonable to consider forestland as a possible element in urban landscaping. Large and small woodlots could be placed in and around the town for firewood production, located so as to serve as windbreaks, and harvested and replanted on a rotating basis. While the trees were growing, the woodlots would provide space for play, walking, jogging, picnics, and contemplation, and as a refuge for wildlife. It would be possible to get away to the woods for half an hour any time, without driving great distances — or any distance at all.

In Davis, it has been proposed that the city government create biomass forest areas around and within the city, using eucalyptus, black locust, and other fast-growing species, interspersed with 1- to 20-acre organic truck farms.[9] This would serve as a buffer zone to protect the city from the drift of toxic agricultural chemical sprays. The city is presently considering the feasibility of the idea.

Circulation and Town Layout

Circulation systems within cities have traditionally been based on a grid pattern with local residential streets connected to larger arterial streets. Streets are for both cars and bicycles, which generally leaves the cyclist at a severe disadvantage. Pedestrian walks are along the sides of most of these streets. The pedestrian must cross the path of the automobile at every block and be subjected to noise and exhaust fumes. Because of the inability of the grid system to handle heavy flows of long-distance, high-speed through traffic, freeways are often added as the city expands.

In some instances this has worked well, particularly where through traffic has been rerouted around a city, to avoid interference with local traffic. It has not worked well in situations where freeways have been built to move commuter traffic to and from work. The freeway has encouraged the continuation of sprawl by

[9]Ad Hoc Committee on Alternative Land Use. "Alternative Land Use Report," presented to the Davis, California, City Council (November 1979).

permitting developers to build in locations that have access to freeways which are not yet congested during commuting hours. As building proceeds, the freeways gradually become more and more clogged for seemingly endless miles. This has led to billions of frustrating commuter hours spent in slow-moving lines of traffic, not to mention the resultant enormous drain on energy supplies.

More energy fed into the transportation system means that more people move faster over a greater range in the course of every day. Everybody's daily radius expands at the expense of being able to drop in on an acquaintance or walk through the park on the way to work. Extremes of privilege are created at the cost of universal enslavement. An elite packs unlimited distance into a lifetime of pampered travel, while the majority spends a bigger slice of their existence on unwanted trips. The few mount their magic carpets to travel between distant points that their ephemeral presence renders both scarce and seductive, while the many are compelled to trip further and faster and to spend more time preparing for and recovering from their trips.

In the United States, four-fifths of all man-hours on the road are those of commuters and shoppers who hardly ever get into a plane, while four-fifths of the mileage flown to conventions and resorts is covered year after year by the same one and a half percent of the population, usually those who are either well-to-do or professionally trained to do good. The speedier the vehicle, the larger the subsidy it gets from regressive taxation. Barely 0.2 percent of the entire U.S. population can engage in self-chosen air travel more than once a year, and few other countries can support a jet set which is that large.

The captive tripper and the reckless traveller become equally dependent on transport. Neither can do without it. Occasional spurts to Acapulco or to a Party Congress dupe the ordinary passenger into believing that he has made it into the shrunk world of the powerfully rushed. The occasional chance to spend a few hours strapped into a high-powered seat makes him an accomplice in the distortion of human space, and prompts him to consent to the design of his country's geography around vehicles rather than around people. Man has evolved physically and culturally together with his cosmic niche. What for animals is their environment, he has learned to make into his home. His self-image requires as its complement a life-space and a life-time integrated by the pace at which he moves. If that relationship is determined by the velocity of vehicles rather than by the movement of people, man the architect is reduced to the status of a mere commuter.

The typical American male devotes more than 1,600 hours a year to his car. He sits in it while it goes and while it stands idling. He parks it and searches for it. He earns the money to put down on it and to meet the monthly installments. He works to pay for petrol, tolls, insurance, taxes and tickets. He spends four of his sixteen waking hours on the road or gathering his resources for it. And this figure does not take into account the time consumed by other activities dictated by transport: time spent in hospitals, traffic courts and garages; time spent watching automobile commercials or attending consumer education meetings to improve the quality of the next buy. The model American puts in 1,600 hours to get 7,500 miles: less than five miles per hour. In countries deprived of a transportation industry, people manage to do the same, walking wherever they want to go, and they allocate only three to eight percent of their society's time budget to traffic instead of 28 per cent. What distinguishes the traffic in rich countries from the traffic in poor countries is not more mileage per hour of life-time for the majority, but more hours of compulsory consumption of high doses of energy, packaged and unequally distributed by the transportation industry.[10]

Rapid transit systems should replace the freeways as the major form of transportation in the future. They are a far more

[10]Ivan Illich, *Energy and Equity* (New York: Harper & Row, 1974), pp. 17–19.

efficient use of energy. But rapid transit systems alone are not going to eliminate heavy use of the auto. People still have to drive to the store, to the rapid transit station, to take children to school, and to find entertainment.

Dependence on the auto will only be reduced when towns are designed to a scale that makes bicycling and walking convenient means of transportation. Overall size must be kept within certain limits, and a balance of residences, places of employment, entertainment, goods, and services must be provided in a design that makes walking and riding a bike safe and pleasant. In order to create pleasant, safe pedestrian routes where dangerous exhaust fumes are absent, auto and pedestrian paths must be kept separate. At the same time, emergency vehicle access must be available to all the buildings, as must access for transporting items that cannot easily be carried. This does not necessarily mean that every residential lot must front directly on a street, but as a practical matter that will probably be required, at least until we have developed real alternatives to driving autos, and have become accustomed to their use.

The most obvious way to accomplish this, and in fact the one that has been used in Radburn and some other garden city plans, is to make all streets in the town feed outward to a peripheral ring road, rather than inward. Bicycle and pedestrian paths, on the other hand, would run inward from each neighborhood to the geographic center of town, where the commercial and civic facilities people visit most often would be located. Vehicle access to the town center could be provided by a single service road bisecting the town, either on grade or below grade, and connecting at both ends to the ring road. With such a circulation system, one could reach any point in the town by auto, or travel between any two points, if necessary, by driving out to the ring road and around to the appropriate street entrance. The route would be fairly indirect, however. The direct routes would be reserved for the bicyclists and pedestrians for whom distance is more crucial than it is for drivers. To keep these distances practical, the size of the town would have to be limited to two to six square miles. Around the town center would be neighborhoods of about 500 to 1,000 people, each surrounded by a greenbelt consisting of agricultural areas, parks, sports fields, and natural areas.

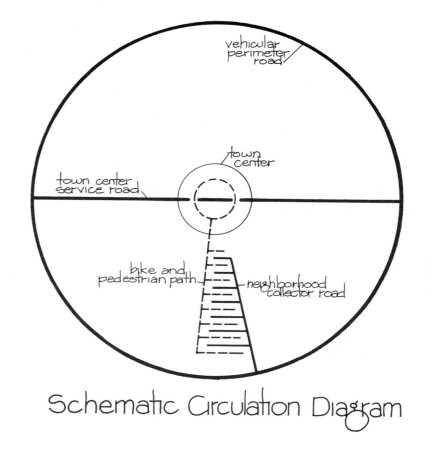

Schematic Circulation Diagram

Laying out a community in this way creates an auto-free living environment. The plan also lends itself easily to other design solutions such as the creation of distinct neighborhoods adjacent to open spaces where food and fuel supplies can be grown and where, if conditions permit, treated wastewater can be used for subsurface irrigation. The plan makes it simple to incorporate natural drainage systems because there is open space adjacent to all buildings. The interconnection of open spaces allows for continuous waterways.

This basic pattern, which appears somewhat rigid in the conceptual drawing, can take on a variety of different final forms based on the terrain encountered in each design situation.

The Village Homes subdivision offers one example of how auto access can be provided for every home while maintaining a generally auto-free neighborhood. Every house in Village Homes faces on a street. The difference is that fences and shrubs have been placed along the street to form a courtyard between the street and the house. This replaces the wasted front lawn found in the typical subdivision. Because a private yard has been created on the street side, we have been able to eliminate the traditional fenced backyard and turn the property behind the home into a common open space. Here we have located the bicycle and footpaths and the creeklike channels which make up the natural drainage system. People can be found there cycling and walking as they go to and from their residences or using the space for vegetable gardening or some other activity. Children tend to play there rather than in the streets.

Another important consideration in laying out a neighborhood is that all structures should be able to take maximum advantage of the sun for space and water heating. The Village Homes subdivision provides an example of how to provide north-south orientation while avoiding the somewhat undesirable visual impact of having straight rows of houses all facing south.

Streets in Village Homes are curved, allowing the houses to be staggered yet still to universally maintain a southern orientation.

There are a couple of points that seem important to the general layout of a subdivision which is designed to reduce auto traffic. Very small commercial centers should be located adjacent to each neighborhood to reduce the number of trips made to the town center. The variety and number of these should be based on the design of the local neighborhood as it grows and determines what its needs are.

In the Village Homes neighborhood there is a small office complex. There are plans for a small eight-room inn-restaurant, a co-op food store, a medical office, and five small shops which could house such enterprises as a bakery, a tofu shop, potter, sprouting operations, tailor, or other small businesses that could thrive with the amount of business available in such a decentralized location.

The appropriate location of schools can reduce dependence on the automobile. Children in the lower grades should be able to attend schools located in the neighborhood. There are several advantages to this. Not only can young children walk safely through the neighborhood to school, but schools would also be convenient so parents could play a larger role in the early years of their children's education. This should create a very comfortable situation for both children and parents.

In lieu of the normal sidewalks on the street, 6-foot-wide paths can be used between groups of houses. These widths in Village Homes seem to work well. These narrower paths can lead into 8- and 10-foot-wide collector paths, designed to carry more traffic.

In the more centralized locations of a town, heavily used arterial paths should probably be 12 to 24 feet wide. As traffic gets to be heavy at intersections, stop signs may be required, or possibly a traffic circle. In very heavy traffic areas, pedestrian walks and bicycle paths will have to be completely separated.

Street widths can be drastically reduced in a development which encourages pedestrians and cyclists because of the reduction in the use of autos. In the last 30 years, street-width standards in the United States have become ridiculously large, resulting in wasted land, to say nothing of the expense involved in development and maintenance.

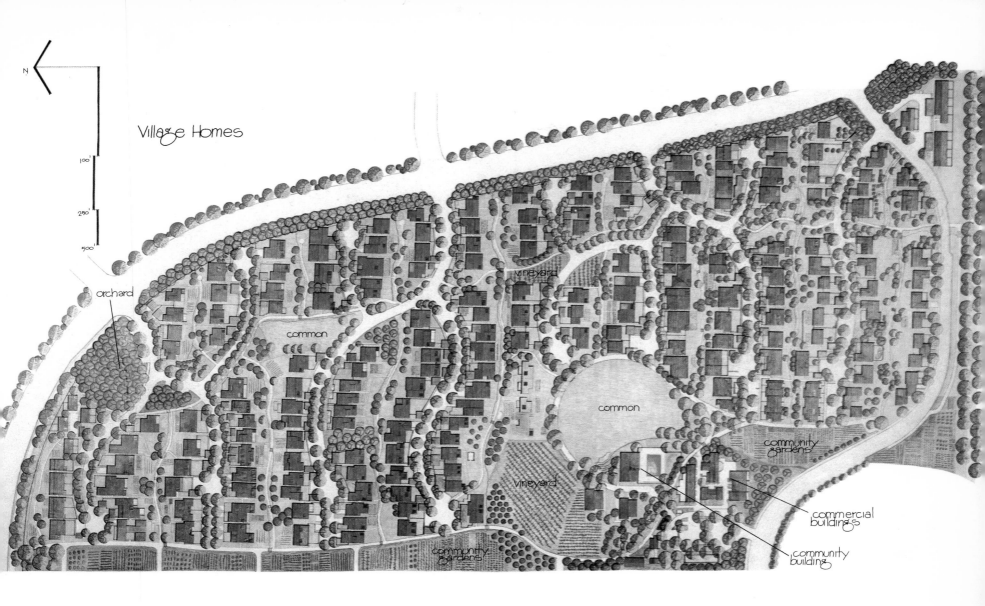

Village Homes

N

100'
250'
500'

orchard

common

vineyard

vineyard

common

community gardens

community gardens

commercial buildings

community building

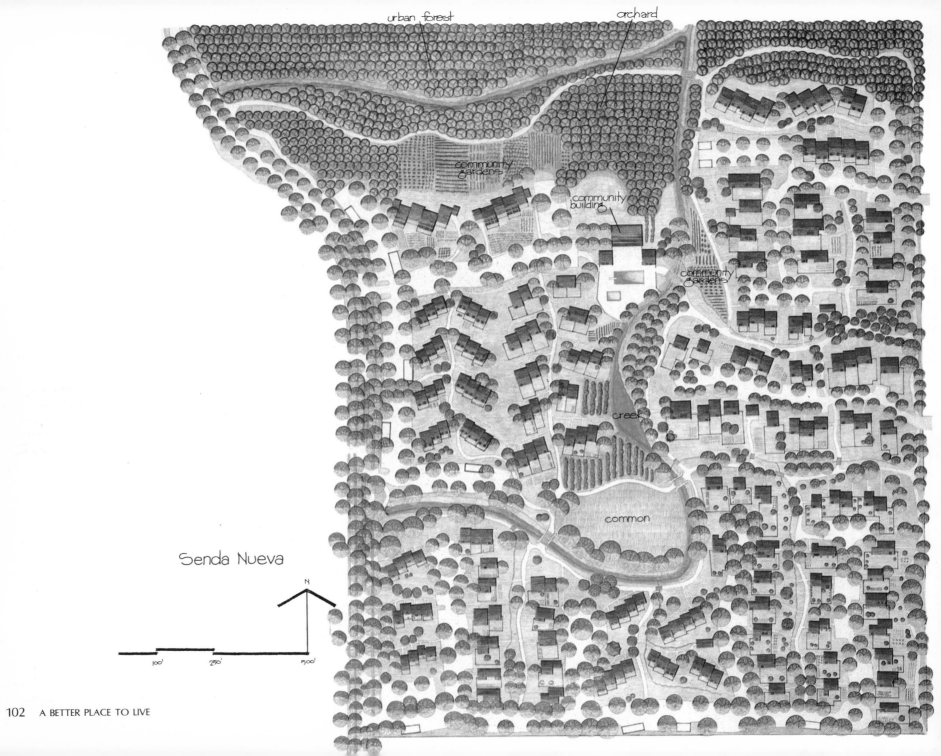

urban forest

orchard

community gardens

community building

community gardens

creek

common

Senda Nueva

N

100'   250'   500'

Village Homes has 20- and 24-foot-wide streets which are city maintained. The 20-foot-wide streets are more than adequate. There is an additional 3-foot easement where no obstructions or vegetation can be more than 6 inches high. This allows emergency access and walking room. Collector streets are also reduced. A minor arterial street adjacent to Village Homes is 38 feet in width. It has two 11-foot-wide auto lanes and two 8-foot-wide emergency strips that also serve as bicycle lanes. At intersections, this arterial street widens to accommodate an extra turning lane.

Auto-free circulation can be taken one step further in neighborhood designs if we are willing to give up direct auto access to all lots. This has been done in a development plan for a neighborhood of about 297 homes on 49.5 acres in Davis, California.[11] The center of the neighborhood would be an open space, with the housing clustered around the outside. Some of the houses would be on regular streets but others would be grouped around central parking lots, with footpaths leading from the parking lot to the more distant houses in the group. Besides reducing the impact of the auto still further, this plan offers more economical land use by reducing total pavement area.

Once planning and developing auto-free living really take hold, people are likely to begin to feel that their private autos are just more trouble than they are worth. This would make possible a still further revolution in town design. We could eliminate all residential streets, parking areas, and garages, with tremendous savings in construction costs and space. The foot-bicycle paths could be built just a little bit wider and more solidly to accommodate small, lightweight emergency vehicles and delivery trucks; elderly or disabled persons could be licensed to drive small electric cars at a top speed of about seven miles per hour on these paths. The space saved would allow the town to be still more compact, making it still easier to get to the town center and the bus terminal.

The point of this section is to show that, although it is very difficult to get along without a car in a world designed for cars rather than for people, it would be not much of a hardship to do without a car in a world designed for that style of life. Probably

[11]The development, to be called Senda Nueva, is being planned by Jon Hammond of Living Systems, Winters, California.

our principal motivation for making the change would be the need to conserve energy. But as I have noted earlier, the private auto has impoverished our lives in ways having nothing to do with energy consumption.

Neighborhoods

The neighborhood has gone almost totally unrecognized as an important element in the design of our urban environment. This is surprising because the neighborhood should be as meaningful a social unit as the individual home and the city. The neighborhood should provide for a certain set of functions, and the diverse elements of the neighborhood should be put together in such a way as to accommodate those functions. Just as a home is designed with certain rooms where family members can go to be alone and other rooms which accommodate group activities, so the neighborhood should be designed to offer opportunities for both privacy and community.

As I strongly advocate specific, well-defined modular garden cities, I also advocate well-defined and comprehensively designed neighborhoods within those cities. A good neighborhood will offer security and privacy, and will aid residents' feelings of identity, and will still satisfy their needs for diversity and a sense of community. The neighborhood can be just a site where houses are located with very little interaction between households, or it can be more of a cohesive unit in which a great deal of interaction takes place between each household and the rest of the community. It can be a social living environment, similar to the villages, tribes, and living groups that humans have formed for thousands of years. It can be the kind of living environment that I believe we are genetically programmed for — one which allows us the opportunity to more easily satisfy our basic social needs of identity, security, and community, and which gives us the social experiences that help us learn to better relate to other individuals.

It seems clear to me that, by comparison with primitive societies, our society is lacking in the quality of human relationships, primarily because we have structured it so that people can get along without much communication or cooperation. This is obvious in suburbs where each household owns a separate lot surrounded by a fence, and all the public facilities, shops, restaurants, offices, theaters, and schools are zoned into another part of town, so there is no necessary contact with anyone in the neighborhood.

In such settings, people tend to find human contact in substitute activities: through lodges and country clubs, churches and popular causes. Some people do fairly well this way, but it is without realizing how much effort goes into creating the interaction that used to come naturally out of the things that people did in groups only a few centuries ago, just to satisfy their basic material needs. Because today's contrived interaction is not essential to the people involved, it has a different quality. The lack of meaningful social relationships for many in today's society is apparent in people's lack of respect for one another, their lack of deep, lasting friendships, and their preoccupation with superficial relationships based on status.

Consequently, there are a lot of people in our society who look successful and do well financially, but haven't gotten very far up the ladder in Maslow's "hierarchy of needs." Our society is set up to produce and cater to these people. Appropriate planning can help to reverse this trend by offering people situations where they can more easily communicate and cooperate, and where they can have easily available options for interaction as they go about their daily activities.

I believe the psychopolitical theories of J. Andre, described in Chapter 2, apply in this situation. Andre feels that people are motivated by both concern for self and concern for others, and that they need to be able to find expression for both of these concerns in their lives. I think that growing up in a society that doesn't require much cooperation has kept people from developing the altruistic side of their natures. Humanity benefits when our environment encourages the development and expression of the altruistic drive, while providing positive outlets for the competitive, self-interested drive through sports and other personal achievement activities.

I have been encouraged by my participation in communication-facilitating techniques, particularly certain group workshops dealing with interpersonal communication. These sessions took various forms, but the basic idea was to put people in a situation where they would get instant, candid feedback from others on whether or not they were dealing fairly and honestly. It was amazing how quickly and how fully most people opened up to each other in such a situation. I was very impressed to see that people who had grown up in a society that doesn't reward open communication and cooperation, or offer much opportunity to practice it, could still learn fairly quickly if given the right environment. It was this experience that later gave me confidence that people could get along, sharing community projects. There would be some initial hassles, but in the long run the interaction would increase people's self-esteem and confidence in their ability to deal with others, enhancing their potential for true friendship with their neighbors.

The importance of making our neighborhoods conducive to a spirit of cooperation and mutual support, instead of isolationism and mutual distrust, cannot be overemphasized. Our state of mind, and even our physical health, are profoundly affected by the social climate of our neighborhood environments.

Consider the example of a little town, Roseto, in Pennsylvania. A small village of Italian-Americans, Roseto was, until very recently, a closely knit community based on old-world cultural patterns. The community as a whole coped with crises and problems, providing a great deal of emotional security to its members. A University of Oklahoma study found that the people in Roseto had a remarkably low death rate, especially from heart attack, and that very few Roseto patients suffered from emotionally related illnesses.

Roseto has, in recent years, grown from a close-knit village into a typical suburban town "complete with Cadillacs, swimming pools, country clubs, and heart attacks."[12] Researchers now say that the sources of social and emotional security are being lost and so is the unusually good health of the residents.

Undoubtedly, there are elements that are essential to a community in order for it to continue to function well over time. The following is a list of what appear to be elements in the support of an ongoing, well-functioning neighborhood community:

[12]*Sacramento Bee,* 2 July 1978.

1. Appropriate Scale

Just as large or small towns have advantages and disadvantages, so do large or small neighborhoods. There's not as much diversity if the neighborhood is very small, but it's easier to know all the people well. Larger neighborhoods offer diversity and can become stronger economically, but as they get bigger, they lose the feeling of community.

Kirkpatrick Sale, in his book *Human Scale,* presents a number of arguments that indicate that 500 people is an optimum number for a neighborhood community in order to have social harmony:

> Anthropology and history both suggest, as we have seen, that humans have been able to work out most of their differences at the population levels clustering around the "magic numbers" of 500–1,000 and 5,000–10,000.
>
> For the first, John Pfeiffer notes that anthropological literature indicates that it is when a population reaches about 1,000 that "a village begins to need policing," and as we have seen, the Dinka villages, like villages in most stateless societies, hold about 500 people on average and almost never more than 1,000. (Rough figures for village sizes in some other stateless societies: 100–1,000 for the Mandavi, 50–400 for the Amba, 300–500 for the Lugbara, 200–300 for the Konkomba, 400–500 for the Tupi.) Evidently in these face-to-face societies, where every person is known to every other—and presumably every idiosyncrasy, sore spot, boiling point, and the final straw—it is comparatively easy to keep the peace and comparatively easy to restore it once broken. Confirmation comes from the New England towns, the great majority of which were under 1,000, where harmony was the regular rule and "concord and consensus" the norm: from the Chinese villages of all periods until the most recent, with rarely more than 500 people, where traditional law of many varying kinds operated independently of dynastic decrees; from Russia, where the traditional *mir,* with seldom more than 600 or 700 people, was the basic peace-keeping unit for more than a millennium, each with its own version of customary law and all without codification or judicial apparatus.[13]

I would agree that the optimum number is 500 people or about 150 homes based on my experience living in Village Homes. It seemed there was a lack of individual diversity and resources when it was under 100 households and, as it approaches 200, it seems that the residents have more difficulty functioning as a group.

2. Boundaries

Clear boundaries make it possible for people to know where one neighborhood ends and the next one begins. They allow the neighborhood to be grasped and appreciated as a unit. This can be done with streets, or greenbelts. The greenbelt, or open space, seems to be both a more obvious, and a more pleasant boundary than a street.[14]

3. Land and Resources

In order to bring a community together in a meaningful way it is important that the community as a whole provide for some of its basic needs.

The traditional neighborhood has very little to offer in terms of providing reasons for the residents to get together. Even those neighborhoods which have a homeowners' association and share a swimming pool offer little incentive. Decisions like determining the hours the pool will be available do not offer enough to create a community spirit.

Some neighborhoods do rally together when faced with an outside threat, but once the threat is gone, the community spirit gradually dissipates. A surburban neighborhood where we once lived was threatened with a poorly planned adjacent development. In organizing to fight the development some very pleasant side effects occurred. There were neighborhood potlucks,

---

[13]Kirkpatrick Sale, *Human Scale* (New York: Coward, McCann & Geoghegan, 1980), p. 488.

[14]Kevin Lynch, *The Image of the City* (Cambridge, Mass.: Technology Press and Harvard University Press, 1960).

parties, and organized games in the park. Suddenly everyone seemed to know everyone else and the neighborhood grew warmer and felt safer.

But once the external threat was gone and the neighboring property was satisfactorily developed, the parties, the fun, and the sense of togetherness gradually disappeared.

If community members have control over some land and some food production, they may develop meaningful social relationships through working together to provide for the satisfaction of important needs. Any number of experiences with community gardens have shown that the gardens are not only good for food; they are also good for developing a sense of community. Self-help housing projects also tend to foster group cohesiveness because of the mutual aid required by the building process.

In Village Homes, the homeowners' association owns 12 acres of agricultural land, an apartment house site, a commercial development site, a community center site, and an acre of undeveloped land. A large number of community residents are involved in the decision-making process, sharing such activities as the planning of buildings and their management. Community get-togethers, such as planting parties and seasonal holiday parties, are emerging and plans are being prepared for the first annual grape festival.

Having these resources allows the community to have control over the nature of the businesses leasing space in the commercial area and control of the park maintenance. It puts the decisions in the neighborhood's hands, not in the hands of an absentee landlord or the more removed city government. It gives the neighborhood the power to make jobs available for teenagers and to provide activities for all ages of residents. The community, with its extra land, can carry out as many projects as it feels are necessary for the well-being of the neighborhood, such as the building of schools, arts and crafts facilities, workshops, and food-storage structures.

The traditional neighborhood design stifles social interaction because there is no land left in reserve for neighborhood activities. In Village Homes, residents have the opportunity to work together for mutual benefits. Homeowners have any number of reasons and opportunities to interact socially. Through

time they get to know one another and they develop friendships. A sense of community with all its attached benefits begins to emerge.

Village Homes was designed in a way that created clusters of eight houses that, in addition to their separate lots, share a common area consisting of about ⅛ to ¼ acre of land. This allows small groups to accomplish even more at a community level, including sharing a common orchard, an outside entertainment area, and spaces for small children to play. While participating as a member of both the overall community of Village Homes and of a common area, I have seen that some people (10 to 20 percent) do not participate at all (yet most of these people seem to be pleased that they are a part of the neighborhood). Sixty to 80 percent of the people participate in all community activities in varying degrees but generally are more active in common area activities; and 10 to 20 percent of the people are very active in all areas of the community. Varying levels of participation should be expected because people's needs to interact socially or to be a part of a group or to be a leader will vary. By having our town and cities broken down into the smaller neighborhood communities, many more people who would like to have leadership roles get such an opportunity.

The degree of interaction that is stimulated by the Village Homes design does expose the inabilities of some members of the population to work together in social situations, but this becomes a benefit to these people in that it allows the opportunity for personal growth. Most of the people I have observed that have had some difficulty participating in groups have eventually grown and learned cooperative skills.

Land and resources commonly owned by a small neighborhood group should do a lot to improve the social skills of the individual residents and lead to the development of a strong neighborhood community that provides satisfying social experience for its residents.

4. Revenue

In order for a neighborhood to have the ability to carry out projects it needs not only land, it also needs revenue. This can come from donations or assessments, or from income from a business source. Assessments are the traditional method of raising money in condominium-type projects. In the traditional condominium project, assessments pay for the building, management, and maintenance of a multitude of different recreational amenities and open spaces, including pools, craft rooms, and social centers. Assessments are much like taxes and even though they allow people to have more control over their condominium development, they are still not desirable if other sources of revenue can be found. Ongoing revenue from the lease of land and buildings owned by the homeowners' association in Village Homes will allow a reduction of the financial burden on the individual and may provide for special educational arts and crafts programs, all the recreational items in regular condominiums, and even amenities like neighborhood health programs.

5. Security and Safety

Security and safety are very important elements in every neighborhood, yet many neighborhoods in the United States are becoming increasingly prone to the ravages of burglars, rapists, vandals, and so on. The usual response is to keep the children close to home and to install canine and/or mechanical hardware protection.

Recently, several researchers have discovered that design can have an effect on crime prevention and that certain neighborhood layouts are statistically more likely to be safe places to live. In his book, *Defensible Space*,[15] architect Oscar Newman points out that one cause of crime is the failure of residents to control the surrounding open space where intruders, if unchallenged, can commit criminal acts. Planning decisions regarding public, semipublic, semiprivate, and private spaces can be made which tend to further the recognition of neighbors and outsiders, and to encourage residents to assert their dominance against unwelcome persons. If a space is clearly designated as private or semiprivate, residents will act to protect it. A "public" space is always "someone else's" responsibility.

Another key to crime-free design is the ability of residents to see what is going on in the open space around individual dwelling units. Newman contends that too many contemporary housing designs fail to provide surveillance of the space that is crucial for residents' security — the nearby open space.[16]

Newman also comments on street widths, noting that a wide street becomes a public space, ignored by the neighborhood, while a narrow street is psychologically assimilated into the neighborhood. In the latter case, residents are more likely to halt a speeding car or admonish a misbehaving pedestrian.[17] Streets in Village Homes are narrow and they are dead-end. In this situation, the street becomes less public and more controlled because the number of persons who may legitimately use the open space is limited.

A sense of community is another important variable in the safety of a neighborhood. Where neighbors know and care about one another, they will also act to protect their fellow residents from a suspicious stranger. Criminal researchers have discovered that neighborhood watch programs have reduced burglaries by as much as 37 percent.[18]

The cluster commons in Village Homes are designed using several techniques to assure that residents may exert control over adjacent open space. Homes are clustered around the common with windows that overlook the space. Residents have planned and maintained their commons, they have a vested interest in the spaces, and they have every right to protect the areas from unwanted intruders. Even the more public greenbelts are less vulnerable to vandalism than an adjacent neighborhood park. Residents directly pay for maintenance of the greenbelts; they have played a part in hiring the gardeners; and they may have participated in planning or building a pool, play structure, or orchard. Therefore, Village residents have a direct interest in defending the open spaces around them. The space is perceived as Village territory, not public territory.

[15]Oscar Newman, *Defensible Space* (New York: Macmillan, 1972).

[16]Ibid., p. 4.

[17]Oscar Newman, *Design Guidelines for Creating Defensible Space*, U.S. Department of Justice, Law Enforcement Assistance Administration (Washington, D.C., 1975).

[18]U.S. Department of Justice, *Law Enforcement Assistance Administration Newsletter*, vol. 6, no. 6 (December 1976).

The design techniques I have described for the provision of safety and security work equally as well in the inner city as in the suburb. An appropriately designed moderate-income housing development in San Francisco called Saint Francis Square provides an instructive example.

Saint Francis Square is located in the middle of a high-crime area in the city, yet the residents feel it is a fairly safe place to live and to raise children. A number of planning elements have contributed to this. First, the 300 three-story units are grouped around three interior landscaped courts and all units have a view of this open area. The apartments are arranged so that groups of six residents share a common entry to their apartments and each unit has its own private garden or balcony. In this way, Saint Francis Square provides semipublic space (the courtyard), semiprivate space (the entry corridor), and private space (the apartment and garden or balcony). Second, the residents don't rent their apartments; they own them through membership in a cooperative. An active co-op association controls and manages the jointly owned common space. A strong sense of community is apparent in Saint Francis Square which results from membership in the co-op and participation in community-wide social events and work parties. The rates of street crime in the area of San Francisco surrounding Saint Francis Square are unusually high, but the majority of residents feel safe walking in the interior courts at night. It has been reported that if a person is attacked at night and calls out for help, the neighbors respond and the culprit is caught or runs away in fright.[19]

6. Privacy

It is very likely that physical privacy is essential to the development of a sense of community in our culture. It has been observed by anthropologist Edward T. Hall and others that where physical barriers do not provide enough privacy, social barriers develop as substitutes.[20]

In a crowded apartment house with poor sound insulation between the walls, neighbors often make a point not to get to know one another so that they can maintain distance through social barriers if not through physical design. Social withdrawal or "hiding" will substitute as a means of giving the harrassed individual the privacy he so badly needs.

Occasionally, we run across individuals who seem to have relinquished their privacy in favor of a more communal life-style. This arrangement rarely lasts very long. Soon the freshman deserts his crowded dormitory for a quiet apartment off campus, or the dropout leaves the commune and looks for a place of her own. For a lasting community spirit to develop, it seems essential to provide group members with an opportunity for privacy.

We felt it necessary to provide plenty of opportunity to satisfy the need for privacy in Village Homes. Every home has space for a fenced, private yard. Sound insulation is stressed between common-wall units. Large expanses of windows are either screened or planned so that they face courtyards or open space. The neighborhood's appointed design review committee monitors new construction to assure that future additions will not detract from an individual's ability to maintain privacy. No second-story windows may look into another's private yard.

7. Diversity

In Chapter 2, I have identified diversity as a necessary component of a well-functioning human settlement; it is just as much a necessary component of a well-functioning neighborhood. Unfortunately, modern neighborhoods have been growing less diverse. Just as we have moved toward large-scale farming exemplified by rows and rows of a single crop, we have moved toward neighborhoods which segregate people of similar social class into endless vertical and horizontal rows of housing units.

[19]Clare Cooper, *Resident Attitudes Towards the Environment at St. Francis Square, San Francisco: A Summary of the Initial Findings,* University of California, Institute of Urban and Regional Development, working paper no. 126 (Berkeley, July 1970).

[20]Edward T. Hall, *The Hidden Dimension* (New York: Doubleday & Co., 1966).

It has been demonstrated that children suffer from neighborhood homogeneity. A study in West Germany compared the reactions of children living in 18 new communities with those of youngsters living in older, more diverse German cities. The children in the new communities did not like their living environments very much. According to the *New York Times,* in the new towns, "amid soaring rectangular shapes of apartment houses with shaded walks, big lawns, and fenced-in play areas, the children for whom much of this has been designed apparently feel isolated, regimented and bored."[21]

To maintain the proper amount of diversity, neighborhoods should incorporate the following:

- housing for various income levels
- space for field games
- natural play areas providing plenty of hiding places
- a large party or meeting facility
- spaces for informal gatherings such as a well-placed bench under an appealing tree
- recreational facilities such as a swimming pool, basketball courts, and arts and crafts center
- agricultural production
- a small commercial center including a neighborhood store, restaurant, and small shops

Though all these items need not be included in every neighborhood, it is well to remember that a more diverse neighborhood will be more full of vitality.

The neighborhood functions well when people feel that they are safe and can rely on help from others. It functions well when they can grow in their ability to get along and work out their differences. It functions well when, through participation in community activities, including work and fun in groups, they experience the inner warmth and fullness which comes from feeling that they as individuals are part of the community and that the community as a whole is part of all humanity. All neighborhoods should be designed to accommodate these functions, for when they are not, part of the human potential may be lost.

[21]Urie Bronfenbrenner, "The Origins of Alienation," *Scientific Monthly* (August 1974)231:53–61.

The Town Center

The town center has the potential of being a friendly and exciting place for the people who work, shop, find entertainment, or reside there.[22] It can tie a group of neighborhood communities together and provide an environment of diverse activities that contrasts with the outlying neighborhoods.

It is unfortunate that most towns and cities have lost most,

[22]I would like to make a distinction between a town center and a metropolitan downtown area. The town center is small, easily accessible by the residents of a community, and is the focal point of much of the community's commerce and social activity. It is frequented regularly by most residents of a community and helps bond the town together.

The metropolitan downtown area, on the other hand, is much larger with much more variety. While there is a sense of belonging for those who work there, the large numbers of strangers coming and going, and the fact that it is spread out, generates much less of a quality of intimacy and belonging for the people passing through.

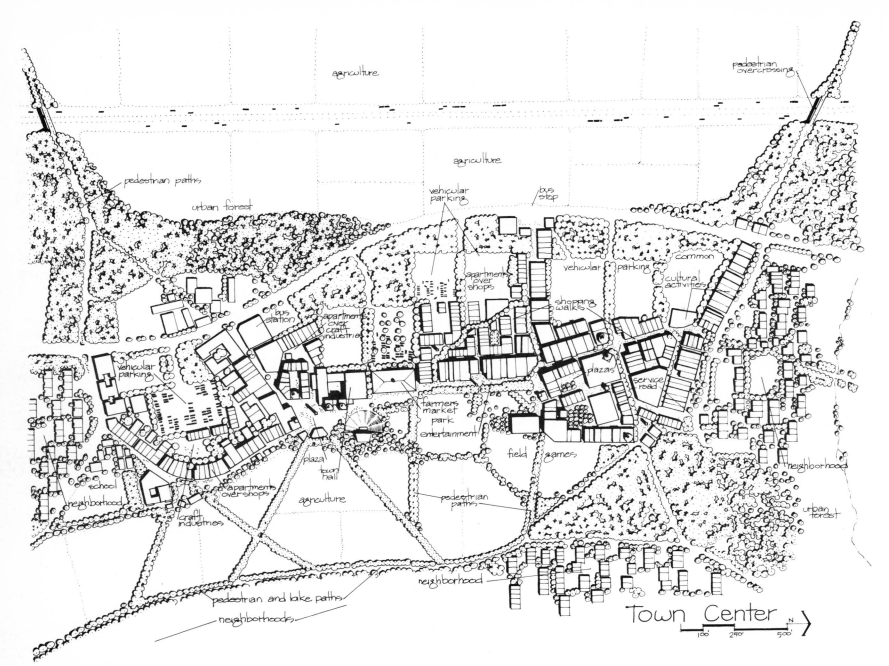

pedestrian
overcrossing

agriculture

agriculture

pedestrian paths

vehicular
parking

bus
stop

urban forest

apartments
over shops

common

vehicular parking

cultural
activities

bus
station

apartments
over craft
industries

shopping
walks

vehicular
parking

plazas

service
road

farmers
market
park

entertainment

field games

plaza

neighborhood

town
hall

school

apartments
over shops

agriculture

pedestrian
paths

urban
forest

neighborhood

craft
industries

neighborhood

pedestrian and lake paths

Town Center

N

neighborhoods

100   250   500

if not all, of the essence of the town center as it existed in many towns 50 years ago in the United States, and still does exist in many European towns. The town center has deteriorated due to sprawling growth and the intrusion of the auto. With sprawling growth, most of the residents live farther and farther from the town center. More convenient shopping centers have sprung up away from the town center. This has reduced the frequency of people's visits to the town center and has thereby reduced their feeling of belonging there. At the same time, heavy auto traffic has made the town center a less pleasant place to be.

We have seen some efforts to recreate a pleasant town center by partially or completely removing the automobile and creating pedestrian malls. This has been very successful in cities like Santa Cruz, California, and Aspen, Colorado, but has been a near failure in others. Some failures may be due to poor design, but in many cases the city is simply too large to have a town-center character. Such cities' core areas can only hope to achieve the qualities of a large metropolitan shopping and business district, which has a positive value but is definitely different from the intimate town center I am speaking of.

For the most part, urban sprawl has resulted in the modern shopping center replacing the town center. The shopping center serves as a place to purchase goods and services, but for the most part, fails to function as a town center for the area it serves, even though the area is often small enough to permit it to do so. This is partly because, as the name implies, the shopping center is just for shopping; it lacks the range of activities and facilities found in a real town center. It is not a workplace except for the shop personnel, nor a center of local government; nobody actually lives there, and there are no schools or public recreation areas. Aside from a few restaurants, there is little or no space for leisure or socializing; this is probably deliberate, so that shoppers will keep shopping.

The shopping center also fails to function as a town center because it is oriented to automobiles, even though its interior malls may be auto-free. Acres of surrounding land, in a prime location for the needed nonshopping facilities, are taken up by parking lots. Even where other facilities exist nearby, they are typically separated by busy streets and long stretches of barren parking lots, quite inhospitable to pedestrians.

To function well as a town center, the area should have shops, stores, businesses, restaurants, sidewalk cafes, theaters, schools, and professional and governmental offices. It should also have open spaces in the form of parks, plazas, bowling greens, horseshoe pits, and so on. With this variety of elements, it can be an exciting and vibrant place to be and to meet people, as well as a place to shop and do business.

This vision of the town center depends partly on good design, partly on a lively diversity of activities, and partly on size, but mostly on the absence of the automobile. Eliminating automobile traffic lanes and parking will make the area more compact and thus easier to get around on foot with no need to be alert for cars. Undistracted by their noise, motion, and brightness, the strolling pedestrian will be better able to appreciate the sights, sounds, and smells of human activity. The air will be cleaner, and the atmosphere of the street will be calmer and quieter; more conducive to browsing, to striking up a conversation, or to settling down on a bench to rest and just observe.

The town center seems to function better if it has its own neighborhood community. People can live in flats above businesses, in small apartments, and in town houses. A few merchants or craftspeople may even combine their places of business and their living quarters. This sort of mixed use adds to the liveliness and homeness of the downtown area, and also makes it a safer place because people are present at all times. The downtown live-in community needs many of the same facilities as the outlying neighborhoods, though in some cases it can use the larger facilities designed to serve the whole town. Since compactness is of the essence, some facilities like community gardens and playing fields would not be appropriate within the town center itself, though they might be provided adjacent to it.

Major activities requiring much space and relatively little contact with the public such as automotive sales and services, major industries, and the city equipment yard would more logically be located toward the outer part of the town rather than at the town center.

To revitalize town centers in existing urban areas and to ensure the building of town centers with new urban growth are major goals of appropriate planning that can result in the increased richness of people's existence. This element of our civilization must not be ignored.

Chapter 6
The Synthesis

To establish a long-range plan for a new community or the rehabilitation of some existent urban area, we must face the task of integrating many different elements into a specific plan. What can we say about this process?

There are factors of several sorts to consider. Some of them relate to the location of the site: its climate, its proximity to other settlements and to natural resources, the availability of water, and the potential for dispersion of air pollution. Others relate to an examination of the site itself which, according to the methods and criteria proposed by Ian McHarg, would analyze and catalog the existing drainage patterns and natural aesthetic features of the site, soil types, solar orientation, and so on, and would indicate which locations on the site are best suited to various uses: agriculture, forestry, sewage recycling, buildings, roads and paths, and parks. These factors would also be used to determine what overall size and density of settlement the site can support.

At the same time, there are a number of conceptual notions about what a settlement should ideally be like, and how it should ideally be laid out — appropriate size for efficient government and a good social atmosphere, appropriate patterns of circulation, proper relation between public and private spaces, between living and working spaces, and so on. Finally, there is a variety of possible technologies to choose from — different ways of handling sewage, different ways of producing energy, and different materials and methods for building construction.

At this point analysis and theorizing can go no further. To integrate these factors successfully into a harmonious, elegant site plan depends on a designer or design team's creative ability and intuitive perception of comprehensive solutions. In the end, wholistic design of wholesome human settlements will require sensitive artists who have a grasp on all aspects of the problem and all elements of the required solution.

I must emphasize, however, that successful design is more than a successful integration of all these ''practical'' considerations. The designers must also draw on their own sense of line, space, proportion, pattern, and symbolism. Their ability to do so will make the difference between a profoundly beautiful and satisfying setting, and one that is aesthetically and subjectively mediocre.

It seems to me that there is an unfortunate tendency in the environmental-awareness movement to subordinate beauty and other subjective satisfactions, and even human comfort and convenience, to the requirements of ''appropriate technology,'' or even to forget them altogether. For example, I have seen solar houses that were meticulously energy-efficient, but looked rather ugly and uncomfortable to live in. This is partly a result of their being first attempts. But I sense in some adherents of appropriate technology an inclination to belittle any desire for beauty, comfort, and utility as "middle-class aesthetics"; as an expression of consumerism and status-consciousness. Chaotic design and makeshift features are becoming almost fashionable in the appropriate technology movement, as expressions of contempt for these standards.

This is not my idea of appropriate design. When we work to conserve energy, protect the environment, and develop an economy based on renewable resources, we do it, in the final analysis, not for the sake of the ecosystem, but for our own sakes and our children's. To achieve these goals by ignoring other essential human needs is to miss the point entirely. To give more attention to heating systems than to meeting social, psychological, and aesthetic needs reflects an engineering mentality, no matter whether the heating systems use fossil fuels or solar energy.

Many years ago, when I was visiting a Frank Lloyd Wright house, I became keenly aware of a pleasant feeling and, at that time, I realized that architecture should be judged by *how people feel when they are using the space for what it is designed for*. This criterion takes in both the functional and the aesthetic aspects of architecture. The functional aspects are fairly straightforward; people will feel less comfortable if the light glares in their eyes, if the temperature is too warm or cold for the amount of physical activity going on, if furniture is too high or too low, if there is too much or too little privacy, or if things are arranged to require unnecessary movements or to make circulation awkward. But there are more subtle and subjective factors that affect people's comfort and mood within architectural spaces, and determine the ambience of those spaces. Some of the factors may be purely symbolic, like an orderly design that symbolizes an orderly and dependable world; a broad porch and a pleasant, accessible walkway that symbolize welcome; or house plants that symbolize life, growth, and nurturing; or some shape that has special meaning within a culture. Other design elements may contribute to a pleasant ambience by evoking echoes of the natural forms among which humans evolved. Others may have meanings, or meet subtle human needs, of which even the designer is only intuitively aware.

This means it is not enough for the designer to be intellectually knowledgeable about human needs and ways of meeting them, nor even to be skilled at integrating a variety of needs into a single harmonious, elegant solution. To masterfully design nurturing spaces, one must also be intuitively sensitive to the ambience of spaces; to the shades of mood and feeling that spaces evoke, and the meanings they suggest. The designer must be able to arrange spaces to evoke the desired feeling, meanings, and mood, just as the poet must be able to arrange words to evoke the desired feelings and understandings in a reader's mind. The designer's task differs from the poet's only in that the elements he or she works with, unlike words on paper, must also perform definite concrete physical and social functions. His or her solutions must integrate ambience and function.

Individuals' emotional and behavioral reactions to the ambience of a space may range from very positive to very negative. The individual may feel uncomfortable, anxious, frustrated, discouraged, or lethargic; he or she may feel comfortable, relaxed, supported, uplifted, or energized, or something between these extremes. In any one situation these reactions vary somewhat from individual to individual and are obviously affected by a person's preoccupation with other thoughts or stimuli, but they are also in part an expression of universal human nature and human experience.

The designer of any space (be it a room, a building, a garden, or a neighborhood) cannot take lightly the responsibility for the ambience of that space. The ambience will be a strong and persistent influence on the moods, feelings, and behavior of the people who use that space, and that influence can be either nurturing or oppressive.

People who are uncomfortable in an environment will first try to avoid it or change it. If they cannot do either of these, they will learn to ignore it. In doing so, if it happens often, they deaden their sense of beauty and lose some of their human sensitivity. I feel that much of our human-made environment has a grossly negative effect on us, and greatly reduces our sensibilities. Eventually, we can easily accept ugly environments; we cannot feel the discomfort any more, or see the ugliness. But the insensitivity we develop continues to impoverish our lives and our relationships with others.

So much of our human-made environment is created without thought for the visual consequences. This may be a sociological time bomb. Humans had been tampering with the physical environment for many years before the long-range detrimental effects of their manipulations became obvious. The same may be true for changes in the subjective environment. I am convinced that we have not yet begun to understand the negative effects of visual environments that have an oppressive ambience. The social problems that plague us today may stem in part from such subjective factors, and their effects may be only beginning.

I am afraid that there are not many people who are skilled at designing nurturing spaces, because the values of the architectural profession do not encourage development of this skill to any great extent. Architectural schools and architectural criticism have encouraged the designer to create striking or unique designs for the sake of their novelty. Buildings featured in architectural journals are often criticized as if they were sculptures rather than places for living and working. These values may give us buildings that are as interesting as pure art, but they have little to do with creating beautiful, comfortable, useful spaces. In many cases, novel designs are actually destructive of the quality of spaces. Mies van der Rohe's design for the Martin Luther King Library in Washington, D.C., for example, has been widely acclaimed by architectural critics, but the librarians have complained of its inappropriate design.

Not many years ago there was a movement among artists toward deliberately ugly works, intended to provoke an unpleasant response. This was a valid artistic statement, but not the sort that would be valid for an architect. The architectural designer should not have the same liberty as the pure artist; it is not acceptable for him or her to create unpleasant environments either intentionally or unintentionally, because people have to live with them; they cannot experience them and then walk away from them as they can from purely artistic works.

When architects create bad spaces it is generally unintentionally a result of error or oversight, but that is no excuse. I suspect that one reason the artist's role is so tempting to architects is that it excuses their mistakes; it puts them above mere functional

design, and frees them from responsibility for the less glamorous but more difficult tasks of understanding, anticipating, and harmoniously providing for a multitude of human needs.

There are countless design theories, philosophies, and styles that express the subjective aspect of architectural design. I will not go into them here except to suggest that some, more than others, may lead to solutions that are better at satisfying basic human needs. Two, I believe, stand out. One is the traditional Japanese style, which emphasizes simplicty, subtlety, use of natural materials and naturalistic landscaping, and the relationship between the building and the garden. The second is the view expressed by John Ruskin in *The Poetry of Architecture*.[1] Ruskin praises the architecture of simple, unpretentious buildings of the eighteenth and nineteenth centuries. European cottages and villas of this era, he says, demonstrate that beauty is born in the simplicity of the design solution, and matures with the aging of a building, as the building serves its function well and shows the signs of use.

I believe there is also a great deal to be said for an order and consistency in neighborhood design that extends to a consistency in the appearance of homes. I am not talking about the monotonous fundamental uniformity of tract homes, poorly masked by random variations in color and style of facade, but rather the opposite: a fundamental variation and individuality in design, overlain with a harmonious thematic consistency, as we see and feel in the ambience of the old European towns and more primitive villages, where consistency developed naturally through emulation and tradition, a limited variety of available materials, and an absence of rapid change in building technology.

I feel consistency in building style has a lot of desirable symbolism. It suggests that good solutions do not change; that they are not arbitrary, and that appropriate materials are not arbitrary. On a deeper level, it symbolizes the possibility that unique individuals can join together into harmonious communities

[1]John Ruskin, *The Poetry of Architecture* (New York: John Wiley & Sons, 1891).

and societies without necessarily losing their basic individuality. It symbolizes respect, consideration, and cooperation toward one's neighbors, and toward the community as a whole. The clashing colors and styles of the typical housing tract symbolize just the opposite: a society whose fundamental drabness and uniformity are so oppressive that people must assert their individuality in trivial but conspicuous ways; a society where it is fashionable to thumb one's nose at neighbors and community, and at their tastes and standards.

Consistency in building style also echoes the world of nature. Consider peach trees; no two are alike, but there is a fundamental consistency in shape, color, and growth pattern that allows one to easily distinguish any peach tree from a palm tree or rosebush, or even from members of more closely related species, like apple or plum trees. Landforms and types of rock also exhibit this patterned variation. If it is true, as I believe, that human perception is adapted by evolution to natural forms, then it is probably also adapted to allow us to detect such patterns. Since we generally find pleasure in the exercise of our capacities, it is likely that we would experience such patterned variation as pleasurable, whether we find it in peach trees or in houses. This may account for the appeal of some of the works of Henri Matisse and of certain primitive artists that show a pleasing design resulting neither from rigid uniformity nor wide variation, but from small variations and imperfections in a general pattern.

To create such a general pattern does not require any great degree of uniformity. Often the mere repetition of certain colors or materials will be enough to unify diverse designs. Also, diminishing affluence and increasing attention to conservation and functional design will naturally bring about some uniformity in materials and design.

Stylistic consistency is most crucial in high-density development. Where buildings are close together, inconsistencies are more apparent and less susceptible to masking by consistent landscaping. People with strong or unusual stylistic preferences and a strong need to express them in their houses should probably be encouraged to do so in low-density neighborhoods or in rural areas.

To establish a consistent style throughout a neighborhood or town requires some entity with authority over building and landscaping on private lots. Cities often have design review boards for this purpose, but they exercise authority mainly over commercial and historical areas, and, to a lesser extent, over established residential neighborhoods. But since their authority in residential areas is based on preventing specific annoyances to neighbors or disruption of an existing ambience, they generally have little control over building style in new developments. In this area the only control is likely to be that exercised by the private developer, who wishes to make lots more salable by guaranteeing buyers protection from eyesores on the block, now or in the future.

There is a legal mechanism for this. Before selling any lots, the developer files a declaration of "Codes, Covenants, and Restrictions" (C,C, & R's). In it, he declares his intent to require every lot buyer to agree to a set of specific restrictions on what he can build on the lot, and often to submit to the general authority of a neighborhood design review board. (The board is usually set up so that the developer appoints all the members at first, but later the homeowners elect them.) Each buyer then signs an agreement, included in the deed to the lot, to abide by the C,C, & R's and to require anyone to whom he or she later sells the lot to make the same agreement. We have a great deal to learn about making such deed restrictions flexible yet enforceable, particularly where very subjective standards are concerned. Also, only a few developers have tried to use this design-control mechanism in very careful or enlightened ways.

I feel, however, that the greatest potential for achieving unified neighborhood design lies not in stricter authoritative controls, but in people becoming aware that there are optimum materials and design techniques for their location and that there are aesthetic advantages and delights of a neighborhood designed and created by using those things that are most appropriate for their location.

But while an overall design continuity is important, I also think it is very important for individuals to be involved in this overall design, and, indeed, in any decision affecting the overall community. This is partly to help the designers successfully meet people's needs, but only partly. Equally important, it gives the residents a sense of their ability to help shape their community, and a feeling that it is truly theirs.

It does, however, complicate the designer's job immensely. This may be why continuity in large-scale designs often seems to be achieved at the expense of user participation. On the other hand, user participation without adequate designer coordination has produced chaotic, unpleasant environments. One must steer a middle course here.

The procedures I used in the design of Village Homes provide a useful example of such a middle course. My general strategy involved beginning with an overall plan and a set of planning concepts, leaving the details to be worked out as development progressed, with as much user input as possible at each stage.

Many of the ideas I put into Village Homes originated among a small group of like-minded people that a friend and I had brought together to plan an intentional cooperative community. At the time, I had no serious thought of developing a community myself. That group eventually broke up, but its meetings and discussions had helped me develop a general concept of what a neighborhood should be like.

Two years later, when the way opened for me to develop a 70-acre parcel of land on the edge of Davis, I developed this concept into a master plan for the site, which I presented to friends, acquaintances, and prospective home buyers and investors to get their reactions. I used this feedback to refine the plan, and began to seek the necessary financing and city approval.

The plan I presented to the city showed streets, lots, open spaces, and sites for recreational and commercial facilities, but left the details of buildings and landscaping to be determined as the project proceeded, with homeowner input. Instead of detailed plans, I showed city officials plans and photos of my previous houses to give them a sense of my design style, and gave them a long explanation of my ideas for the subdivision and the thinking behind them. This was very different from the usual procedure, and I think the city showed great understanding and flexibility in allowing me to proceed without showing detailed designs or even specifying exactly what community and commercial facilities would be included.

When lot sales began, each potential buyer was shown the master plan and the accompanying documents, including the C,C, & R's and the report of the California Department of Real Estate. The unique nature of the project was also explained to them. They were told that I would design much of the open-space landscaping after interviewing homeowners, and that the homeowners themselves, acting through a homeowners' association, would have final authority over the nature and design of the recreational and commercial facilities, with me acting only as their consultant. They were told that I would design landscaping for the smaller common areas only after consulting with the adjacent homeowners as a group, and that this group might arrange with the homeowners' association to handle the area's maintenance themselves. They were also told that their own house design and lot landscaping would be subject to approval of the design review board, under the C,C, & R's.

With this information in mind, the buyer could decide whether or not he or she liked and agreed with the basic concepts, knowing that he or she could have input into much of the final design. Even so, in the first stage of the development, there were one or two buyers who did not really understand what they were getting into and were unpleasantly surprised at the nature of the neighborhood. In later stages, when prospective buyers could see actual streets and houses and talk to homeowners, there were fewer misunderstandings, and the project attracted buyers more and more in agreement with its intent.

I felt I had to retain partial or final authority over some of these design decisions not only to maintain a unified overall design, but also to allow me to carry out my responsibilities as developer — to return a profit to investors, and to meet deadlines imposed by the California Department of Real Estate and the lending institutions. For example, it was required that each phase of the development should be entirely completed within a certain number of months, including the landscaping of the small common areas. Because of this, I often could not wait for input from the buyers of the last few lots surrounding a common area before designing the landscaping.

This process inevitably produced conflict. In several situations there was resentment on the part of interested and creative homeowners whose ideas were not used. In other situations where I felt strongly about a design question, I was overruled by the homeowners' association, which I had given final authority, though I was convinced the association's action would hurt the overall design. I think conflicts like these are a small price to pay for achieving a degree of both user participation and design unity. In this era of individuality and independence, we need to rediscover that conflicts can be resolved, that cooperation can be achieved, and that it is worth achieving, for both practical and psychological reasons.

I think similar procedures could be used in designing new garden cities and redesigning old existing urban spaces into viable communities. A designer, or design team, familiar with general social, environmental, and aesthetic considerations can talk with people representative of those he or she is planning for to get a sense of their particular needs and desires. Then, based on the available technologies and the characteristics of the site, and drawing on his or her knowledge of design concepts, the designer can develop a master plan and a set of architectural and landscaping guidelines, leaving detailed design to be determined during development with further input from actual residents. Before development begins, however, the master plan and guidelines can be refined through feedback gained in further talks with representative users. I think this method will prove to be extremely useful in designing useful, satisfying, and healthy human environments.

Chapter 7
The Appropriate Planning Area

In the previous chapters, I have discussed separately various elements of appropriate urban planning—agriculture, housing, drainage, circulation, and so on. For almost every one of these elements, it was clear that a variety of solutions was possible, and that for any particular urban plan, the best solution for each element would depend on the peculiarities of the site and its relationship to existing development. Nevertheless, a general pattern emerged, with a few basic characteristics that I would expect to see in any wholistically designed community. This garden city pattern has widespread applicability, I believe, for designing or redesigning almost any urban environment to meet today's needs.

A New Tool for Urban Planning

In this chapter I want to show how this general model can be adapted to a variety of sites and situations. Up to this point, it has probably been easiest to visualize the model in terms of a new town built from scratch on an undeveloped rural site. Here, however, I will talk about other cases. I will explain how a new garden city might be developed on a site with unusual topogra-

phical features, on a site adjacent to an existing town, on a partly developed urban site, or on a site that includes a smaller existing town. I will also talk about how the same pattern could be applied to redevelopment and rehabilitation of a existing town, an existing city, and an existing partly developed suburban area. In every case, however, the basic problem is to avoid piecemeal planning or planning by default, and to take a more comprehensive and far-sighted approach.

The two most important features of the garden city pattern are: (1) heavy reliance on pedestrian and bicycle circulation, and (2) a high degree of self-sufficiency. Both of these have important implications for town size. The town must be small enough to keep distances within the town short enough for walking and bicycling, but at the same time it must be large enough to satisfy most of its residents' needs within the community, providing food, energy, and a variety of jobs, housing, goods and services, recreation, and social opportunities. I think these two requirements set fairly definite upper and lower limits on the size of an appropriately designed town: it should not be larger than six square miles in area, nor smaller than two. An area larger than six square miles requires two towns, each one separate and complete in itself, even though the two may be adjacent.

What I am advocating, then, is a *modular approach to*

urban development and redevelopment. The garden city, with its fairly fixed size, is the module—the building block for urban development and redevelopment.

A modular approach to development will require a modular planning strategy. To this end, I wish to propose a new planning tool which I call an Appropriate Planning Area (APA). An APA would be a compact area of two to six square miles, intended for development or redevelopment along the lines I have suggested in the previous chapters. The planning process should be flexible enough to permit adaptation to site characteristics, but these size limits should be firmly observed in all cases to keep the APA large enough for self-sufficiency but small enough for walking and bicycling. Any planning area larger than this should be divided into several APA's. Thus the APA would be a sort of regional planning module, adaptable to new development or redevelopment, and to small towns or large cities.

Creation of Appropriate Planning Areas is within the authority of any city or county under existing law, though the procedure would differ somewhat in different situations. A city or county could designate an APA as part of its general plan. In a large city or urban county, the general plan would include a number of APA's along with overall plans for regional resource use and environmental protection, and for public transportation systems linking the APA core areas with each other and with existing population centers. Just as the general plan itself declares the city's or county's intent to guide future development along certain lines, designation of an APA would declare the city's or county's intent to see the area develop into a comprehensive, self-contained community with features such as the following:

- a core area offering a full range of goods and services, located within 1½ miles of all residents in the APA
- an internal circulation pattern emphasizing pedestrian and bike traffic, and minimizing human contact with automobile traffic
- production within the APA of much or most of the food required by its residents
- provision for commercial and industrial enterprises that would provide work for a high proportion of the APA residents

- a housing mix that includes affordable housing for all income groups expected to work within the APA
- a full range of primary and secondary schools
- a full range of recreational opportunities
- street design and general planning to minimize costs and energy demands for construction and maintenance of public and private improvements in the APA
- use of available renewable energy sources and energy conservation measures to make the APA as nearly energy self-sufficient as possible
- ecologically sound patterns of agriculture, waste management, and resource use (including water use)

This list of features is not intended to be final or exhaustive, and not every APA would achieve all of them with great success. Not every element of the theoretically ideal town will be possible and appropriate in every APA, as you will see in the case examples that follow. My basic point is simply that the designation of an APA should be a clear statement of general planning intent to make development in the APA address the whole range of planning problems I have discussed in the previous chapters, and do whatever is possible toward solving them.

Designation of APA's would be a formidable planning task in itself, particularly where they would include or be adjacent to existing development. APA's cannot be laid out arbitrarily, since part of the goal is to make new development complement existing development and take advantage of whatever potential the existing development has for incorporation into a wholistically designed community or a comprehensive regional plan. Planners must try to make sense out of existing development and to maximize its potential through careful designation of APA's with suitable sizes and boundaries. Thus, it is unlikely that a planning agency would designate an APA without already having some idea of a plan for its development. Perhaps adoption of a preliminary plan for the APA should be part of the designation process.

The APA planning process would differ from current planning procedures in two main ways. First, it would direct attention in planning to a number of social, environmental, and economic factors that have been virtually ignored in current

planning. Second, it would develop a comprehensive plan for an area at a much earlier stage of development. This would lead to better planning, since planning issues can be better addressed when a plan is developed as a whole than when it is pieced together from unrelated proposals submitted over a number of years by many different developers. With a comprehensive plan already laid out, government evaluation and approval of developers' proposals would be simpler and quicker, which would save money and time for both the government and the developer. The developer would also benefit from knowing more clearly in advance what sort of proposal the government would find acceptable. The reduction of red tape and time delays, and the assurance of good environmental decisions, could ease some of the tension and open the door to a more unified effort between the traditional opposing forces of the development industry and the environmentalists.

I think it is crucial that we adopt this kind of planning and development immediately, all across the country. We have devoted a great deal of attention to promoting solar heating in buildings because of the potential energy savings. But the potential savings in transportation are even greater; the private auto alone accounts for 20 to 25 percent (depending on the region) of total energy use. APA-style development has a greater potential for reducing auto use than any other measure, and reducing it not by making driving more costly, but by making it less necessary; by providing an alternative way of living that is actually more pleasant than the present auto-oriented life-style. And it is not just a question of saving energy; it is a question of how comfortably people will be able to live as energy becomes more and more scarce and expensive.

When I say we should adopt this kind of planning all across the country, what I mean is that we should permit urban and suburban development *only* within designated APA's. This would not apply to isolated rural homes, or to the construction of a few individual homes per year in very small towns where no substantial growth is foreseen. But no rapid growth and no tract development should be permitted except under the APA planning process.

I think the most simple and effective step toward implementing such a planning process across the nation will be simply to convince local governments and citizens that it is both practical and desirable. I think they can be convinced; these days most people in the United States are aware of the need to save energy. No doubt it will become easier as soon as enough prototype communities are built to serve as examples. But it must be done county by county and city by city, with concerned local citizens taking the initiative.

This will take time, and I am not sure we can afford the time. We are building new neighborhoods every month, whose design we will have to live with for decades or centuries. The more old-style, energy-demanding neighborhoods we build, the more we will undermine whatever energy savings we can make in other areas, and the more people we will saddle with high future energy costs. Therefore, state and federal governments, even if they do not become directly involved in promoting this kind of planning, should do all they can to remove obstacles and smooth the way for local governments to do so.

A small but important obstacle to this kind of planning is that someone has to lay out money for preparation of the comprehensive plan a number of years before there is any development income to cover it. In some cases, developers or landowners might organize to finance a comprehensive plan, if they felt they wouldn't be allowed to develop without one. In many cases, however, city or county governments would have to provide the initiative, and counties in particular often have limited funds. One solution might be for the state or federal government to make planning loans to planning districts set up by cities or counties, to be repaid not out of general revenues but out of future development fees. Alternatively, comprehensive planning might be deemed to be sufficiently in the public interest to justify grants instead of loans.

Another important role for state and federal governments will be in supporting and financing some initial pilot projects. A single completed, well-designed, smoothly functioning garden city — with planners and officials willing to talk to visitors about their experiences in building and running it — will be the greatest asset in convincing other local officials that appropriate planning is both necessary and practical.

New Garden Cities

Although peculiarities of site and situation will make every garden city in some sense a unique problem, there are some considerations that apply to all of them.

For economic reasons, it is important to develop public services for a new town gradually, as the town itself develops. With a comprehensive plan for the fully developed town in hand, it may be tempting to build the full-scale public facilities at once with borrowed money, to be paid back from development fees as the town grows. Under today's high interest rates, however, the interest on this borrowed capital would be staggering, and would significantly increase the price of homes. Any delays in town development would make these interest costs even higher.

In its initial stages, the new town should take advantage of any existing services in the area. Counties normally provide fire and police protection to rural areas; if there is an existing city nearby it may be willing to provide these services on contract. Children, particularly those in the upper grades, can be bused to nearby schools until the town is large enough to support its own schools. If there is any existing development in the APA, there may already be a water or sewer service district that can continue to serve the developing town for a time. The town may also rely on nearby towns for jobs at first; in some cases, it may be worthwhile to run a temporary commuter bus service to a nearby town.

It will be tempting to locate new garden cities near existing cities or towns just to be able to take advantage of such services, but the temptation should be resisted unless there is some other good reason for locating there. Otherwise, we will be passing over many of the sites with the best potential for self-sufficient development and energy conservation.

Development of the town's own services and facilities should proceed cautiously and frugally. For example, when the town sets up its own fire and police forces, they can be housed temporarily in an inexpensive structure which will eventually become an equipment storage building for the public works department. The first fire truck can be a used one. The city government can initially share this building and later work out of a building that will ultimately be rented to private businesses for office space, either in the town center or in one of the neighborhood centers. A permanent police station, fire station, and city hall need not be built until the city is about three-fourths complete. Similarly, the town's first school for all grades up to or including junior high can be a building which eventually will house only a few grades, or serve only one or two neighborhoods.

Even in the town's permanent public facilities, there must be a real effort for simplicity, frugality, and functionality. Some of the features I advocate for noneconomic reasons, such as narrow streets and surface storm drainage, will coincidentally save money, but we must deliberately try to economize in all other areas as well. Designing more economically will take a conscious effort because public officials, engineers, architects, and planners as well as citizens have developed their standards during a period of affluence.

A county in which a new garden city is to be located will want some sort of guarantee that the town will incorporate within a reasonable time or when it reaches a certain size. Ordinarily, a developing area cannot be incorporated unless the residents vote to incorporate, and where they are reluctant to do so, the county is saddled with the cost and responsibility for providing services and utilities on a scale beyond what it is equipped to handle. The most direct solution would be for the county to simply require incorporation before it permits development to begin. It would also be possible, however, to include a provision in the subdivision C, C, & R's that the town will be incorporated at some specified time. This way each new resident would give his or her consent to incorporation as part of the lot purchase transaction — it would be written into the deed, and no vote would be necessary at the time of incorporation. With this assurance, the county should be willing to provide services until the town grew large enough to provide its own efficiently, which would greatly simplify development. The county might do this by establishing a special service district for all services within the APA.

It is usual for cities or counties to require subdivision developers, as part of the subdivision agreement, to donate to the public certain parcels of land within their subdivisions and certain improvements to those parcels — streets, sewer and water lines, land for parks, etc. — and to contribute through a development fee to city facilities outside the subdivision, such as central sewage

plants. While it is important for the local government not to make development needlessly difficult by requiring too much too soon, it is also important that these contributions from the developer not be allowed to lag behind the general pace of development, to avoid the danger of inflation or a developer's bankruptcy, which would leave the town without necessary public properties. Therefore, there must be a careful plan of development for the entire garden city project, stating just what is required from the developer at each stage. This would be an agreement between the developer and the county which would also protect the developer from capricious changes in the requirements, and allow him or her to plan ahead with confidence.

Equal attention must be given to development of the town's economic base. Not even the most ideal garden city will be entirely self-sufficient. Each will have to "import" some goods and services. To pay for these "imports," it must "export" something. Since commuting is to be avoided in appropriate planning, the garden city cannot rely on exporting labor like today's bedroom communities. Therefore, it will require local business and industry that either produce goods for "export" or provide services — accounting, research, or computer services, for example — to outside businesses.

Garden cities will have one great drawing card for business: they will offer a pleasant place for employees to live, in a lively community, with a beautiful setting, clean air, little crime, housing at competitive prices, and the excitement of building one's own town. Finding businesses looking for a new location, and selling them on the garden city's advantages, however, will still require some active recruitment, at least for the first generation of garden cities. In remote locations, this recruitment of industry can probably be left to the developer, because nothing will help him as much to sell homes as the availability of employment. In other locations, it might be better for the regional planning agency to conduct the search for industry.

What is to prevent a new town, once developed, from growing beyond its intended size? This is particularly important in a comprehensively planned community because additional growth would tend to undermine the benefits of the original good planning. For example, it could occupy land intended for food or biomass production, or for recreation. Development outside the distance convenient for bicycling would tend to generate amounts of automobile traffic that would cause congestion in streets and parking areas designed only for light use. Therefore, local governments undertaking APA-type planning must take steps to keep the new towns from growing beyond the optimum size.

Growth limitation has been a very controversial issue in those towns that have considered it; in Petaluma, California, it was the subject of litigation that went as high as the U.S. Supreme Court.[1] But this is partly because in existing towns, growth limitation represented a radical change in planning policy. Landowners, developers, builders, and general businesspeople who had long expected to prosper from the previously planned growth felt they had a legitimate grievance when a proposed growth limitation threatened to destroy their expectations. In a new town planned from the very beginning to grow only to a certain size, no one could claim he or she had been taken by surprise. In addition, the voters in a new town would tend to be aware of the town's development plan and the reasons behind it, and the disadvantages of further growth would be clearer to them than to the voters in a conventional town.

Still, it would be wise in many cases to set up some further barriers to growth beyond the intended size. One method would be to tie up development options on land outside the planned borders of the town. In Yellow Springs, Ohio, a private group — the Committee for a Country Common — has been partly successful in using this method to create a belt of undevelopable farmland around the small town.[2] In a new town it should be easier because the options could be acquired before development began to make them valuable. This could be done either by the special service district or by the developers themselves. Once all the necessary options were acquired, they could be placed in trust so that the land could only be developed with the approval of some large majority of the voters. This would provide a strong barrier to development, but provide a way to make exceptions in case of some strong unforeseen need in the future.

[1]City Attorney's Office, Petaluma, California, personal communication.
[2]Yellow Springs, Ohio, Village Planner's Office, Jeffrey Bothwell, Village Planner, personal communication.

Case I—A Foothill Town

The owner of 1,000 acres on the edge of California's Sacramento Valley has hired a consulting team of which I am a member to produce a development plan for her land. The problem is an interesting one, and provides a good example of how a garden city could be designed from scratch on an undeveloped site.

The land consists mostly of variably sloping hills with poor agricultural potential. There is a town of 2,000 people three miles to the north, and a town of 40,000 eight miles to the south. There is prime agricultural land to the east and north, and steep rolling hills to the west, rising toward a range of low mountains. The site is beautiful, with attractive views in all directions. It is next to a freeway, but most of the site is separated from the freeway by a low ridge and is absolutely quiet.

Much of the land to the south has been subdivided into parcels of 5 to 20 acres. If not otherwise developed, this site would probably be similarly subdivided, and have a total population of about 300 people. A garden city developed there could have a population of about 7,000. There is substantial pressure for growth in this general area, and with the surrounding towns adopting growth-control policies, a new town here would be helpful in relieving this pressure. The site has the definite advantage of being off agricultural land, whereas the existing towns nearby have already spread over some of the finest cropland in the world.

The freeway runs along the flat valley floor, and an irrigation canal runs parallel to the freeway about ¼ mile west. Beyond the canal is the low ridge. The strip between the canal and the freeway is ideal for heavy industry that generates noise or heavy traffic, or requires access to the freeway. The low ridge could be planted with a forest of fast-growing black locust trees to provide biomass and further protect the town proper from noise.

At right angles to this strip is a broad arroyo that cuts through the ridge and the rolling land to the west, created by a seasonal stream running down from the hills. Since this is often flooded during the winter rainy season with an inch or so of water, it is not suitable for building, but its alluvial soil makes it ideal for orchards and vineyards that would create a greenbelt through the middle of the town. The town center would be located on one side of this greenbelt.

This site lends itself well to the circulation patterns I have proposed in this book. The site is hilly, but the valleys generally drain toward the arroyo from either side. Most of the bike-footpaths leading to the town center can simply follow the seasonal streambeds along the bottom of each valley. Gravity-flow sewer lines would logically follow the same routes. The valley drained by each of these seasonal streambeds would become a neighborhood, with its smaller paths feeding down to the main one by the streambed. Roads for automobiles would come in from the perimeter, following routes just below the ridgetops, and streets would branch off from them into the neighborhoods. The ridgetops would generally be left in their natural state or forested, and each valley bottom would be devoted to neighborhood agriculture.

As I was on the site doing preliminary design, I was struck by how different this was from the way engineers usually lay out subdivisions. Instead of beginning with a street layout, we began with the existing drainage pattern and let everything follow from that. One of our last considerations was how we would get the roads to the houses. I think the resulting town will look and feel much more in harmony with its natural setting.

Sewage treatment on this site poses an interesting problem. A series of three large septic tanks could serve 8 to 10 houses each, but because the soil over most of the site is shallow with rock beneath, the septic-tank effluent could not be dispersed with leach lines; it could not soak into the ground. It could, however, be collected in pipes and carried by gravity flow to a central location for surface treatment in sand beds.

This treatment system requires a number of grass-covered sand beds about 18 inches deep and 200 feet long; with the beds side by side, the area would be about 400 feet wide. The idea is to release the septic-tank effluent into first one bed and then the next so that each bed receives intermittent doses. As each dose travels very slowly through the slightly sloped bed, it is filtered by the sand and mixed with air which allows further decomposition. The grass takes up some of the water and dissolved nutrients, and can be periodically mowed for livestock fodder or for composting.

At the far end of the sand beds, the effluent flows into a marsh for further decomposition. After this it is clear and odorless enough to be used for irrigation of vine and tree crops, though it still contains valuable plant nutrients. On this site, however, because the relatively poor soil would already be saturated during the rainy season, the winter effluent would either have to be piped to the better land to the north and east, or stored in a large holding pond until spring. In the spring, summer and fall, however, the effluent could be used to water and fertilize the forest on the ridge, and the orchards and vineyards in the lower part of the arroyo. In the beginning the shallow soil on the ridge would not hold much moisture, and frequent light waterings would be required. Continual cover cropping between the trees, however, would gradually improve the soil so that it could be watered more heavily, and the forest would grow more richly. Growing and plowing under cover crops in the arroyo would similarly build up the soil there.

One of the many beauties of this scheme is that, since the site slopes downhill to the east, the system could be designed to operate almost entirely by gravity flow and require very little pumping.

There are several possibilities for supplying the town with electricity. The best would be adding hydroelectric generation to the Monticello Dam mentioned in Chapter 4, which is only eight miles away. About five miles away are mountain ridges with sufficiently strong winds for efficient windmill generation.[3] Photovoltaic cells are another possibility, as is thermal generation by burning wood grown in the forests on the site.

In a garden city of this size, the fire department could also serve as the local police force; the fire chief would also be police chief. Marina, California, a town with a population of 16,000, has adopted this system in order to save money, and it is working very well. One man serves as the director of the Department of Public Safety, which provides both fire and police services. One firefighter, in charge of equipment, answers all fire calls and is met at the scene by police officers who are also trained fire fighters. According to the director, the system is working well and has proved to be extremely cost efficient.

[3]California Energy Commission, Biennial Report (Sacramento, 1979).

grazing

canal

grazing

orchards and row crops

natural drainage

pedestrian paths

neighborhoods

orchards and row crops

vehicular roads

water treatment

hilltop park

high school

city park

freeway

pedestrian paths

town center

natural drainage

orchards and row crops

vehicular road

reservoir

grazing

natural drainage

neighborhoods

Foothill Garden City

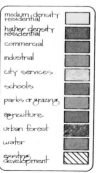

medium density residential
higher density residential
commercial
industrial
city services
schools
parks or grazing
agriculture
urban forest
water
existing development

N

1500'   1000'   1/4 mile

perimeter vehicular roads

town center

regional bike pedestrian path

town center

perimeter vehicular roads

residential areas

natural drainage

town center

natural drainage

regional bike pedestrian path

residential areas

regional industrial

natural drainage

railroad

route 65

City of Roseville

town center

regional bike pedestrian path

natural drainage

regional bike pedestrian path

town center

residential areas

town center

residential areas

perimeter vehicular roads

route 80

Railroad

City of Rocklin

town center

Roseville Region Garden Cities

1000'   3000'   1 mile   N

Case II—Roseville

Roseville, California, provides a good example of a situation where it would be appropriate to develop several entire garden cities on undeveloped land adjacent to an existing city.

Roseville is a town of about 25,000 people, located on Interstate 80 about 20 miles northeast of downtown Sacramento. It is almost connected to Sacramento by sprawling, spotty development. Roseville itself is a sprawling town covering about six square miles, with only about half of that area developed. The developed areas are scattered, and there is no clearly defined town center. The city suffers from being split into several sections by a highway and by three major rail lines that intersect the town. A large but only partially developed industrial park corridor exists a few miles to the north along rail and highway routes.

Since it is a mixture of developed and undeveloped areas, Roseville itself is an example of a growing urban area which could be developed into a single, balanced garden city. However, tremendous growth is projected for the whole region around Roseville, because of its convenience to transportation routes and recreational opportunities, and because the land (rolling countryside on the edge of the Sierra foothills) is not particularly good for agriculture. The development of additional new towns adjacent to Roseville is therefore appropriate, as Roseville is already near the maximum desirable size for a garden city.

The situation is of immediate interest because Hewlett Packard, an electronics firm, is starting construction of a large manufacturing plant in the industrial corridor about four miles north of Roseville's city center. Hewlett Packard anticipates hiring 4,600 employees for the first phase of plant development, scheduled for completion in 1985. The plant's work force will be expanded to 22,000 workers by the year 2000, becoming one of the largest industrial facilities in the state.

In a draft environment impact report (EIR) prepared for the city of Roseville, Hewlett Packard downplayed the impact plant employees would have on the local housing market. The firm projected employing significant numbers of persons already residing in the area, and it estimated that over 50 percent of other employees would commute from Sacramento or areas to the

south along the interstate. Nonetheless, it is clear that substantial pressure for new housing will be created by the huge facility—a fact recognized by local planners who are just now attempting to begin coordinated planning.

An investment company has recently proposed development of a 3,300-acre parcel north of Roseville, directly to the east of the future manufacturing plant. Currently, 2,700 acres of this land is being annexed to the city of Rocklin (just northeast of Roseville). Preliminary plans submitted by the developer suggest development of 6,000 housing units. With an overall density of 2 units per acre, and little community planning, the proposed development will continue the existing pattern of auto-oriented sprawl. To minimize the extension of public services, Rocklin has required that development begin at the easternmost end of the parcel that is closest to the center of Rocklin and farthest from the site of the new plant.

Let us assume that in addition to the 22,000 workers to be employed by Hewlett Packard, another 10,000 will be employed by other basic industry attracted to the area, and let us further assume that each of these 32,000 jobs in basic industry will create two jobs in supporting businesses like grocery stores, dry cleaners, insurance agencies, and so on. This would mean 96,000 new jobs created during the next 20 years in the Roseville-Rocklin area. Even allowing for significant numbers of households with two wage earners, we could expect the jobs created to support 60,000 or 70,000 new households.

Assuming 2.5 persons per household, every 10,000 of these households would contain enough people to populate a garden city of the size I propose. Even if, as Hewlett Packard predicts, a majority of its employees will commute from outside the Roseville-Rocklin area, there would be enough new households within the area to support development of one or two new towns. With less commuting, however, four to six new garden cities could be developed.

With thoughtful comprehensive planning, the growth generated by new employment could provide a base for better planning of the entire Roseville area. The county could designate Roseville itself as one APA and Rocklin as a second. The approximately 3,000 acres recently annexed by Rocklin could become a third APA, clearly distinct from either Roseville or Rocklin. Additional APA's would logically be designated to the west of Rose-ville, and north along both sides of the industrial corridor.

The APA's in the currently underdeveloped areas could be developed as garden cities each with their own commercial and service centers, and open spaces for food production and recreation. The garden cities would be separated by ½- to 1-mile greenbelts in the form of biomass forests and agriculture irrigated by reclaimed water. This would have the beneficial effect of producing a cooler microclimate for the area during hot summer months. Industrial development would be concentrated in the industrial corridor which would be surrounded by the cluster of towns for easy access by workers walking or on bicycles.

In Roseville and Rocklin proper, new development could be planned to include not just streets and houses, but clear bike paths, community gardens and agricultural areas, recreational facilities, and a small shopping and social center for each neighborhood—elements of a comprehensive, self-sufficient community so far lacking in Roseville's development. The plan could also encourage development of a clear, centrally located auto-free core area, with easy access by bicycle from all parts of Roseville.

The Roseville situation can also be used to illustrate the potential of the APA concept in addressing the problem of affordable housing (and indirectly, the problem of providing employment). An adequate supply or potential supply of housing for employees at all income levels is an increasingly important siting consideration for many large employers (including Hewlett Packard, which left the Santa Clara Valley largely because of the extremely high cost of housing there).

When the APA process is used, required EIR's and most public hearings and approvals would be completed prior to adoption of an APA plan. Once the plan is approved, housing developers could begin work rapidly, without having to repeat the full costly, time-consuming review process. They would save significant amounts in time, interest, and other project approval-related costs, so they should be able to sell homes for a lower price than would otherwise be possible.

Such an unusually streamlined development process will likely attract many housing developers, even if the plan contains specifications on the price ranges of the types of housing to be built. It is important that development be permitted by a large number of different developers and builders simultaneously in several adjacent APA's.

With many developers, small builders and housing projects, competition would ensure that prices were held to a reasonable level. It would also guarantee that developers did not take advantage of a streamlined development process by merely increasing their profits.

Case III—Southport

The Southport area on the outskirts of Sacramento, California, is a good example of an area with some existing development that has the potential of becoming a garden city.

Downtown Sacramento and the state capital are located on the east bank of the Sacramento River. The city and its unincorporated suburbs have spread far to the north, east, and south, but across the river in Yolo County there is only a pocket of unincorporated, partly industrial development within the bend of the river, including West Sacramento, Broderick, and Bryte. South of this, across the barge canal, is the Southport district, containing only some scattered residential development—small, older rural homes along the back roads, plus a few subdivisions built more recently. The rest is cropland. About 1,500 people live there, though it has a potential population, using the densities I advocate, of 18,000 to 24,000. Yet it is only a few miles from the center of Sacramento; from Southport's fields one can see the tops of tall buildings downtown rising above the trees that line the river.

The only future plan the county has for this area is a rectangular grid of 60-foot-wide streets that individual developers can fill in with smaller streets and residential lots, turning Southport into a standard high-density, sterile, amorphous, automobile-oriented bedroom suburb for Sacramento workers. This development is being delayed at the moment mainly because the sewage system serving the area is already at capacity and the county has not worked out a way to finance enlargement of the facility.

A member of the Yolo County Board of Supervisors proposed development of a more careful plan that would address

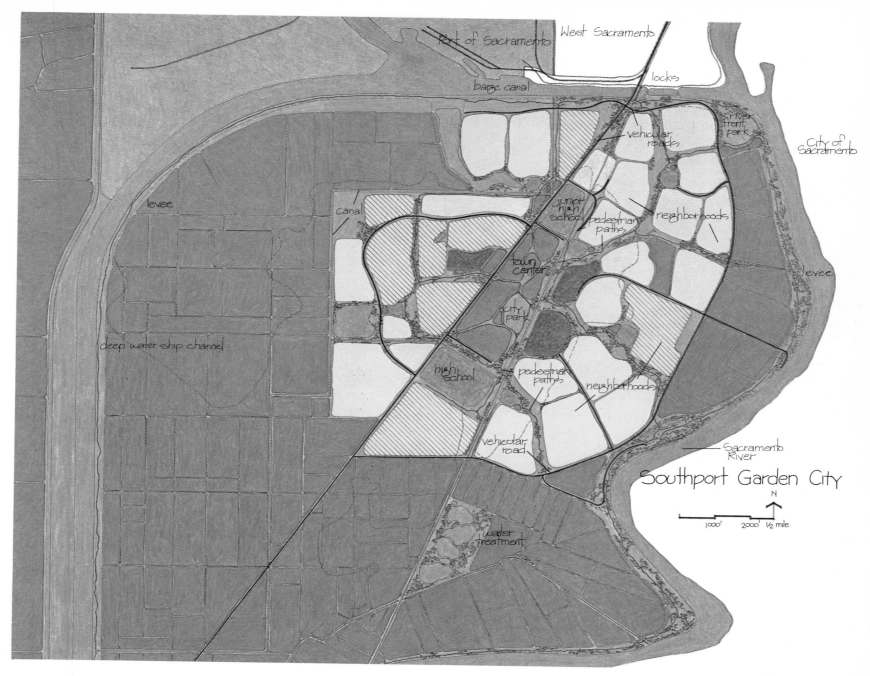

Port of Sacramento   West Sacramento

barge canal

locks

vehicular roads

river front park

City of Sacramento

levee

canal

junior high school

pedestrian paths

neighborhoods

town center

city park

levee

deep water ship channel

high school

pedestrian paths

neighborhoods

vehicular road

Sacramento River

Southport Garden City

N

1000'   2000'   ½ mile

water treatment

many of the issues I have discussed. Unfortunately, the county planning staff opposed this, saying that the existing plan was adequate and that anything more would be a waste of money. The board, very aware of its limited budget and with confidence in its planners, rejected the proposal. This may not be the final word, however. At this writing, the board has recently hired a new planning director who has a reputation for innovation, and there is a group of citizens beginning to gather support for better planning of the area.

Southport has unusual potential for development as an APA because it is within bicycling distance of two existing employment centers: downtown Sacramento with its businesses and government buildings, and the port of Sacramento with its docks for ocean-going ships and its associated industry. The first is about four miles by bicycle from the center of Southport; the second, about two miles.

This means Southport would not need to include any industry as such to provide enough employment for all its inhabitants. Yet it would not be a bedroom community in the ordinary sense of the word, because it would have its own commercial core offering a full range of goods and services, and would grow a great deal of its own food in its greenbelts and in fields to the south. These enterprises and others would probably provide jobs within the community for half of Southport's workers. And for those working outside, in downtown Sacramento or in the port, the distance would be so short that one could hardly call it commuting. I must emphasize again that this is an unusual case; proximity to industry does not make a location desirable for a garden city if that industry is not within bicycling distance.

Southport is bisected by an existing highway running from northeast to southwest, roughly parallel to the river. The town center could be developed in a linear fashion on the east side of this highway. Parking areas would be located closest to the road; next would be the buildings requiring frequent vehicle access, with their backs to the parking area. Beyond those would be pedestrian malls and buildings requiring infrequent vehicle access, followed by parks and playgrounds. Bicycle and foot traffic from existing residential development west of the highway could be led across it to the auto-free core area via overpasses or underpasses at several points. This is, of course, less than ideal; it would be better if the central access road to a garden city core area did not have to carry through traffic.

The remaining area east of the highway could be developed more in line with the conceptual garden city plan. Between the core area and the river would be residential neighborhoods and greenbelts, with a network of bike-footpaths leading west and north to the core area. Existing roads form a ring around this residential area that joins the main road at either end. Streets in the residential area could lead outward to this ring road, to avoid interference with the central bike-foot circulation.

From the north end of the core area, a major bike path could cross the barge canal and proceed north along the river levee to enter downtown Sacramento via the Capitol Avenue bridge. A shuttle bus could also run between downtown Sacramento and Southport's core area, with lockable bike parking at the Southport stops. Making only a few stops at each end, this bus could provide very rapid commuting.

Developing Southport in this fashion could be the first step in redeveloping other Sacramento suburbs into more appropriately planned communities. The suburbs to the north and east of Sacramento tend to be true bedroom communities, and redeveloping them as APA's would involve adding the agriculture and light industry they now lack. A pleasant community so convenient to downtown Sacramento as Southport would attract many downtown workers now living in the bedroom communities and commuting as far as 20 miles to work. This in itself would save a great deal of energy, but it would also make housing available in those bedroom communities for people working in the new enterprises to be developed there.

Southport land is of good agricultural quality, ideal for food-producing landscaping. The community could also include small French-intensive-method truck farms and orchards providing fresh organic produce both for Southport itself and for the downtown markets just a few miles away. The entire community could be surrounded by a narrow agricultural strip, but the largest agricultural areas should probably be to the south. This would

keep the residential areas as close as possible to the employment centers within bicycling distance to the north. Small agricultural areas scattered throughout the town's neighborhoods, however, should help to make the plan acceptable to present residents who settled in Southport for its rural atmosphere.

Such development would mean that only those residential neighborhoods to the south would be adjacent to large enough agricultural areas to use septic tanks for sewage disposal, and even there septic tanks might be impractical because of the high water table. Therefore, one of the central sewage systems described in the earlier section on waste management would have to be used, with the sewage being carried to the south where the treated effluent could be used to irrigate Southport orchards, or fields farther south.

At present, Southport is part of larger water and sewer service districts run by the county. If Southport were incorporated as a city or organized as a unified service district, it would probably contract with these existing service districts for water and sewer services until Southport had a large enough population to justify providing such services itself.

Police and fire protection for Southport are presently provided by the county, with no facilities actually in the Southport area, and there is only one school in the area. Development of these services could probably follow the same pattern as for a garden city developed from scratch.

Since Southport is practically surrounded by water, there would be little danger of its developing beyond the optimum size. Title to the land planned as open space within the town itself, however, should be set up in such a way as to guard against any future pressure for its development.

This plan is a good example of how the conceptual design from Chapter 4 can be adapted to the peculiarities of a particular site. Agriculture has been concentrated at one end of the plan, and the industries that would provide a large portion of the necessary employment are located outside the planning area itself. Even so, the basic concept—a unified, self-sufficient community with bike and foot traffic predominant—remains reasonably intact.

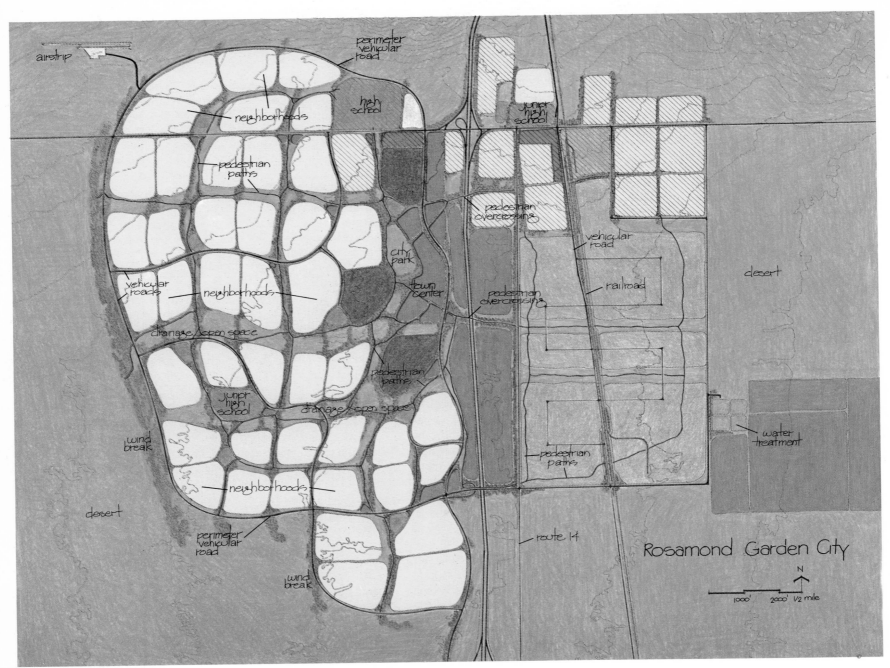

airstrip

perimeter
vehicular
road

neighborhoods

high
school

junior
high
school

pedestrian
paths

pedestrian
overcrossing

vehicular
road

city
park

railroad

desert

town
center

pedestrian
overcrossing

vehicular
roads

neighborhoods

drainage/open space

pedestrian
paths

junior
high
school

drainage/open space

pedestrian
paths

wind
break

water
treatment

neighborhoods

desert

perimeter
vehicular
road

route 14

Rosamond Garden City

wind
break

N

1000'   2000'   1/2 mile

Case IV—Rosamond

The unincorporated town of Rosamond in southern California (population 3,000) provides a good example of how an existing small town might form the nucleus for a garden city. I was contacted by the owner of a square mile of land there who wanted me to prepare a plan for developing it. After talking it over, we suggested that Kern County should develop a master plan for orderly development of Rosamond into a larger town. The county supervisors have scheduled a public hearing on this proposal. I think Rosamond is a good site for development along the lines I have suggested for an APA.

Rosamond is located in the Antelope Valley, on the southern edge of Kern County. It is the closest town to Edwards Air Force Base, and is on a major highway about 60 miles north of Los Angeles. Since it is separated from the Los Angeles Air Basin by the San Gabriel Mountains, the air quality is high. Sunlight is plentiful. Strong breezes allow good natural cooling at night, even in the hottest weather, and provide a possibility of wind-powered electric generation. The terrain is flat, ideal for bicycling. The major argument against growth there is that, like most of southern California, Rosamond must import water from northern California at a very high expense, both financial and ecological. If there is to be any growth in southern California, however, this is the kind of place for it.

There is already pressure for population growth in the area because of expanding operations at Edwards Air Force Base. Without planning, this growth will probably be dispersed among Rosamond and other small towns in the area, the larger city of Lancaster 10 miles to the south, and the rural areas between. Already, isolated subdivisions and mobile-home parks have sprung up at random locations in the desert, where not even the most rudimentary public, commercial, or community facilities are available without driving several miles. None of the small towns is likely to grow very fast, so anyone looking for urban conveniences will have to live in Lancaster. But Lancaster, suffering from inconvenient layout, unsightliness, and sprawl as a result of bad planning, already has a population over 30,000.

It would make much more sense, it seems to me, to concentrate most of this growth in one or two locations, to produce, over the next decade or two, new garden cities large enough to offer their own urban amenities. Rosamond is a very logical site, and after talking with a handful of its citizens, I got the impression that most of them would be glad to see it grow to a population of 20,000 or 30,000 and then stop. They like a small town with open space around it, but they know they need a larger population to support a department store, several good markets, a hospital, and a good school system, as well as other amenities, and to attract some light industry to provide jobs.

To do this, Kern County could set up a special Rosamond planning district which would hire a consultant to draw up a master plan and a tentative development schedule. Current Rosamond residents, potential residents, landowners, and representatives of companies that might like to locate there would be invited to discuss their views and preferences with the planners at several stages in the planning process. Eventually, the master plan for Rosamond would be adopted by the county as part of a general plan which would, at the same time, discourage random isolated development in other parts of the county.

The fact that Rosamond has the basic city services — water, power, sewer, and street systems — is in some ways an advantage and in others a handicap. People are more likely to be attracted to an area where there are some services and shopping facilities already available. New development can be added more easily because developers do not have to invest such large amounts of money at the start as they would for a whole new town. But the design of the enlarged town will suffer if it has to accommodate too much to the existing pattern of circulation and services.

In Rosamond's case, this is not a great problem because the existing town is a small part of the projected final development. The new neighborhoods could all be developed on one side of the existing town, rather than surrounding it. The present town would become a neighborhood on one side of the new town, and its downtown area would become a neighborhood commercial area and social center. The present town would take up about one-fifth of the garden city's area, although its present population is, at most, one-tenth of the garden city's projected population, because the present density is low and there are some undeveloped spaces within the existing town.

Thus, four-fifths of the town could be developed with an uncompromised circulation system of the type I consider ideal: a network of bike-footpaths leading inward to the new town center by short, direct routes, and a separate network of cul-de-sac streets served by arterial streets leading outward to a peripheral road. This would tend to encourage walking and bicycling in the old part of town as well, even if the circulation system there were not changed at all, partly because that would be the most convenient way to get to other parts of town. To reach other neighborhoods or the new core area by car, residents of the old section would have to drive out to the peripheral road and around to the appropriate arterial street entrance, just like residents of newer neighborhoods, while they could go much more directly by foot or bike.

However, the safety and convenience of bike travel in the older part of town could be greatly increased by creating a few main bike routes that are direct and well paved, with few stops and few intersections with automobile traffic. Methods of creating such bike routes are discussed in detail in the section of this chapter dealing with redevelopment of existing towns that have already reached garden city size. The low-density and undeveloped spaces in the old town should facilitate these and other changes to bring the old town closer to the garden city neighborhood ideal.

The county already operates a fire station in Rosamond, and the county sheriff also has an office there. Rosamond would probably take these over when it incorporated and set up its own fire and police departments, and could build larger permanent facilities later. The town already has its own school district and two schools, one for the high school and one for all other grades; others could be built as needed.

Gas and electricity in Rosamond are presently provided by a private utility company. Gas service could probably be omitted entirely in new development, because solar (which could meet 90 to 95 percent of heating needs) and wood heating would eliminate the need for gas. Until the town became large enough to build its own generation facilities, it would doubtless continue to buy electricity from the private utility, but the long-term goal should be to make the town independent of "imported" electricity. To this end, a city utility company could be set up, having control over some land in the surrounding desert where it could build a wind-powered electric generating station, or a "solar farm" with arrays of photovoltaic cells or mirrors for a solar boiler, along with some kind of energy storage system.

The distribution of electricity in the new part of town could be handled in a number of ways. The distribution network might be installed, owned, and operated by the private utility, or it might be installed by the private utility under contract with the special services district, to be owned and operated by the city.

The important thing is that the city should own and operate its own on-site generation facilities with enough capacity to meet its own electric needs. Local generation would make the townspeople more sensitive to the real costs and environmental risks of the various alternative generation methods, and give them a clearer incentive for using electricity frugally. It would also guarantee them a reliable supply of electricity independent of any shortages that might arise elsewhere in the country due to waste or poor planning.

Rosamond's present sewage-treatment plant is large enough to serve a population of 28,000. Since the plant is already there, a conventional sewage collection system will involve less additional cost than the septic-tank system that would ordinarily be cheapest. If special toilets and flow-restricting devices on sink and shower faucets are required (which should be done anyway to conserve water), this plant should be sufficient for the new town's needs. If the residents could be persuaded to be as careful about not putting toxic chemicals into the drains as they would be with a septic-tank system, and if industrial wastes were kept separate, the effluent from the plant could be used to irrigate orchards or biomass crops south of town, making the desert agriculturally productive using only recycled water and nutrients.

The APA in Small-Town Rehabilitation

The effects of establishing APA's in existing urban areas will not be nearly as dramatic as in locations where new garden cities can be built. But they do offer existing communities a planning tool that will help localize the planning process and facilitate the urban remodeling that will eventually have to take place as the present high-energy urban design becomes less and less affordable.

Let us first consider towns no larger than a single APA. They range in size from a few thousand people to towns a little larger than the optimum 20,000 to 30,000 population and six-square-mile area. One of the first issues the town will have to deal with is what size it would consider optimum for itself and whether or not it is willing to impose growth controls to maintain that size. The town will then have to consider how it will (1) balance and complete both the neighborhoods and the town as a whole by adding whatever elements are missing — industry, agriculture, shopping areas, parks, garden space, housing in a certain price range, or whatever; (2) make bicycling and walking as safe, convenient, and pleasant as possible; and (3) establish a clear and final boundary around the town.

If the town sets a growth limit and it still appears that there are economic reasons for future growth, and if the region is ecologically appropriate for further growth, the question should not be whether or not to allow the town to grow beyond the optimum size, but whether or not to establish a second APA and develop a separate community next to the existing one, or a little distance away.

Growth control has been controversial in the past, with opponents arguing that it infringes on the freedom of the landowner and developer, and proponents arguing that it protects the residents' right to preserve the town character that attracted them to live there in the first place. The U.S. Supreme Court has upheld growth control methods used in Petaluma, California, and growth control has spread to a number of communities throughout the United States.

My home town — Davis, California — provides a good example of the problems and potential of APA-style redevelopment in a small town. Davis is located on Interstate Highway 80 about 15 miles west of Sacramento. During the last 20 years Davis has experienced a great deal of growth, partly due to expansion of the Davis campus of the University of California, and partly because the college and the small-town atmosphere make it very attractive to Sacramento commuters. These two factors still create significant growth pressure, although development has been sharply limited for the last 5 years by a growth-control ordinance which restricts the number of single-family home building permits issued each year.

Davis is already larger than is desirable for an APA, and in other circumstances, dividing it into two APA's and allowing each to grow would be a good solution. But the layout of Davis does not lend itself to division, and moreover, the area around Davis is all prime agricultural land, where development should be avoided if at all possible. This is a good example of why regional planning must look far enough ahead to avoid locating "growth generators" such as highways or industries so as to create pressure for development where development is not appropriate.

The layout of Davis is not ideal for a single APA, either. The town is rather elongated from east to west, and the two hubs of activity — the campus and the core area — are not in the center of town, but rather on one side. On the positive side, Davis has a delightful commercial core area plus small peripheral shopping centers in each part of town. Davis is already fairly bicycle-conscious because of the university, particularly because parking on campus is very limited. There are also buses running to and from campus when school is in session. The automobile still predominates, however; I doubt if 1 trip in 20 outside the university campus is by bicycle. I think good comprehensive planning for bicycle circulation could increase this figure to 1 in 2.

Davis has already taken some steps toward encouraging bicycling. It has established bike lanes on many streets, and has developed off-street bike paths in some places, particularly near campus and in new subdivisions. It has rejected proposals to add

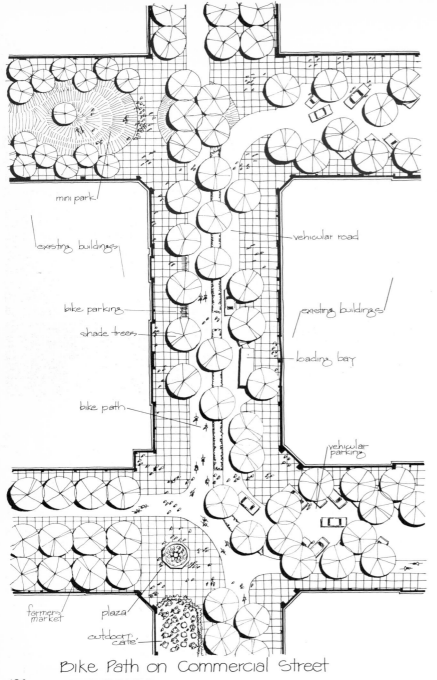

mini park

existing buildings

bike parking

shade trees

bike path

farmers market

plaza

outdoor café

vehicular road

existing buildings

loading bay

vehicular parking

Bike Path on Commercial Street

sidewalk   bike path   vehicular road   loading bay   sidewalk

Section

more lanes to an automobile underpass connecting downtown Davis with Interstate Highway 80, but has instead added a separate small underpass there for bicycles.

These bike routes are still more or less makeshift, however. In places they become narrow or badly paved, make inconvenient detours, run dangerously along heavily traveled auto lanes or cross streets frequently. In most parts of town, there is no equivalent for bicycles of the major through streets that allow automobiles to go long distances without stopping for cross traffic. In the core areas, bikes have to compete with heavy auto traffic and with cars moving in and out of parking spaces, mostly on streets without any separate bike lane. The congested traffic detracts from the area's attractiveness for pedestrian shoppers as well. Similarly, in the peripheral shopping centers, bikes have to compete with heavy auto traffic at the entrances and in the parking lots.

I do not say this to disparage Davis' present system of bike routes. With all its shortcomings, Davis' bike-path system is one of the best in the country, and is considered a model by planners all over the nation. It has required a great deal of hard work and dedication on the part of many concerned individuals to bring the city this far in providing for bike traffic. The point I want to make is that even in this model system, the amounts spent to provide safety and convenience for bicyclists are the merest pittance compared to the amounts spent on streets and parking for automobiles, the sacrifices made to provide bike routes are

negligible. Even in Davis, the bicyclists who are making an effort to help solve our energy problems are treated as second-class citizens compared to the drivers who help to perpetuate the problem.

To achieve a significant increase in the percentage of trips made by bicycle, the whole of Davis must be made more safe, pleasant and convenient for bicyclists and pedestrians. I see several main steps as necessary to accomplish this:

First, a number of streets in the core area should be closed to auto traffic for several blocks and converted into pedestrian-bicycle malls, to create a virtually auto-free area several blocks square. Many downtown Davis blocks have a central alley which could be used for deliveries to businesses; in others the central lanes of the street might be left open from one end for deliveries only. Parking would have to be provided on the periphery of this auto-free area.

The closed streets could be planted with large trees to keep the core area pleasantly cool in the hot Davis summers, and continuous awnings or arcades could be installed along the sidewalks to provide rain protection in the wet winters. Park benches and picnic tables could be provided, permits could be granted for sidewalk cafes and street vendors, and courts could be set up for lawn bowling and shuffleboard. Owners of many downtown buildings would probably alter the second stories to provide shops and offices with balconies overlooking the quiet, pleasant, busy malls. (This has already been done in several cases where the second stories overlook interior courtyards, but never on the street side, for obvious reasons: who wants a balcony with a view of noisy, congested traffic?)

Second, the city should create three or four major bike routes leading directly to this core area. They should be fairly straight, separated from the auto lanes of streets (and preferably

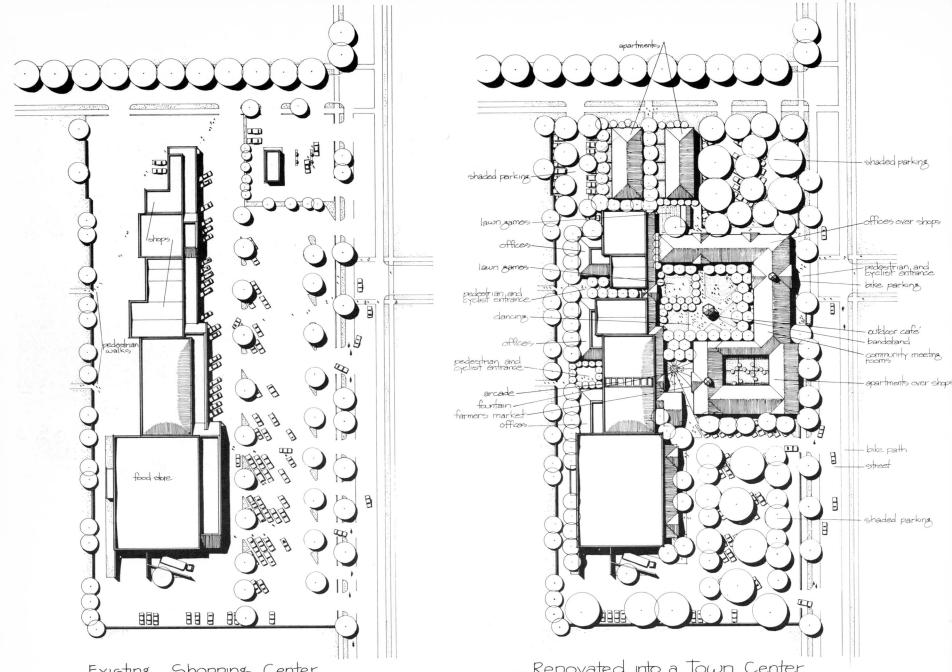

Existing Shopping Center...

...Renovated into a Town Center

shops

pedestrian walks

food store

apartments

shaded parking

shaded parking

lawn games

offices over shops

offices

pedestrian and cyclist entrance

lawn games

bike parking

pedestrian and cyclist entrance

dancing

outdoor café

offices

bandstand

community meeting rooms

pedestrian and cyclist entrance

apartments over shops

arcade

fountain

farmers market

bike path

offices

street

shaded parking

not even alongside major streets, so bicyclists do not have to breathe exhaust fumes), and without more than two or three intersections with auto traffic in their entire length of two to three miles. The intersections should have traffic lights so that auto traffic would have to stop periodically for bikes to cross. These major routes, or branches of them, should also extend to every outlying neighborhood shopping center, and to each public school. Secondary branches — not necessarily off the streets, but avoiding streets with through auto traffic — should lead from these major routes into every residential neighborhood.

Third, the neighborhood shopping centers should be redesigned to be more convenient for bicyclists, and to function better as community social centers, which they already are to some extent merely because people's paths cross there. Bicycle entrances and parking should be separate from auto entrances and parking. Outdoor areas for play, lounging, eating, socializing, and general hanging out should be provided, largely by conversion of some parking space to these other uses. Rooms for meetings and classes could also be provided. Meeting space is presently scarce and expensive in Davis — expensive mainly because the rooms available are mostly in churches or other buildings that have to be opened and supervised specially for any meeting or class. In a shopping mall that would not be a problem.

Finally, ample bicycle parking should be provided, both in the city core area and in the peripheral areas.

Creation of major auto-free bike paths in previously developed areas will also be necessary in several other types of APA's, so the possible methods are probably worth discussing in some detail here.

Davis has already established several bike-path segments that run for considerable distances with little interruption. Some run through existing parks or alongside major streets that have few cross streets entering from the bike-path side. Around Village Homes and in another recently developed area, they run through long greenbelts equidistant between major parallel streets; side streets run toward the greenbelts from each major street, but few streets cross the greenbelts. These clear-travel bike-path segments are all toward the outskirts of Davis, however. To continue the

routes through the older sections to the core area will require major changes.

One way to establish a clear major bike path would be simply to close a street to auto traffic, so that most streets originally entering that street from either side would become cul-de-sacs for autos. Half the width of a typical side street would provide a very generous bike path; the other half of the pavement width could be torn up to form a park strip with benches, play areas, and gardens. In this case, the owners of homes fronting only on the converted street would have to be compensated for their loss of direct vehicle access to their lots.

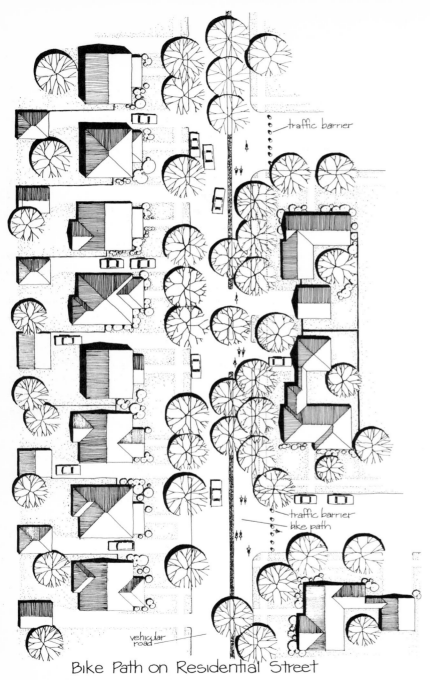

traffic barrier

traffic barrier
bike path

vehicular
road

Bike Path on Residential Street

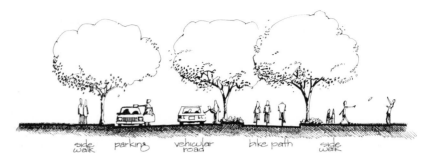

side
walk   parking   vehicular   bike path   side
                   road   walk

Section

Another option would be to narrow the street and run the bike path along one side of it, with the cross streets on that side becoming cul-de-sacs. Driveways on that side crossing the bike path might or might not be permitted.

With either of these methods, intersections between bike and auto traffic could be further minimized by using overpasses and underpasses to carry the bike path over or under major streets. At all on-grade intersections, traffic lights should be provided.

Secondary bike routes leading to these main routes could proceed along existing streets without closing the streets entirely to auto traffic, but simply installing, every block or so, an auto barricade of pylons that bikes could pass through, to make auto traffic take different routes. The street would still be a through route for bicycle traffic, however, so cross traffic at each intersection should be required to stop for bikes, rather than vice versa.

Establishing such a system of clear bike paths would mean that in general, autos could not go as directly from one point to another as they could in a pure grid system where all streets go through. Such grid systems are usually found only in the older parts of towns, however, because planning has already moved away from them, toward the use of cul-de-sacs, U-shaped streets, and traffic barricades intended to keep through traffic on a few main streets and out of residential neighborhoods. Even where pure grid systems exist, drivers often take somewhat indirect routes in order to use through streets and avoid stop signs. So the inconvenience for autos from creation of a clear bike-path system would not be great, and would be most noticeable for short-distance trips — and these are the trips for which driving should really be discouraged anyway.

The final step I would suggest in appropriate planning for Davis is the creation of a greenbelt between ½ and 1 mile wide surrounding the city, where only farming and some very limited development would be permitted. Toxic pesticide sprays would be prohibited, in order to protect the adjacent residential areas from drifting chemicals. This greenbelt would put a definite and final limit on the city's geographic size. It would generally lie just outside the fully developed parts of the city and would include areas with some scattered development. In places, arms of the greenbelt would reach inward toward the center of town.

One simple way to create such a greenbelt would be to establish a new zoning category for the undeveloped land. Under this zoning, the land could either be used for farming, or it could be developed in a particular way. If developed, only a small portion closest to the city could be built on; the developer would have to sell or dedicate the outlying portion to the city. The city would use the undeveloped land for biomass forest, or lease it in plots up to about 40 acres in size for intensive organic truck gardens, orchards, and vineyards to supply the city with fresh wholesome produce.

In addition to its growth limitation ordinance and its development of bicycle paths, Davis has adopted several other energy efficient measures which would be valuable in most any other urban rehabilitations.

A home occupations ordinance allows a business which requires only one nonfamilial employee and a small sign to locate in any residential neighborhood. This eliminates some commuting and saves the owner from having to heat and cool two buildings — a home and an office.

Conditional-use permits are liberally given to any physician or dentist who wants to convert a residence into office space. This allows needed services to be provided right in the neighborhoods within walking and biking distances.

A restriction against the use of clotheslines was often written by developers into the C, C, & R's of new subdivisions, but that doesn't happen anymore. The city council passed an ordinance making such requirements illegal so that now all residents may use the sun to dry their clothes. Clotheslines must also be provided in new apartment buildings.

A city retrofit ordinance cuts down on home energy use by requiring homeowners to upgrade insulation of water heaters and attics and to weather-strip doors and windows before selling their houses. (Similar ordinances are now being adopted by many other California communities). It is projected that such action will cut energy use in the home by as much as 30 percent and save the homeowner as much as $150 at 1979 energy prices.[4]

Conservation is also mandated in new construction. The city's "Energy Conservation Building Ordinance," calculated to reduce energy consumption in the home by 20 to 30 percent, was adopted in 1975. It sets insulation standards and limits the amount of windows allowed in new residences. To earn more glazing area, the builder has to add the elements required to make the home a passive solar house: southern exposure of most of the windows and perhaps additional heat-storage capacity. Another requirement that says most windows must be shaded from the sun in the summer significantly cuts air conditioning requirements.

City planning department policies further boost the use of solar technologies by requiring that 80 percent of the lots in new subdivisions be oriented north-south and that all new homes in these subdivisions have solar hot-water heaters. The street trees planting program has been changed, replacing evergreen trees with deciduous ones in locations where winter sunlight is desirable while insuring that streets are shaded in the summer.

The city is now investigating the idea of going into the business of centralized power generation. It has applied for a grant to build a solar electrical-generation system to be located on its landfill site, and a citizens' committee is currently studying how to develop the biomass greenbelt that I described earlier.[5]

---

[4]California Energy Commision Staff, "Achieving Energy Efficiency in Existing Buildings," legislative issue memorandum (Sacramento, 1 April 1980).
[5]For copies of the Davis ordinances, contact the City of Davis, Community Development Department, 226 F Street, Davis, CA 95616.

The APA in Urban Redevelopment

Existing larger cities and densely developed suburbs will be the most difficult to transform into healthy, energy-efficient, nurturing environments. Certainly, large cities may employ many of the same measures used by smaller cities to effect positive change. But it will be difficult to change the things that are not only very poorly designed, but are also very established in the city. For example, certain traffic patterns may be very poorly planned, but they may also be so complex and so vital to the everyday operations of the city that changing them will require costly major restructuring. This will have to be done gradually and will require serious long-term planning and commitment. I think there will be increasing support for such efforts, however, as life in our present cities becomes increasingly difficult, expensive, and unpleasant, and as the costs of driving elsewhere for weekends and vacations increase prohibitively.

The first step in the restructuring process, as I see it, should be to divide the existing city into Appropriate Planning Areas. Like APA's used for planning isolated garden cities, these urban redevelopment APA's would have a rather fixed size of two to six square miles, determined by the aim of maximizing diversity, self-sufficiency, and efficiencies of scale, while staying within the limits imposed by reliance on walking and bicycling within each APA instead of driving.

As I have indicated earlier, the APA is a sort of regional planning module. If one wanted to develop a large city from scratch, one could simply put together a cluster of such modules, as many as needed for the projected population. In practice, there would seldom be much reason to create very large clusters of modular towns, since the ability to decentralize is a major point of this planning concept. It is useful, however, to imagine what a metropolitan area composed of clustered modular towns would be like, in order to see more clearly what we should aim for in redevelopment of existing metropolitan areas.

In a metropolitan cluster planned from scratch, the modular towns would be separated from each other by mile-wide greenbelts of forest and agriculture, and their core areas would be linked to each other by a public transportation system. The central module would serve as cultural center for the whole, containing such specialized facilities as universities, museums, and performing arts centers, as well as any highly specialized shops or commercial services. It would not be a downtown area in the usual sense, however, with a concentration of jobs and a shortage of housing requiring workers and students to commute from the outlying areas. Each modular town in the cluster would have its share of business and industry, and even the cultural center would have its share of housing to provide for the workers and full-time students using its facilities.

There would probably still be a certain amount of commuting. A person living in one modular town, presented with a particularly attractive job offer in an adjacent town, might choose to commute rather than to move from an established home. (If another member of his or her family worked in the first town, moving would be still more difficult.) But the attractions of working near home, with members of one's own community, would lead many people to avoid commuting, either by moving to the towns where they worked, or by finding jobs in the towns where they lived. In today's cities, many workers simply do not have that option; they *must* commute.

With any significant portion of the population pursuing a noncommuting life-style, others will tend to follow their example; there will be a snowball effect. With commuting at a minimum, the public transit system could be a relatively modest affair — perhaps a small fleet of buses with outside racks for bicycles. Buses would travel only between town centers, and passengers would walk or ride bikes from there to their destinations. With so few stops, the buses could make a very quick round trip, so they would both provide faster service and move more passengers per hour than conventional buses that make many local stops.

Redevelopment of existing cities will undoubtedly fall short of this ideal in several ways. For one, there will be more commuting, simply because workplaces tend to be concentrated in certain parts of the existing city and homes and schools in others. This imbalance could be reduced — for example, by converting some downtown office buildings to apartments, and by adding office buildings, workshops, and light industry to residential areas wherever possible. But eliminating commuting entirely would require demolishing and rebuilding so much existing construction that it would be prohibitively costly.

With redevelopment to encourage bike and foot travel within each APA, and the use of express buses between APA centers, however, the style of this commuting would be drastically changed so that it would be less costly and objectionable. Use of private autos for commuting will tend to be discouraged by high gas prices, but it should be further discouraged by such administrative measures as tolls or parking taxes, since it does so much to degrade the urban environment.

It will also be difficult or impossible to make redeveloped urban APA's entirely self-sufficient in food production, simply because of the lack of open space. Home vegetable gardens and productive landscaping could take an urban APA part of the way, but to create the agricultural greenbelts necessary for real self-sufficiency would require demolishing whole neighborhoods. I think it is important, however, to create some areas for agriculture and open space within and surrounding each urban APA. These areas may range from part of a block to a strip two or three blocks wide.

Our experience in recent decades with urban renewal, however, should be enough to convince us that these areas cannot be cleared in one fell swoop, by wholesale demolition. Except in very special cases, the costs are simply too high. We have to consider not only the value of the buildings demolished, but the very real and very severe psychological costs and hardships involved in the destruction of homes and communities.[6]

It might be possible, however, to accomplish the same thing very gradually over a period of several decades, turning developed areas back into agricultural land by a sort of reverse development process without disrupting people's communities or lives. Over a period of ten years or so, many of those living in an area designated for open space would move away of their own accord. Others wishing to stay in the community could be helped

to find other homes nearby. As they did so, the city could buy their houses; the older ones could be demolished to provide community gardening space, and those in better condition could be rented until the time came to clear the designated area entirely.

Lest we overestimate the difficulty of this, we should remember that many of those now living in our cities are there only because of economics and job availability. Offered the chance of living and working in a new garden city, many would probably be happy to leave. In some cases, a neighborhood designated for clearing could be given the chance to choose a new garden city neighborhood where they would have first choice of housing, so that those of the community who wished to stay together could do so.

The first step in the redevelopment of a large urban complex would be to divide it into appropriate planning areas. Each APA should have the potential for establishing a centrally located core area, and for bringing foot and bicycle traffic into this core separately from auto traffic. Ideally every part of the APA should be within 1 to 1½ miles of this core area. In many cases, then, an APA would be set up around an existing concentration of business or industry, or a large shopping center. Development planning for the APA should aim to minimize auto traffic there and provide access and conveniences for pedestrians and bicyclists, and to provide the full range of core-area facilities and services, adding whatever is lacking in the existing development. Smaller commercial areas within the APA could be similarly adapted as neighborhood centers.

At the same time, there should be an attempt to provide the best possible balance of existing elements within each APA. Insofar as possible boundaries should be drawn so that initially each APA has a variety of jobs, housing in all price ranges, schools, shopping, and open space. Ideally, the boundaries should fall where the community is already broken by railroads, waterways, major streets and highways, greenbelts, or developed areas that for one reason or another lend themselves to demolition for open space.

I have included here a diagram showing how Sacramento, California, might be divided into appropriate planning areas. I am

[6]Mark Fried, "Grieving for a Lost Home: The Psychological Costs of Relocation," in *Urban Renewal: The Record and the Controversy,* ed. James Q. Wilson (Cambridge, Mass.: MIT Press, 1966), pp. 359–79.

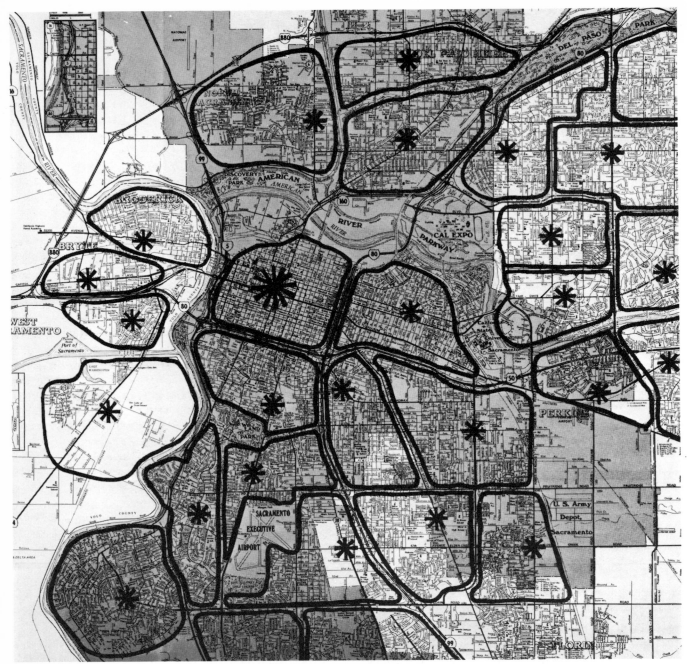

not seriously proposing this particular plan; it is just an example I prepared in about an hour with a marking pen and a map of Sacramento. You might find it interesting to try the same thing with a map of some city you are familiar with. It is an instructive exercise because it forces you to think about what potential the various areas have for redevelopment as APA's, and what that redevelopment would entail.

In actual practice, this division should be carried out by the city planning department working with an advisory committee of citizen volunteers, and finalized after public hearings. The entire plan should be considered and approved as a unit, however, since the boundaries selected for any one APA also affect the possibilities for adjacent APA's.

The next step would be to establish in each APA a citizens' planning group of five to seven members to develop a long-range plan for the area, addressing all the points mentioned in the APA guidelines at the beginning of this chapter. This group would operate under the authority of the city council, and its members would either be appointed by the council or chosen by a special election within the APA. They would all be citizens of the APA, and ideally would include any who might have served on the advisory committee that helped determine the APA boundaries. Public hearings on the long-range APA plan would be held within the APA, and the final version would be approved both by the city council and by the voters in the APA itself. The process of developing the APA plan would be as important as the product; it would do much to develop the citizens' awareness of the APA as a political, economic, and social unit to which they belong.

The APA plan would include a rezoning of the land within the APA, which would encourage the sorts of private development and redevelopment that would tend to increase the diversity, balance, and self-sufficiency of the APA. Local businesses and businesses interested in locating in the APA would have much to contribute to both the planning and the actual development of the town center. The longest range goal would be the reverse development of selected pieces of land within the APA back to open space for intensive agriculture.

Working under the APA planning group would be still other citizens' committees, one for each neighborhood in the APA. These would provide input to the overall APA plan, particularly in developing detailed plans for their own neighborhoods. They would work on ways to provide neighborhood meeting space, recreation areas, miniparks, community gardens, shopping centers, and small business where appropriate. They would also help plan the neighborhood bike routes as part of the overall APA circulation system, and would give individual, personalized attention to the problems of people living in areas needed for open space, particularly the elderly.

The city government could help these citizens' volunteer planning groups by providing technical advice and assistance — possibly from its own planning staff, but preferably by providing funds for each APA to hire its own consultants. The cost to the city would be partly offset by the fact that the various local planning groups would reduce the work load on the city's own planning department. The neighborhood development consultant, working with citizens at the local level, would be a new profession, quite different from the planner working with a large redevelopment agency in opposition to the people of the areas affected. Instead of making decisions for people, these consultants would provide technical assistance citizens need to make their own decisions.

Consultants would be versed in three areas of knowledge and might be known as the new community architect, the new community organizer, and the new community agriculturalist. I consider the work that I performed in establishing the Village Homes neighborhood, the kind of work this new type of professional would undertake. In the process of designing the Village Homes neighborhood, I worked with many prospective residents evolving a plan which would reflect their concerns as well as my own. The common areas between the homes were again developed with the residents. At a series of meetings, I contributed my knowledge in design and landscape materials and meshed that with the needs and expertise of each group of eight families. In the design and building of the individual homes, I again played as large or small a role as was needed by the individual client.

The new community organizer and agriculturalist also play a part in the Village Homes community. I originally filled these roles; now they are being assumed by resident volunteers as well as by the manager and gardeners paid by the homeowners' association.

The community organizer will face his or her most difficult challenge in a neighborhood not built under the garden city philosophy. Most neighborhoods are planned without any community spaces, almost as though there was a conscious intent to keep the neighbors apart. The community organizer must be a professional with an exceptional ability to work with people, to bring them together, and to help them form a common vision even under the most nonconducive physical conditions.

We need new community agriculturalists to teach us those skills which were second nature to many of our grandparents, but which we have unfortunately lost. Anyone who has tried to revive these skills knows that it takes some knowledge to successfully prepare your own soil, build a fly-free compost pile, grow vegetables, prune fruit trees, and successfully control pests.

The success of communities in the future will depend upon the growing availability of these new professionals who, rather than overpowering their clients with their indisputable knowledge, are able to gain professional satisfaction through working with people.

In new garden cities, the cost of consultants and the planning and development work could easily be included within the development cost as it was in Village Homes. In existing neighborhoods, financial assistance from state and federal governments, as well as from local governments, would be necessary. Funding would be justified as one of the government's best possible investments for saving energy and solving urban social problems. Some of these funds could also be used to hire unemployed people within the APA for redevelopment work.

The APA in Partly Developed Areas

This brings us to the final type of case in which the APA planning method should be used: the half-developed suburban area. Such areas surround many of our cities and even smaller

towns; areas in which fully developed subdivisions and large open fields are mixed more or less at random. Such "leapfrog" development rarely occurred before the automobile. It took longer to get from place to place, so development tended to be strictly concentric in order to keep distances within the city short. After most families owned cars, this no longer seemed as important, and it often seemed advantageous to develop cheaper land a little distance from the existing city. Planning agencies did little to prevent this, especially where rapid growth made it likely that land passed over would not remain undeveloped for long anyway.

I do not feel I need to discuss in detail the application of APA planning to these areas. It will be a mixture of development and redevelopment, including elements of the various situations already discussed in this chapter. Most half-developed areas are bedroom communities; in these areas the goal must be to develop local business and industry, a town center, and a bicycle and pedestrian pathway system, and to permanently set aside large and small parcels of land for agriculture, livestock, and forestry. Some half-developed areas are primarily commercial; in these the emphasis must be more on developing the residential community. Specific planning will depend on the land and the pattern of existing development.

These areas deserve our immediate attention, however, because it is in these areas that we have the greatest leverage for making large and rapid changes in the overall makeup of the nation's urban areas. The opportunities are greater than in either new development or redevelopment. Imposing the new patterns on fully developed urban areas through redevelopment is possible, but difficult and costly. In new development, on the other hand, it is very easy to follow an ideal, but new development will only take place at the rate required by population growth. But in a partially developed suburban area, it may be possible to achieve some approximation of the garden city model over the whole area, with a small amount of additional development and very little redevelopment. The planning of the additional development is crucial; it will turn what is already there into either a pleasant, self-sufficient garden city, or another sterile, energy-consuming suburb.

What makes this situation particularly frustrating is that

much of the support for bad planning in these areas is coming from environmentally concerned people. Aware of the need to conserve energy and resources, and to preserve agriculturally productive land, they advocate high-density infill development, cramming as many people as possible into existing urban areas. They take this position, I think, because they have been unable to look very far beyond our present planning patterns. They are still thinking in terms of commuting, in terms of centralized production and nationwide distribution of both goods and energy, of mammoth agribusiness and unproductive landscaping, of concentric growth, and of cities so unpleasant to live in that their inhabitants must escape each weekend for rest and relaxation. If we had no other option, then high-density infill would make sense; it would be the logical way to make the best of a bad situation. But we are not locked into our present patterns. We have alternatives. If there is one idea I would like you to carry away from this book, it is simply this: we have alternatives. The more we realize this, the clearer it becomes that infill development is just one more step along our present dead-end road.

It is a dead-end partly because it is no longer practical —

economically, environmentally, or socially. But it is also a dead-end because it is inhumane; our humanity requires open space, communities of comprehensible size, and contact with nature. As Lewis Mumford so eloquently put it:

> Sky, mountain, ocean, and river are part of man's constant environment; they form the elemental basis of our animal existence; they were associated with man's history, with his thoughts, long before he uttered an intelligible sound or learned to keep a fire burning. No urban existence that pushes the primeval background out of sight, that makes it remote and unavailable, that deprives people of intimate contact with it, hunting, fishing, rambling, exploring, collecting, boating, is likely to produce adequate men and women, able to cope with the realities of life and death. The coalescing of urban communities into one vast man-hive, a tendency to which Patrick Geddes gave the deservedly ugly name of conurbation, cannot be treated as a permanent urban phenomenon; it is a sign of that lack of political discipline which precedes and announces decay.[7]

[7]Lewis Mumford, *City Development* (London: Secker & Warburg, 1947), p. 161.

Chapter 8
Grass-Roots Action

In thinking about large-scale planning, it is easy to fall into the mistake of assuming it can only be brought about by powerful large-scale organizations—huge development companies, or state or federal government. You have to keep reminding yourself that you as an individual are not impotent in the process of creating ecologically and socially sensible communities. In fact, without the active participation of individuals, small businesses, local groups, and local governments, the transformation will never occur. Experience has shown that in reducing energy consumption, for example, state and federal governments are almost helpless. They can remove obstacles and provide incentives and assistance, but actually reducing and redefining patterns of energy consumption can only be done by individuals and communities.

The appropriately designed communities I advocate here are designed to encourage and facilitate appropriate life-styles, but appropriate life-styles are not entirely dependent on design. It is possible to adopt many elements of these life-styles right now. You can live closer to your work (or work closer to your home), ride a bike for local trips, develop more social life close to home, grow food in your yard, separate your trash for recycling, buy organic produce, dress warmer in winter and cooler in summer, and avoid unnecessary consumption in many ways. A single household can independently take many significant energy-conservation measures—installing solar space heating or water heating, insulating a conventional water heater or improving home insulation and weather stripping, installing a woodstove, setting thermostats lower in the winter, using plants for shading to minimize air conditioning needs, and buying a smaller car.

All of these individual actions are beginning to become more commonplace, and less restricted to an unconventional minority. And people are doing these things not simply for economic reasons, although the economic pressures are becoming more apparent; they are also doing them partly for moral reasons. They believe that these are the things individuals must do if our society is to survive.

Food-buying co-ops, farmer's markets, and home-weatherization workshops are examples of the next step, that of joining together with others to produce change. No one is helpless. In 1972, a group of welfare mothers in San Bernadino, California, banded together to form a Community Development Corporation and began to work for housing rehabilitation and neighborhood revitilization. Led by a dynamic black grandmother, Valerie Pope, the group began in 1976 to hire and train minority youth to produce solar equipment. Many of the first trainees were unable even to read a ruler; now they are productive members of a community-based industry.[1]

Cooperative action is particularly appropriate in neighborhoods because people who live in the same neighborhood are a natural, clearly defined group with many common interests and concerns. The mere fact that they live close to each other makes communication and cooperation easier.

Anyone can take the initiative in bringing a neighborhood together. It requires knocking on some neighbors' doors and asking them to get behind some project of obvious benefit to the neighborhood as a whole. In some high-crime areas, community-watch projects have provided the reason for neighbors to come together as a unit. Organizing to lobby the local government for neighborhood improvements, or, in new neighborhoods, to influence the planning of adjacent development, can perform a similar function. Once the neighborhood has formed a communication network and people have come to know each other, it is easier to initiate other joint projects. A great deal of purely social interaction is also likely to develop within the neighborhood.

Homeowners' associations, which already exist in many subdivisions, can be a useful vehicle for more financially ambitious projects, such as purchasing land within the neighborhood for community gardens, or developing a community center or swimming pool. In some subdivisions, the Codes, Covenants, and Restrictions (C, C, & R's) that give the homeowners' association its authority may be written so as to restrict it to very limited operations, perhaps only the management of existing facilities. However, C, C, & R's often include provisions for amendment, and as cooperative neighborhood improvement projects become more common, courts may begin to take a more liberal interpretation of C, C, & R's. In Village Homes, we took care to write the C, C, & R's to permit even unconventional projects such as developing rental housing or commercial properties within the subdivision, or purchasing land miles away for camping and firewood.

If there is no existing homeowners' association, or if its functions are too restricted, a neighborhood association with voluntary membership can be formed, with use of the facilities it develops limited to members. Like a subdivision homeowners' association, it can use dues or capital assessments to raise money for projects. When I lived in the Sleepy Hollow section of San Anselmo, California, a neighborhood club there built a meeting room for the neighborhood this way.

City and county governments also have a great deal of power to effect change. Over the past few decades, there has been a tendency toward centralization, leaving local elected officials economically more dependent on state and federal decision makers. I think this economic dependence has also led to a kind of psychological dependence and impotence. I once heard a member of a local board of supervisors say, "How would I know what to do about the energy crisis? The president doesn't even know what to do!" A statement like this exposes the supervisor's own feelings of inferiority and powerlessness, while in fact he has more ability to influence the energy situation in his own community than does the president. More local politicians must realize this if needed changes are to occur.

Because building permits are generally required for any type of construction from new commercial facilities to backyard swimming pools, the local building department has substantial control over the individual structures that make up a community. In some areas, federal and state building codes can be amended by a city or county. When they must be adopted verbatim, local enforcement policy can have a large effect on their impact, and local ordinances can add more stringent requirements. They can require, for example, that buildings be more energy efficient or use solar heating or solar water heating. One seacoast community in California has even limited the issuance of permits for air conditioners in new buildings, on the premise that if the building were designed and constructed correctly, air conditioning would be unnecessary.[2] Municipalities can assist the use of solar technologies in their jurisdictions by guaranteeing solar access.

Local planning departments and planning commissions can

[1]Office of Consumer Affairs, *The Energy Consumer,* U.S. Department of Energy (February/March 1980).

[2]Ordinance no. 306, An Ordinance of the City Council of the City of Del Mar, California, adding article V to Chapter 6 of the Del Mar Municipal Code.

exercise an enormous amount of control over the design of the community through land use planning and zoning. They can allow home business, encourage developers to use more appropriate street layouts, require bicycle paths, and even influence the type of vegetation used in a neighborhood. They can determine the location of schools and businesses.

The city of Visalia, California, has actually designed a neighborhood somewhat along the lines of the garden city plan I propose. Rather than depending on private developers to plan appropriate new development, the city planners did it themselves. A variety of housing, commercial facilities, and schools are all connected by greenbelts and bike paths in the proposed development. Drainage is handled by surface channels and ponds which require no energy for pumping. Streets are narrow and shaded, to keep the town cool in the hot San Joaquin Valley summers. Having the city do the planning should save the private developers who actually build the project time and therefore money. Lengthy hearings and an environmental impact report will not be required as long as the developer carries out the plan as it was developed by the city.[3]

The appropriate management of municipally owned facilities can cut energy use and reduce the costs of city and county government. Buildings can be insulated, public pools can be retrofitted with solar heaters, and smaller, more energy-efficient vehicles can be purchased. The city of Los Angeles, California, is replacing its incandescent and mercury vapor street-lights with high-pressure sodium units for an estimated savings of $3 to $4 million a year.[4]

In promoting individual energy-conservation efforts, local government must make a tactical choice between the carrot and the stick; between offering incentives to change, and imposing requirements. The carrot is certainly the more palatable solution. Unfortunately, there are situations where only the stick will work. Although a number of local governments have attempted volun-

tary conservation programs, I have not yet heard of any voluntary effort that has obtained more than 50 percent compliance. In fact, getting half of the population to cooperate is considered a major victory.

One major problem seems to be that while conservation and solar energy measures are already cost-effective, and will become even more so as resource costs increase, current pricing of conventional energy does not reflect that cost-effectiveness to the consumer. Electricity is a good example. The cost of building power plants has increased tremendously in recent decades, in addition to the rising fuel costs. In areas where electricity is used for domestic water heating and space heating, it is already cheaper to install solar heating than to build and run power plants to provide the same amount of energy. But electric rates are not based on the cost of adding new power plants; they are based on the average costs for the whole system, including old power plants built cheaply many years ago. This keeps the price of electricity below the real cost of producing it, which makes electricity appear more cost-effective to the consumer than it really is.

Various ways of overcoming the average cost problem have been proposed. The Tennessee Valley Authority (TVA), for example, is experimenting with subsidizing solar systems and woodstoves for home heating. TVA officials say the subsidies merely pass on to these homeowners what they save TVA by making new generating capacity unnecessary.

Since rates are set by public utility commissioners, they are outside the direct control of local governments, though local governments and citizen groups can appear as advocates before the commission. As mentioned earlier, some local governments have chosen to simply mandate conservation or solar energy measures. For example, San Diego County, California, has changed its building code to require solar water heating in all new construction where electric heating is the only alternative, and to eventually require it even where gas is available. County Supervisor Roger Hedgecock, who proposed the mandate, says that in this era of energy shortage, the solar requirement is just as much in the public interest as are the structural safety requirements of the building code.

[3]Northeast Area Specific Plan, City Planning, Visalia, California.
[4]Los Angeles Mayor's Office, ''Energy'' pamphlet (Los Angeles, Spring 1980).

To build public awareness and support for conservation and solar requirements, it can be helpful for a community to take a look at the relationship between its economy and its power supply. Franklin County, Massachusetts, did so and learned that the total cost of the energy used in the county almost doubled between 1975 and 1979.[5] The study also showed that at least 85 percent of this money was spent outside the county. From this, Franklin County residents discovered that energy self-sufficiency would have a double benefit. If they could develop local resources for energy production, it would mean this money would be kept within the county, and create jobs there. In addition, locally generated energy supplies would insulate the county from fuel shortages and rising prices.

The study also indicated that the county could become almost independent of "imported" energy through conservation strategies and alternative energy sources. Citizens there have chosen this option and are now in the process of exploring how to implement it.

In most cases, a community that wants to tackle energy problems automatically hires an outside consultant to do a "study." This is unfortunate. A great deal of time is wasted in looking for funding from a federal source to hire the consultant. When the consultant is hired, he does the job and leaves, leaving behind a document that only he truly understands to sit on the shelf and gather dust. The outside consultant has no vested interest in the community and little desire to make sure his study is understood and acted upon by the local government. I think a major reason that our city government in Davis has done so much to implement conservation is that Davis energy studies have been written by local residents who stuck around to make sure that something happened as a result of their work.

It can be difficult, of course, for a group of laypersons to do an energy plan or study. The problem is complex, it is difficult to know where to start. Fortunately, there is now available an excellent guidebook on the subject. Called the *County Energy Plan Guidebook*,[6] it provides a comprehensive, nontechnical tool with which to create local renewable energy plans.

Volunteer citizen planning can even be extremely effective at the state level. An example is SolarCal, a California citizen group proposed by Tom Hayden and established by Governor Jerry Brown in 1978. SolarCal was charged with producing a plan which would provide maximum feasible solar commercialization in the state. While the plan was produced by laypersons volunteering their time instead of a high-priced, professional consulting team, it has been termed "the most outstanding solar energy program we have yet encountered" by Robert Stobaugh and Daniel Yergin, editors of *Energy Future: Report of the Energy Project at the Harvard Business School*.[7] Not surprisingly, the plan views support for local citizen action as one of the state's most important functions.

As a next step, in 1980 Governor Brown established the SolarCal Local Government Commission on Conservation and Renewable Resources. The commission is made up of 42 city councilpersons and county supervisors. Members of the commission volunteer their time to develop and implement energy programs in their own communities, then share their experiences with other local governments. A small staff is funded by the California Energy Extension Service to provide technical assistance to the group, set up meetings, maintain a liaison between local governments and other agencies, and facilitate networking. Since the establishment of this group there has been an explosion of energy-related local action in California. I think personal communication and interaction stimulates policymakers in a way that is extremely beneficial.

Through zoning requirements, land-use planning, growth control, building ordinances, and a multitude of other mechanisms, the citizen, through his or her city or county elected official is able to influence the entire complexion of the community. Local

[5]Office of Consumer Affairs, U.S. Department of Energy, *The Energy Consumer* (February/March 1980).

[6]Alan Okagaki, with Jim Benson, *County Energy Plan Guidebook: Creating a Renewable Energy Plan,* Institute for Ecological Policies (Fairfax, Va., July 1979).

[7]Robert Stobaugh and Daniel Yergin, eds., *Energy Future*: *Report of the Energy Project at the Harvard Business School* (New York: Random House, 1979), p. 327.

elections and local issues should never be taken lightly. It is at this level that you have the greatest ability to make your voice heard, not only through your vote but also through participation in the public hearing process and personal communication with your local elected representatives.

It is possible, though very difficult, for citizens to go beyond influencing the design of an existing town and to become instrumental in the development of a new town. In fact, the only attempts to build energy-efficient garden cities in this decade have been initiated and carried out, not by professional developers, but by groups of concerned citizens.

Cerro Gordo, a proposed new town near Cottage Grove, Oregon, was the first of two such citizen-initiated projects. Several thousand people all over the United States have been involved, at one time or another, in the development or support of this ecologically sound, no-cars-allowed, community-oriented new town of 2,500 people. Unfortunately, the project has encountered enormous difficulties of all kinds. It has proven impossible to fill the needs of all of the people involved, financial problems have arisen, and residents of nearby Cottage Grove have decided they don't want any new neighbors, thereby holding up approval of the project by the county. After 10 years of effort, the plan for the town is complete and several buildings are on the site. Even though some problems still exist, the project is proceeding.

Solar Village in Marin County, California, is a plan for a 1,200-acre new town conceived by community activist Clark Blasdell and designed by architect Sim Van der Ryn. Several thousand Marin County citizens have organized to try to obtain a former air force base as the site for the project. The Solar Village concept was placed on the ballot for an advisory vote in November 1979 and it obtained not quite half the votes. At this writing,

there is still a great deal of active citizen support for the project, and the Marin County Board of Supervisors is looking favorably at it. Since there have been no other uses of the air force base accepted by the county, the Marin Solar Village Corporation, now staffed with a board of directors, a board of advisors, and professional consultants is ready to present another Solar Village proposal. It is anticipated that the county will then open requests for proposals.

Innovative projects and new ideas do not generally emerge from the established business community. To gain acceptance for new ideas, we need models. We need to prove they will work, that they are marketable, and that someone can make money on them. After that, new concepts will spread rapidly.

The building of solar homes in California began as a grass-roots movement, with individuals and a few small business-people who felt a commitment to find solutions to the energy crisis. Seven years later, one of the largest builders in California, M. J. Brock, is building, marketing, and rapidly selling passive solar homes.

A similar tale can be told about community energy planning. Our small college town, Davis, began in 1973 to establish a model for what could be done in a community to reduce energy use. Seven years later, communities all over California have citizen task forces scrutinizing the Davis model for possible application in their communities and our town is overrun with tourists, photographers, and news reporters.

New towns will almost certainly follow the same pattern. It will take a strong grass-roots movement to obtain the first few models. Once these are established, and the idea has proven itself successfully, it is almost certain to be replicated many times over. The future lies in the hands of active citizens who are willing to lead the way.

Conclusion
Beyond Piecemeal Planning

Because of the magnitude of the urbanization that will occur in the years to come, it is essential that we improve our urban planning process.

The Department of Housing and Urban Development estimates that there will be an average need for at least 2 million additional housing units every year for the next couple of decades.[1,2] This means that within 20 years we will have to increase our housing supply by 40 to 50 percent.

Currently, most housing development is occurring in subdivisions on the peripheries of existing cities, and this new growth is adding to the complexity of these cities' problems. Much of the remainder of the housing which is being developed is on previously undeveloped land within urban areas. Urban infill, as the latter kind of development is called, is being touted by many

planners as the solution to the problem of how to control urban sprawl. Even if there were no good arguments (and there are many — ecological, energy related, social, and political) for leaving much of this land in some form of open space, this approach can at best provide a short-term solution to the problem, without serious overcrowding, because of the limited amount of land remaining within urban boundaries.

Inevitably, we must answer the question of how we should develop beyond existing urban limits. Should we continue adding concentric rings of subdivisions, industrial parks, and shopping centers around the peripheries of cities using the piecemeal approach, or should we look for better solutions? Should we continue to view urban planning as a process separate from the rest of society's problems or should we look at urban planning as it relates to the entire set of contemporary problems?

Please ask yourself: isn't it likely that a continuation of our past performance will bury us in the environmental and social problems already being experienced at a crisis level? I think that if we fail to understand the relationship between the design of the built environment and how society functions in it, and also fail to use that knowledge for restructuring it in an enlightened way, then we are headed for a future burdened with continual deterioration in the quality of life for most, if not all, of the human population.

[1]John C. Weicher, Lorene Yap, and Mary S. Jones, "National Housing Needs and Quality Changes during the 1980s," unpublished report by the Urban Institute (Department of Housing and Urban Development), Office of Policy Development and Research (Completed in April 1980).

[2]John Pitkin and George Masnick, "Analysis and Projection of Housing Consumption by Birthcohorts: 1960–2000," unpublished report by the Joint Center for Urban Studies, Massachusetts Institute of Technology and Harvard University (Completed in March 1980).

Our first priority must be to scale down the institutions and physical settings that surround us so that we can more easily relate to them. The gigantism of cities, industry, and government that has overtaken us and has made most of us human population apathetic and alienated, must give way to a society revolving more around neighborhood communities, small towns, and local business and government. At this level, we can address the problems that have been impossible to solve by our highly centralized government bureaucracy and the conglomerates controlling industry and agriculture.

Our first step must be to start changing our environment so we can improve our well-being as a society. Kirkpatrick Sale explains:

> A person surrounded by subways and blaring radios, beset on every side with clamor, confusion, filth, boredom, and hopelessness, might well strike out in rage when provoked; a person surrounded by calm, decorousness, purposefulness, and comfort is less likely to. Behavior basically depends on the setting, the time and place and society in which it happens. Obviously, the desired effort is to find those settings in which the benevolent side of our human nature is encouraged and the malevolent side dampened: that will not ensure constant and unvarying harmony, it seems safe to say, but it certainly will go a long way to permitting it and fostering it.
>
> And without question such settings, as our examination of stateless societies has shown, are those of the small community.
>
> The increased participation in all aspects of life that is fostered by the small community is also beneficial. In social terms this allows an individual to ventilate grievances and to make changes, escaping the pressures that tend to build up in people who feel powerless or useless or ignored. And in political terms participation allows people to see that the process of decision-making, having included them, is fair, and that the decisions themselves, having been influenced by them, are fairly arrived at — the very two reasons, not so

incidentally, that historically people have obeyed laws and honored social norms.

> To the extent that it can provide organizations and systems at sizes where individuals may feel some sense of control, it diminishes the kinds of psychological and social dislocations that arise when people face large, depersonalized, and violent ones. And to the degree that it can develop a community-controlled, self-sufficient, and participatory economy, it is likely to remove many of the causes of crime, because that should provide everyone with not only the general economic satisfactions but the fullest and most rewarding kinds of employment.[3]

Murray Bookchin discusses the task ahead:

> To restore urbanity as a meaningful terrain for sociation, culture, and community, the megalopolis must be ruthlessly dissolved and replaced by new decentralized ecocommunities, each carefully tailored to the natural ecosystem in which it is located. One might reasonably say that these ecocommunities will possess the best features of the polis and medieval commune, supported by rounded ecotechnologies that rescale the most advanced elements of modern technology — including such energy sources as solar and wind power — to local dimensions. The equilibrium between town and country will be restored — not as a sprawling suburb that mistakes a lawn or patch of strategically placed trees for nature, but as an interactive functional ecocommunity that unites industry with agriculture, mental work with physical, individuality with community. Nature will not be reduced to a mere symbol of the natural, a spectatorial object to be seen from a window or during a stroll; it will become an integral part of all aspects of human experience, from work to play. Only in this form can the needs of nature become integrated with the needs of humanity and yield an authentic ecological

[3]Kirkpatrick Sale, *Human Scale* (New York: Coward, McCann and Geoghegan, 1980), pp. 484, 485–86.

consciousness that transcends the instrumentalist "environmental" outlook of the social and sanitary engineer.[4]

If we can see what is wrong with the communities we're building now and start making changes, the future will bring many choices of healthy living environments ranging from rural homesteads and a multitude of different village-type communities — some larger, some smaller, some more isolated, others clustered, many perhaps born out of the rehabilitation of our sprawling suburbs — to metropolitan centers such as San Francisco or New York, possibly enhanced by the creation of adjacent open space and other types of redevelopment.

It may seem that this vision will be difficult to achieve but I believe it will not be, if we realize that it will take time, and if we are willing to make a commitment to providing *a better place to live* for ourselves and our children and the generations to follow.

If we choose this course and begin to apply our efforts to its implementation, we may find that living becomes more meaningful. What is more essential for the survival of the human species than for our generation to work toward improving the quality of life for our children and what could give a deeper feeling of inner satisfaction than working toward that goal?

[4]Murray Bookchin, *The Limits of the City* (New York: Harper & Row, 1974), pp. 137–38.

Photography Credits

Index